Making Speeches

Making Speeches

The Speechmaking of Margaret Thatcher, 1975–1990

Tom Hurst

BLOOMSBURY ACADEMIC

LONDON · NEW YORK · OXFORD · NEW DELHI · SYDNEY

BLOOMSBURY ACADEMIC
Bloomsbury Publishing Plc, 50 Bedford Square, London, WC1B 3DP, UK
Bloomsbury Publishing Inc, 1385 Broadway, New York, NY 10018, USA
Bloomsbury Publishing Ireland, 29 Earlsfort Terrace, Dublin 2, D02 AY28, Ireland

BLOOMSBURY, BLOOMSBURY ACADEMIC and the Diana logo
are trademarks of Bloomsbury Publishing Plc

First published in Great Britain 2025

Copyright © Tom Hurst, 2025

Tom Hurst has asserted his right under the Copyright, Designs and
Patents Act, 1988, to be identified as Author of this work.

For legal purposes the Acknowledgements on p. ix constitute
an extension of this copyright page.

Cover images © Hulton Deutsch / Contributor via
Getty Images and The Thatcher Foundation

All rights reserved. No part of this publication may be: i) reproduced or transmitted in
any form, electronic or mechanical, including photocopying, recording or by means of
any information storage or retrieval system without prior permission in writing from the
publishers; or ii) used or reproduced in any way for the training, development or operation
of artificial intelligence (AI) technologies, including generative AI technologies. The rights
holders expressly reserve this publication from the text and data mining exception as
per Article 4(3) of the Digital Single Market Directive (EU) 2019/790.

Bloomsbury Publishing Plc does not have any control over, or responsibility for, any
third-party websites referred to or in this book. All internet addresses given in this
book were correct at the time of going to press. The author and publisher regret
any inconvenience caused if addresses have changed or sites have ceased
to exist, but can accept no responsibility for any such changes.

A catalogue record for this book is available from the British Library.

A catalog record for this book is available from the Library of Congress.

ISBN: HB: 978-1-3501-5857-3
         ePDF: 978-1-3501-5858-0
         eBook: 978-1-3501-5859-7

Typeset by Integra Software Services Pvt. Ltd.

For product safety related questions contact productsafety@bloomsbury.com.

To find out more about our authors and books visit www.bloomsbury.com
and sign up for our newsletters.

For my father.

Contents

List of Figures	viii
Acknowledgements	ix
Introduction	1
1 'Defy[ing] analysis'? Thatcher's speechwriting process	15
2 'Policy hostages'. Speechmaking and the policy-agenda	35
3 'We are playing to our geographical strengths'. Thatcher's electioneering platform	53
4 'The trip itself is the message'. Thatcher's platform	67
5 'We have issued a speech text which does not relate to the one spoken by the Prime Minister, in every respect'. The press and post-delivery speechmaking	81
6 'Tight and taut'. Speechmaking and the electronic news media	95
7 'Changing the climate'? The speechwriter's political influence	113
Conclusion	131
Notes	148
Bibliography	189
Index	195

Figures

1	John Hoskyns, head of the Number 10 Policy Unit, 1979–1982	18
2	'This is <u>not</u> a script for me'	47
3	John Gummer, an influential member of Thatcher's 'Home Team'	48
4	Thatcher speaking to the immediate and national audience	68
5	Margaret Thatcher shares a joke with Ronald Reagan	74
6	Bernard Ingham, chief press secretary, 1979–1990	90
7	Brian Walden, one of Thatcher's favoured television interviewers	96

Acknowledgements

Some people enjoy spending their leisure time in the gym, playing football or going to concerts. I have spent my leisure time writing history. Although fun, writing in one's spare time does present challenges. Consequently, this book has in large part been made possible by a range of individuals who, in one way or another, have supported me in its completion.

I owe thanks to Vincent McInerney who agreed to my working part time for one year, and to the John Antcliffe Foundation, who funded my Archival By-Fellowship at Churchill College, Cambridge. The project would not have been feasible without these generous acts.

I am grateful to the archival staff at the Churchill Archives Centre, especially to Andrew Riley whose unparalleled knowledge of Thatcher's papers has enabled me to make sense of the archives. Andrew was good enough to comment on an early draft of the book and to be a constant source of good cheer and encouragement. Similarly, the Margaret Thatcher Foundation, an organization that has made a wealth of material available online, has made this project's completion possible.

Numerous people have provided useful suggestions during the writing of this book. Of course, any mistakes are mine alone. I am particularly thankful to Professor Paul Readman and Dr Robert Saunders, both of whom gave up time in their busy schedules to read and comment upon the manuscript. I owe a huge debt of gratitude to Professor Richard Vinen who has, for more than fifteen years, been incredibly generous with his time, encouragement and advice.

My parents, Mandy and Jerry have provided emotional and practical support. Indeed, it is impossible to put into words the support provided by my father. Grainne, my wife, deserves special thanks. During weekends and evenings, she has provided advice and inspiration and, when necessary, kept my nose to the grindstone. She has also done more than her fair share of childcare. My two sons, Ted and Harry, have tolerated, without complaint, the periods of time when I have been writing instead of accompanying them on various outings. Without my family I doubt that this book would ever have been written.

Introduction

When Margaret Thatcher died, on 8 April 2013, the press responded with a mixture of recollections, hagiography and criticism. Throughout the coverage, spanning the entire political spectrum, were Thatcher's public utterances. *The Daily Telegraph* and *The Guardian* published articles detailing Thatcher's famous phrases. Both were entitled 'In Her Own Words'.[1] The *Socialist Worker* printed posters celebrating the news of Thatcher's death, repeating the words she had uttered on the steps of Downing Street in April 1982, 'Rejoice, Rejoice'. The *Sun* was correct when it suggested that Thatcher was 'loved and loathed for her memorable one-liners'.[2] Little wonder that her premiership – the sixth longest in history – took on a peculiarly personalized character, as the term 'Thatcherism' suggests. What Thatcher did, and did not say in public, demands attention.

Studying public, political speeches is not new.[3] Indeed, Thatcher's electoral dominance itself played a part in British political historians paying closer attention to political language.[4] However, such studies can, at times, take on a rather abstract form. Little attention is paid to the mechanics of speech writing. To fully understand Thatcher's speechmaking one must understand who was in the room at the time of the speech's creation, who was trying desperately to avoid nodding off to sleep in the early hours of the morning (and thus face Thatcher's wrath), and who was on their hands and knees sellotaping pages of a speech together. To do so allows one to appreciate the degree to which speechwriting was an integral part of the process of policy formation and, consequently, raises questions over conventional conceptions of 'Thatcherism' as it reveals that Thatcher's words, and the policy that they shaped, were often written by individuals who were not considered, indeed often did not consider themselves, 'Thatcherites'.

Contrary to existing assumptions, this book will show that the platform remained an important facet in the British political landscape of the 1970s and

1980s. A quantitative analysis of Thatcher's speechmaking reveals that, despite Thatcher's tendency to address 'national issues', when and where Thatcher spoke was of great significance. It is not surprising then that Thatcher's rhetoric was tailored to her immediate audience whose reactions to her words not only held the potential to shape her speeches mid-delivery but were used by the national media as a barometer of approval and featured in national coverage accordingly. This national media coverage continued to shape Thatcher's speeches, and the political messages they articulated, post-delivery. Despite the party and the government's best efforts, Thatcher's words, and the political messages they articulated, reached the wider national audiences in a mediated form, distorted by the political and stylistic concerns of the various news media channels. If, as Williamson suggests, a politician is 'what they say', and Thatcher's words were shaped by a range of individuals – 'wordsmiths', journalists and audience members – questions must be raised about who 'Thatcher' was, and what 'Thatcherism' means.

This is not to say that an emphasis on 'context' has been eschewed in the following work. Drawing on current studies of Thatcherism that stress Thatcher's relationship with her 'enemies', Thatcher's words will be shown to have operated as part of a wider political dialogue.[5] In so doing, existing explanations of Thatcher's success that stress her 'luck' with her enemies, be they General Galtieri, the Labour Party or the National Union of Mineworkers (NUM), will be questioned. By using text mining software to interrogate Thatcher's public statements Thatcher's political language can be assessed in a quantitative fashion. This enables the tracking of Thatcher's use of political labels over the period 1975–90. It is demonstrated that the shaping of political labels, and the political benefit Thatcher derived from them relied, in large part, upon the political context in which they existed and less on Thatcher or her speechwriters' authorial intentions. The claim made by Thatcher that she 'changed everything' is therefore problematized; did Thatcher shape Britain, or did Britain shape Thatcher?

What is a speech?

Speaking in public can, of course, take many different forms. It is therefore necessary to clarify what constitutes a 'public speech'. How, for example, does '*a* speech' differ from 'speech'? What are the differences between public statements made by Thatcher at the annual Finchley Fair and those delivered at the Winter Gardens in Brighton? At first glance, this seems a superfluous question. *The Complete Public Statements of Margaret Thatcher* asserts that 'most [of Thatcher's] statements [...] individuate themselves. A speech, is a speech, is a speech'.[6] In the same vein a 'remark' is distinguished from 'a speech' by being 'unscheduled and unscripted'.[7] Such a definition appears both reasonable and obvious.

However, on closer inspection the apparent distinctions separating Thatcher's various public pronouncements begin to blur. Whilst a 'remark' is defined by its unscheduled nature, 'a speech' cannot be defined by its status as a scripted piece of oratory. If this were so, many of Gladstone's public statements could not be described as speeches, which of course they were.[8] Similarly, if 'a speech' is characterized by its scripted nature, then many of Thatcher's statements, which were unscripted yet significant, would go unrecognized. Take the speeches Thatcher delivered in the House of Commons, many of which, according to the conventions of the House, were unscripted, memorized or at least, not tightly scripted. Thatcher's set-piece interviews too were usually the result of careful briefings and were semi-scripted, predetermined answers. Similarly, many press conferences following international summit meetings opened with a virtually unscripted statement, unprompted by questioning. The fact that such utterances were unscripted, semi-scripted or delivered in the context of a press conference should not detract from their status as public, set-piece speeches.

Moreover, 'a speech' cannot simply be defined as an unprompted statement. The St Francis Speech (1979) for example, although loosely scripted by Ronnie Millar (playwright, and speechwriter for Heath, Thatcher and Major) was delivered in the guise of an answer to a question. On several occasions Thatcher's speeches included unscripted answers to questions posed by her audience. In her speech at Fornham All Saints during the election campaign of 1987, Thatcher engaged with a member of the audience over the issue of unemployment. The *Birmingham Post* recorded the incident:

> Mr Jones piped up: 'What about the people that cannot work?' Mrs Thatcher replied: 'If you want to get unemployment down, vote Tory'.[9]

Thus, what constitutes 'a speech' is largely subjective. However, to assess Thatcher's use of speechmaking, and to set it in context, it is necessary to define the meaning of 'a speech' in its broadest context. 'A speech', in contrast with 'a remark', will be understood as denoting a premeditated public statement.

Scholars, speeches and sources

As Paul Readman has suggested, historians' current concern with political language is not as novel as some claim.[10] In 1974 for example, Quentin Skinner assessed Bolingbroke's opposition to Walpole by analysing 'Bolingbroke's professed political principles'.[11] Maurice Cowling, a historian of the 'high politics' variety, took political speeches seriously. Cowling defined 'high politics' as 'primarily a matter of rhetoric and manoeuvre'.[12] British political historians have taken political language seriously, and have done so in a variety of ways. Yet it was the dominance of Thatcher's three governments that played a part in the prioritization of language in the study of British political history. After all, it was 'the apparent about turn of the forward march of Labour [and] the Right's electoral successes on both sides of the Atlantic during the 1980s and 1990s' that James Vernon suggests, 'have led many to reassess their understanding of politics.[13] Gareth Stedman Jones' *Languages of Class* (1983), conceived as a means of finding 'different ways of asking why the Labour Party is in a mess', can be read as just such a reassessment.[14] Having 'abandoned a Marxist paradigm', Stedman Jones recalls, he was able to move 'beyond the devotee's fetishization of theory' and thus focus on forming the 'advance guard of a general movement in historical studies directed towards questions of language, meaning, and representation'.[15]

That some historians of the Conservative Party began to acknowledge the importance of language was itself a consequence of the party's ideology being taken seriously. This shift was, in part, the product of Thatcher's ascendance to the party's leadership. During the 1960s and 1970s Conservative history tended to be written by those such as Robert Blake and Maurice Cowling, sympathetic to the Conservative Party but distrustful of doctrine. Blake underplayed the ideological nature of Thatcher's leadership of the Conservative Party.[16] So enamoured was Cowling of Wilson's style of leadership – characterized by many as lacking principles – that, in 1967, he dedicated *1867, Disraeli, Gladstone and Revolution* to 'the Prime Minister'.[17] The rise of Thatcher, although personally supported by both Blake and Cowling, introduced a new dynamic to the conception of the Conservative Party. The party seemed to be defined by enthusiasm; ideas mattered. When Thatcher made her only visit to Peterhouse College, Cambridge, she was alleged to have brushed aside Cowling's sounding a note of caution with the words 'we don't want pessimists in our party'.[18] This new dynamism attracted scholars of the Left. It is perhaps telling that the political label 'Thatcherism', signifying a coherent ideological position, was popularized

Introduction   5

by *Marxism Today* – a title whose contributors began to take seriously the Conservative Party's ideology.

It was 'New Political History' – perhaps now an ironic term given that it had already been pronounced 'rather old news' in 1996 – that, shaped by the earlier 'linguistic turn', ushered in a widespread and comprehensive appreciation of language in the writing of British political history.[19] The prioritization of language has led to a fragmentation of the field. For Philip Williamson in *Stanley Baldwin*, New Political History's appreciation of political language has been fused with a more orthodox concern for 'politicians who mattered'. After all, as Williamson reminds his readers, a 'politician's effectiveness' depends greatly on 'speeches – in public presentation and argument'.[20] For others, attention is directed towards reconstructing the discursive world in which such figures operated. Matthew Roberts' work, for example, looks at *Constructing a Tory World-view*, whilst Karen Musolf's *From Plymouth to Parliament* (an account of the political language of Nancy Astor, MP for Plymouth Sutton, 1919–45 and the first woman to take her seat in the House of Commons) concerns itself with 'focussed encounters with specific eras, themes, events, or movements'.[21] Such work can be read as 'rhetorical histories', they can, 'in brief ... be called analytical narratives'.[22] This has 'moved history decisively towards the recovery of narrative and away from the supply of explanation'.[23] Thus, as Jon Lawrence has suggested, historians of politics 'disagree not just about the usual issues of theory and methodology' but, fundamentally, about 'subject matter'.[24]

Thatcher's public language has, since at least 1975, proved fruitful material for political commentators. Journalists and political scientists writing during the 1970s, 1980s and 1990s, especially those emanating from the Left, took Thatcher's public pronouncements seriously.[25] Similarly, the first academic histories dealing with the period 1975–90 are not without reference to Thatcher's public language.[26] Yet all tended to use her public language out of necessity, not preference. Speeches, interviews and public asides are used in contemporary works and later histories and autobiographies because of a lack of archival sources, the first of which, due to the thirty-year rule (which in 2013 became the twenty-year rule), became available in 2009.

With the fall of Thatcher's government in 1990, political scientists and journalists moved on and the key protagonists of the period began to publish their memoirs. The autobiographies of those who had already left the main political stage, such as Whitelaw, Tebbit, Prior, Nott and Carrington, were joined by others such as Thatcher, Howe, Ridley and Lawson, and later by those whose political life survived Thatcher's departure from Number 10, men such as Major, Hurd and Waldegrave.[27] Although it is difficult to assess the minutiae of the memoir-writing process and the exact goals each author hoped to achieve (Chris Collins, ghost-writer of *The Downing Street Years* noted how 'there is a sacrament of confession, and the priest is sworn to confidence. Ghosting puts me in mind of it'.[28]), each author, in one way or another, engaged in what Peter Clarke called 'the battle of books'.[29] Whilst such memoirs provide a wealth of information for the historian, they tend not to shed a great deal of light on Thatcher's speechwriting process. Ferdinand Mount's (Head of the Policy Unit, 1983–5) complaint in *Cold Cream* that none of 'my speeches were mentioned in any of the later histories of the [1983] campaign' stands testament to the self-conscious manner in which the memoirist, or the interviewee recalls the past.[30]

In some ways, this has contributed to the lack of any explicit discussion of the creation of Thatcher's speeches. Robin Harris (member of Thatcher's 'Home Team', *c.* 1985 onwards) recalls:

> [P]eople did not tell anybody that you had been involved [in drafting a speech]. It was regarded as a great betrayal. Later, after she [Mrs Thatcher] had left office, I was prepared to say that I helped.[31]

Moreover, all memoirists write in the knowledge that most of their readers will not be stimulated by a blow-by-blow account of the speechmaking process. As a result, discussion of speechwriting tends to be confined to election campaigns, major annual political events or, as in the case of the Bruges Speech, events which have, in hindsight, been seen as historical 'turning points'.

Thatcher's personal papers relating to her first year in government were released in 2009. Thereafter, Thatcher's personal papers were released annually. Documents pertaining to her final year in Number 10 were made public in 2020. With each annual release of archival material, the Thatcher era became better established as a distinct field of historical study. Universities from London to Singapore began to offer courses and modules devoted to the study of the subject, and scholars began to ask new questions of the period.[32] Encouraged by New Political History's interest in language – an interest that was given methodological shape in reaction to Thatcher's electoral dominance of the 1980s – some scholars sought to open fresh lines of enquiry by assessing Thatcher's public language.[33]

This analysis of Thatcher's public language however rarely paid attention to documents pertaining to the creation, delivery and reception of Thatcher's speeches.[34] Perhaps this ambivalence towards such archival material is due to the

Introduction

7

sense that, since the publication of Moore's final volume of his official biography of Thatcher, the archives have little new to offer the historian.[35] Perhaps it is the belated result of the leakiness of Thatcher's governments. Ken Stowe's plea to Thatcher in May 1979, 'that there must be no leaks [from the Cabinet], and no gossip' went unheeded.[36] Many of the 'new' finds 'revealed' by the release of archival material – and accompanied by much excitement in the press – were already known. More likely, it is the result of the methodological inspiration 'New Political History' draws from scholars such as Quentin Skinner and the 'Cambridge School'.[37] By setting 'discourse' within its historical context, the 'Cambridge School' paid little attention to the practical, prosaic business of creating the language itself.[38] This was, in part, a consequence of a lack of source material. Skinner was unable to leaf through Bolingbroke's speech drafts – even if he had wanted to, which seems unlikely.[39] However, a study of previously overlooked documents in the archive – the handwritten, annotated or torn speech draft – makes possible the study of Thatcher's (and many other politicians') speechmaking process. By tracing the 'nuts and bolts' of Thatcher's speechmaking it is possible to trace not only the development of Thatcherism as an idea, but the practical operation of politics, usually assumed to have taken place around the Cabinet table.

Methodology

Reviewing *Margaret Thatcher: Complete Public Statements, 1945–1990*, Joseph Meisel notes that the work represented 'a massive quantitative and technological leap beyond all such efforts that have come before'.[40] The collection was published on a CD-ROM and was thus freed from the limitations of the printed page. Consequently, 7,564 of Thatcher's public statements were included – three times as many as Rhodes James included in *Winston S. Churchill: His Complete Speeches, 1897–1963* (1974) and covering two-thirds of the number of years.[41] The digital format not only provides the historian with a 'mass of material', but also the apparatus to allow its navigation.[42] Like many historians, Meisel prizes the accessibility and searchability of digitized databanks, 'boons' which, Luke Blaxill points out, 'facilitate and accelerate traditional qualitative research rather than allow new kinds of quantitative research'.[43]

This work embraces the opportunity to apply a quantitative approach to the study of political language. A corpus has been built containing Thatcher's 1,593 premeditated statements and Antconc (freely accessible software) has been employed to interrogate the corpus.[44] This allows trends in Thatcher's language to be identified – trends that a 'close reading' of Thatcher's speeches would have failed to reveal. Take, for example, Thatcher's use of the term 'Thatcherism'. Antconc's 'word list' function (which allows the historian to ascertain how often a particular word was used during a specific period of time) reveals that she used the term just nineteen times during her premiership. This raises questions over Thatcher's – and commentators'– relationship with the term 'Thatcherism'.

Corpus analysis techniques enable more than simply the counting of particular words. The 'key word in context' (KWIC) function allows specific words to be searched, and displayed in their context, as a list. In so doing it is clear that Thatcher's engagement with the term 'Thatcherism' evolved over time. In opposition the term was seen as a political slur, later it was treated in a more positive light (though Thatcher was never comfortable with the word).[45] Such conclusions, and the statistical evidence that underpins them, would be beyond the reach of the orthodox 'close reading' of political speeches.

For meaningful conclusions to be derived from an analysis of Thatcher's words a series of subsamples have been built. Thatcher's statements have been grouped according to the year of their delivery (with 1979 including two supplementary corpora to allow for a distinction to be drawn between her speechmaking in opposition and in government) and grouped according to geographical location. Such subsamples enable Thatcher's words to be analysed in context, and for this analysis to be conducted over a broad chronological span. That Thatcher used the word 'union(s)' in relation to the Labour Party just six times during 1976 and 1977 is of limited interest. However, when this total is compared to the first five months of 1979 when Thatcher used the term ten times, one can begin to reveal rhetorical techniques that contributed to the Conservative Party's electoral success. Thus, the analysis of vast numbers of speeches, made possible by text mining software, enables this book to address the perceived shortcoming of 'New Political History', namely that 'agency and causation ... [are] eschewed in favour of the recovery and analysis of political cultures and discourses'.[46]

Using text mining software to analyse corpora is not, however, the principle methodological approach of this work. This is not only a reflection of the author's limit technical ability, but also an acknowledgement of the limitations of such an approach. Blaxill is correct to assert:

> [T]he central assumption at the heart of corpus linguistics is that, because a speaker or writer's choice of words is not random, counting them and observing patterns formed by them can be revealing.[47]

Introduction 9

Observing patterns in Thatcher's public language is indeed revealing, but it can only reveal so much. A quantitative analysis of Thatcher's words makes it difficult to reconstruct the way in which various audiences accessed, and understood, her words. Just because Thatcher delivered a particular political message from the platform did not mean that this same message would be broadcast to wider audiences. Furthermore, the meaning that Thatcher hoped to convey was not necessarily shared by her audience(s). Take, for example, Thatcher's use of her 'language of conviction'. Whilst corpus analysis enables Thatcher's consistent use of this language to be identified, it does not reveal that the political advantage that this was able to generate declined as the 1980s wore on.

Similarly, whilst textual analysis reveals the rhetorical patterns of Thatcher's speeches, it cannot answer questions concerned with the authorship of these words, and the way in which these words were related to policy formation. A reading of the drafts of Thatcher's 1981 Conference Speech reveals the way in which competing speechwriters struggled to shape the final draft and, with it, the government's policy platform. It is for this reason that memoirs, party, and government papers have been consulted, and supplemented with oral interviews, to identify the key individuals who were responsible for scripting Thatcher's words, and to reconstruct, as much as any historian can, the political context in which these 'wordsmiths' wrote.[48]

Of course, such sources must be treated with care. The recollections of numerous individuals overstate their contributions to Thatcher's speeches.[49] Yet, the discrepancy between recollection and reality is not the product of a faulty memory, or of a large ego – although these may apply – so much as Thatcher's speechwriting process. Thatcher's speeches were composed by a variety of individuals, many of whom were only vaguely aware of the contributions of others. Apparently 'faulty' recollections of Thatcher's speechwriting in fact offer valuable insights into the way that Thatcher's speeches were composed.

This book addresses Thatcher's speechmaking in its broadest form, from the drafting of Thatcher's words, through to their delivery, and ultimately to their interaction with the wider political context. A range of questions have been asked of a variety of sources using methodological techniques ranging from the 'close reading' of archival documents through to the analysis of purpose-made corpora. In so doing, this book goes some way in 'transcend[ing] the divisions'[50] within British political history in terms of both subject and methodology.

Arguments

Reviewing Tim Bale's *Margaret Thatcher*, an eclectic collection of works assessing Thatcher drawn from across academic disciplines, Robert Saunders asks whether 'Thatcher studies have reached critical mass'.[51] This is a question worth pondering. After all, there now exist more than thirty biographies of Thatcher.[52] In terms of biographical works then the answer to Saunders' question must surely be an emphatic 'yes'. Already, by 2000, John Campbell had taken the biographical study of Thatcher almost as far as it could go; Charles Moore's official biography seems to have left nothing of significance to say for future biographers. This is not to say that there is nothing left to interest students of Thatcher and Thatcherism, or for historians of twentieth-century British political history more generally. An assessment of previously overlooked documents associated with Thatcher's speechmaking process provides fresh perspectives of familiar topics.

No study of Thatcher's public language, or Thatcher in general, would be complete without engaging with the debates surrounding the term 'Thatcherism'. However, this book avoids the now well-rehearsed positions that are so common in accounts of Thatcherism. Little, it seems, can be added to positions whose basic tenets were set out forty years ago; does the term 'Thatcherism' describe a coherent political doctrine, or was it shaped by Thatcher's own set of beliefs, or are neither of these the case? Can 'Thatcherism' be better defined as a pragmatic political strategy to secure and hold power?[53] Textual analysis has allowed this book to raise questions about Thatcher's use of, and relationship with the term. This line of enquiry seems more rewarding than the current obsession with defining the term which has captured the attention of many commentators.

Accounts of Thatcher and Thatcherism are shaped by familiar chronological episodes, themselves related to the narrative of the rise of the Right. Few studies, apart from biographies, bridge the pre- and post-1979 period.[54] There is a good reason for this. Leading the opposition is a very different prospect to leading the government. But such a dichotomy runs the risk of restricting an analysis of Thatcher's policy platform to a discussion about whether it was developed in opposition, or in government, and whether it was ideologically or pragmatically inspired. A study of Thatcher's speechmaking in 1975–90, and its relationship to policy formation, offers a more nuanced perspective. It reveals that Thatcher used speechmaking to test ideas and to push boundaries. Some ideas floated in opposition sank without a trace. The idea of a referendum on the subject of curbing trade union powers, discussed by Thatcher during the winter of 1978–9, was not implemented.[55] Other ideas were incorporated into the party's policy platform and introduced during the early 1980s. Some ideas were suggested in opposition but lay dormant for years, until the political climate allowed their realization. Studying Thatcher's speechmaking from 1975–90 enables chronological continuity to be introduced to the study of the development of her policy-agenda.

References to the composition of Thatcher's Cabinet and Shadow Cabinet make regular appearances in histories of her career, and take on a greater significance than similar references made in accounts of other twentieth-century party leaders. They serve as markers in a supposed narrative of the development of Thatcherism. They also belie an assumption – which ironically Thatcher's leadership did much to call into question – that 'real' politics takes place around the Cabinet table.[56] Such a conclusion is only partially correct. Speechwriting provided a space in which the policy-agenda was debated and set. Thatcher and her speechwriters were aware of the political significance of 'speech acts'[57] or, as Norman Tebbitt called them, 'policy hostage[s]'.[58] Thatcher used her words to change the policy-agenda, either immediately or over time. Those studying the formation of a Thatcherite policy-agenda, either in opposition or in government, would thus do well to pay attention to the role of speechmaking, and the individuals involved in this process.[59]

For those who did not inhabit positions in Whitehall or the Cabinet, but were invited to contribute to Thatcher's drafting process, speechmaking offered, amongst other attractions, access to a level of political influence which would otherwise have been unattainable. An assessment of Thatcher's speechwriting process reveals a range of individuals – political appointments as well as civil servants – who played a key role in shaping Thatcher's words, and thus the policy-agenda it informed, who have until now been relegated to the footnotes of history. Far from representing a homogeneous group, 'Thatcher's People' were drawn from a varied array of social backgrounds and political persuasions. Several individuals who wrote for Thatcher were not diehard 'Thatcherites', in fact several were the very opposite: Chris Patten for example. Indeed, the fact that he wrote for Thatcher may illustrate the way in which Thatcher saw her 'wordsmiths' as fulfilling a technical, rather than an ideological activity, or it might indicate the degree to which the 'Thatcherite agenda' in fact encompassed positions that were shared across the party; trade union reform for example.[60] Either way, speechmaking reveals the dichotomy of 'wets' and 'dries', terminology encouraged by Thatcher herself, running throughout accounts of Thatcher and 'Thatcherism', as an analytical tool that distorts as much as it reveals.

An assessment of how 'those who mattered' interacted with Thatcher, and each other, reveals that speeches, and the policy they influenced, were often born out of chaos. Broad principles governing the creation of different types of speeches developed organically over time. They could not, however, survive Thatcher's constant interference in the speechmaking process, a product of her deep insecurity when it came to speechmaking. Unsure of her own ability Thatcher would constantly demand that speech drafts be rewritten, and that new 'wordsmiths' be drafted in to help. Instability existed at the centre of the speechmaking process. Though Thatcher's public language projected an image of decisive leadership, the fragility evidenced during speechmaking revealed her regularly in 'a last-minute frazzle about her speech', hardly the hallmark of an 'Iron Lady'.

Studies of 'Thatcherism', and twentieth-century politics more generally, have tended to view Thatcher's period in office as a distinct era, shaping but not shaped by, its political context. Recent work has challenged this view. It has been suggested that a potentially beneficial direction for future research might be to decentralize Thatcher by studying the 'enemies' against whom she defined herself.[61] This is certainly a worthy activity, and one which is already underway.[62] However, an analysis of Thatcher's speechmaking suggests an alternative approach. The political labels that Thatcher deployed to interact with, challenge and defeat – the 'Labour Party', 'the unions' and 'General Galtieri' – were at least partially creations of Thatcher's own rhetoric. The suggestion that Thatcher was 'lucky' in her opponents is too simplistic. The success, or failure, of these political labels depended as much on existing contemporary meanings as on the intentions of the author. Thatcher's political language, and its ability to achieve its predetermined goals, can only be understood when set in its contemporary political context. A study of her speechmaking process thus, ironically, decentres Thatcher, and raises questions about the concept of a distinct 'Thatcher Era'.

Reflecting upon the interaction between Thatcher's set-piece speeches and the media environment in which they existed, Ingham recalled how 'Television was […] the most persuasive medium, if you got it right'.[63] 'Getting it right' could involve avoiding the 'detailed discourse' of the set-piece speech and by definition, that of radio journalism.[64] Here, Ingham seems to validate implicitly the widely held perception, originating from analysis of the platform's place in the British political landscape, published during the 1890s, but still referred to today, that there existed a 'Golden Era' of speechmaking.[65] Following the democratic reforms of the 1800s, the era of speechmaking flourished in Britain. Later scholars have continued the narrative citing the rise of electronic broadcasting media, especially

Introduction

that of television from 1945 onwards as triggering the platform's demise.[66] By the 1970s and 1980s the set-piece speech, and the platform from which extra-parliamentary speeches were delivered, seemed something of an anachronism.

Such a position sits uncomfortably alongside Thatcher's approach to speechmaking. She spent an inordinate amount of time on the speechwriting process, which could drive her to tears and drive her speechwriters from their beds – hangovers and all. Speeches would be practised into the early hours of the morning, videotaped, watched back and practised again. The platform became ever more sophisticated, albeit from an amateurish starting point. By the late 1980s Thatcher would speak from a purpose-built hydraulic lectern, and a platform that could include lasers, music and carefully designed camera angles. The platform from which Thatcher spoke was certainly different from Gladstone's, but far from being in decline, the platform (and the immediate audience surrounding it) became an integral part of the wider dissemination of Thatcher's speeches across all media channels both during and between general elections.

No one channel of political communication dominated the setting of the news-agenda. Television did not dominate the media landscape to the extent that is regularly assumed. The press rivalled television's ability to set the news-agenda. Radio, though commonly overlooked in accounts of electronic broadcasting, remained significant. All three media tended not to carry verbatim reports of Thatcher's speeches, and thus had the potential to distort the political messages she wished to communicate. Yet, the speechwriting process reveals that Thatcher's speeches were written to exploit the contemporary media landscape. Consequently, Thatcher's speeches remained an effective form of political communication, with the ability to set the news-agenda and affect change. The set-piece speech and the platform from which it was delivered had evolved, but had not declined.

Ronnie Millar, one of the few 'wordsmiths' to write for Thatcher from her earliest days in opposition through to her teary departure from Number 10, recalled the tortuous process of speechwriting. 'The birth of a Thatcher speech', he recalled:

> was a complex and mysterious process [...]. It sort of 'emerged', like the old Conservative Party method of electing a leader. Its origin was part design, part accident and part a host of disconnected and related factors.[67]

Previously overlooked sources pertaining to the construction of Thatcher's words have been considered, and the under-utilized technique of corpora analysis has been used to assess Thatcher's words, to assess this 'mysterious process'[68] in its broadest form. The speechmaking process is revealed to be a key, though hitherto ignored, element in Thatcher's development of policy, both in opposition and in government. Consequently, previously overlooked figures, sidelined in orthodox accounts of Thatcherism, are brought to the fore. In so doing, what is meant by the political label 'Thatcherism' has been questioned, as has Thatcher's and later academics', relationship with the term. The conception of a distinct era, shaped by Thatcher, has been challenged. By setting Thatcher's speechmaking in the media landscape of the 1970s and 1980s the supposed dominance of the electronic media, especially television, has been questioned, as has the corresponding narrative that assumes that the platform, and the immediate audience surrounding it, represented little more than a relic of a previous political age. An assessment of Thatcher's speechmaking then produces conclusions that challenge some of the fundamental assumptions underpinning studies of Thatcher and Thatcherism, and of contemporary British politics more generally.

1

'Defy[ing] analysis'? Thatcher's speechwriting process*

On the afternoon of 25 April 1979, midway through that year's general election campaign, Thatcher was on her knees. Having just removed the curlers from her hair, the soon-to-be prime minister was crawling about her hotel room, brandishing a pair of scissors. The room was a mess, with sections of her upcoming speech strewn about the floor. Sections would be cut out, daubed with glue and applied to other pages. This editing process was conducted at speed. Thatcher was running behind schedule and should have already been on her way to Leith Town Hall, where she was due to deliver the speech. Little wonder then that Ronnie Millar declared that Thatcher's speechwriting process 'defie[d] analysis'.[1]

This chaos is not reflected in Thatcher's recollections of speechmaking. Although she acknowledges that she 'not infrequently' finished writing her speeches in 'a tremendous rush',[2] often involving 'several of us spend[ing] the early evening before the speech crawling around the floor of my room [...] sticking together bits of text with sellotape',[3] she does not give the impression of turmoil. Her recollections of the speechwriting process, characterized as they are by terms such as the 'Home Team'[4] and 'the general rule',[5] suggest that there existed a methodical, rational approach to speechwriting.

Despite Millar's warning, this chapter will analyse the process that led to the 'emerge[nce]'[6] of Thatcher's speeches. Viewed from a broad perspective, Thatcher's speechwriting process was governed by conventions which, although flexible, created an ordered process. Viewed from a narrow perspective, however, the speechwriting process was characterized by 'chaos'.[7] Chaotic speechwriting was not unique to Thatcher. Edward Heath's refusal to engage in speechwriting

16   *Making Speeches*

led to an 'endless process of putting it [speech drafts] in the [prime minister's] box and asking "do you want to talk about it?"'[8] This led to desperate scenes of 'trying to wake the prime minister up at Chequers an hour before the car was due to leave', to take the prime minister to the venue where he was due to deliver his speech.[9] Yet the chaos involved in Thatcher's speechmaking was of a type peculiar to her own personality, and her insistence on close personal involvement in the process. Thatcher's inability to write full speech drafts, a skill that she was unable to master despite fifteen years of practice, not only reveals a vulnerable political leader, at odds with her public persona as the 'Iron Lady', but also slowed the writing process and drove her to consult a wide range of contributors from both the centre and the periphery of political power. By assessing these contributors, this chapter will reveal a range of individuals who, although central to Thatcher's speechwriting, have often been overlooked by current scholarship.[10] In so doing, the definition of 'Thatcher's people', the individuals who conceived, constructed and articulated 'Thatcherism', will be refined.

Thatcher's first party-political speech as leader of the Conservative Party was delivered on the evening of 11 February 1975. Its construction did not suggest any definable speechwriting process. Thatcher prepared for the statement by 'scribbl[ing] some thoughts in the back of [her] diary'.[11] In some ways, this was the product of necessity. Thatcher, in a letter to Edward Boyle (MP for Birmingham Handsworth and holder of various government positions during the 1960s) complained that she had 'too few people of high calibre'[12] on whom she could rely to aid her with tasks such as speechwriting. One aide remembered how, in opposition, Thatcher was 'relatively unknown', and for much of her period in opposition, seemed unlikely to remain the party's leader beyond the next election. As a result, she 'did not have the powers of patronage that an established leader of the opposition would have, let alone a Prime Minister'.[13] Consequently, the recruitment of speechwriters proved trickier in opposition, especially in the early years of opposition, than it would later become.

Yet, years after taking office, Thatcher continued to script her own words for such impromptu statements. On 28 April 1983, Thatcher left Downing Street with Michael Scholar (private secretary to the prime minister, 1981 to 1983). Thatcher was due to begin an official visit to the Midlands the following day.[14] That night she was due to speak to the local Conservative Association. 'As the car drove out of Downing Street', Scholar recalls, Thatcher 'opened her portfolio to look at what she was going to say there and she expected to find a speech, and there was no speech. There were just a few notes.'[15] Thatcher reacted with fury: 'What do we pay all these dumb bunnies for!? [...] I have a speech to so many hundred people and this, this is all they give me!'[16] For the rest of the car journey Thatcher scribbled 'notes on the back of envelopes'.[17]

Thatcher's outburst was unwarranted. It was usual practice, Robin Harris (director of the Conservative Research Department [CRD], 1985–8) remembers, for Thatcher to write a 'small speech' based upon notes provided by political appointments.[18] The same could not be said of 'middling' political speeches, such as the Women's Conservative Party Conference Speech and the Scottish and Welsh Conservative Party Conference Speech.[19] These speeches would be based upon a full speaking text. During the early days of opposition, Thatcher tended to play a significant role in the drafting of such speeches. However, as Adam Ridley (economic adviser to the Conservative Shadow Cabinet, 1974–9) recalled, Thatcher 'contributed less and less' to the early stages of speechwriting as the demands on her time grew.[20] By the late 1970s, the initial drafts of 'middling' speeches would be written by somebody other than Thatcher, usually Chris Patten (director of the CRD, 1974–9) or Nicholas Ridley. Thatcher would then engage with the writing process at a later stage.

Once in government, Thatcher was able to deploy the resources of the Prime Minister's Policy Unit, the head of which played a leading role in producing 'middling' speech drafts. Take, for example, Thatcher's Central Council Speech of 1981. John Hoskyns attended every one of the three speechwriting meetings organized by Thatcher between 26 February and 17 March. The resultant rhetoric, delivered in the wake of the 1981 budget, was characteristically 'Thatcherite'. Attention was drawn to the 'growing internal decline' which, she suggested, began in 1945 and which was 'brought on ourselves by self-deception and self-inflicted wounds'.[21] Thatcher articulated a common theme, advocated by many of 'her people', that 'British decline' could only be reversed if the policy-making orthodoxies, enshrined within the establishment, were overturned. 'I do not greatly care', she continued:

> [W]hat people say about me: I do greatly care what people think about our country. [...] This is the road I am resolved to follow. This is the path I must go [sic]. I ask all who have the spirit – the bold, the steadfast and the young in heart – to stand and join with me as we go forward.[22]

Here, the sense of 'mission', so often identified by commentators as a hallmark of Thatcherite rhetoric, was evident. The minds of many within the party establishment 'boggled' at the 'high drama' evoked by such rhetoric, and the 'radical period of change' it advocated.[23] Given this, it is not surprising that such language had been drafted by the heads of Thatcher's Policy Unit. These men are understood to have epitomized 'Thatcher's people', detached from the party, the wider establishment, or both.[24]

However, such a characterization should not be pushed too far. Hoskyns, although a self-defined 'outsider', was a former officer of the Rifle Brigade and a Wykehamist.[25] Hoskyns' successor, Ferdinand Mount (head of the Number 10 Policy Unit, 1982–3), was also deeply embedded within the establishment. From Oxford to the CRD and then into journalism, Mount's career path was well worn by fellow old Etonians.[26] John Redwood, who replaced Mount as head of the Policy Unit in 1983, was not from a privileged background, but nonetheless progressed from Magdalen College, Oxford and All Souls, to the City, where he became a director at N. M. Rothschild and Sons. Whereas Mount inherited a baronetcy from his uncle, Brian Griffiths' (head of the Number 10 Policy Unit, 1985–90) father was a chauffeur. Nevertheless, Griffiths graduated from the London School of Economics (LSE) and went on to become dean of City University Business School. He was not born into 'the establishment', though he did become a member. Hoskyns and Mount viewed themselves – or at least claimed to view themselves – as 'outsiders', despite the fact that they were born

Figure 1 John Hoskyns led Thatcher's Policy Unit from 1979 until 1982. Like many of Thatcher's early supporters, he saw a rejection of 'the establishment' as being important in creating one's political identity. (Photo by Avalon/Getty Images)

into 'the establishment'. In so doing they were typical of many who surrounded Thatcher, who saw a rejection of 'the establishment' as being necessary for their self-image as belonging to the 'dispossessed right wing'.[27] To define the men who were responsible for the first drafts of many of Thatcher's 'middling' speeches as being detached from 'the establishment' is superficial and of limited value.

The writing of the 1975 Conservative Party Conference Speech, Thatcher's first Conference Speech as leader, defined the process by which her 'major' political speeches were produced. Having discussed the speech with Patten, and others from the CRD, and concluding that they 'were just not getting the message [... she] wanted to despatch',[28] Thatcher decided to write the speech herself, albeit with the inclusion of annotated sections from another draft penned by Alfred Sherman.[29] Although, writing two decades later, Thatcher claimed to have found 'no difficulty' in writing the first draft, the novice party leader was filled with self-doubt.[30] 'Was it a speech?'[31] she asked herself. Unsure of the answer, Thatcher embarked on a process of redrafting. In the same blue biro used to write the first draft, Thatcher re-read the text and proceeded to mark her own work. Ticks were awarded for passages that she felt were exceptionally well-written. Another two redrafts followed, one conducted in black felt-tip and another in a garish pink. Much of the redrafting took place over supper at the house of Woodrow Wyatt (*News of the World* columnist and former Labour Party MP). Although it is difficult to identify Wyatt's influence – some of the language must surely have been his – the draft that Thatcher brought to Blackpool was, as Millar recalls, 'the Leader's original'.[32] Into this draft Patten, Ridley and later Millar, stationed in Thatcher's hotel suite, had to then 'weave' their own rewrites into 'some sort of coherent whole'.[33] This activity proved so challenging that Millar was still putting the finishing touches to the speech twenty minutes before it was delivered.

Out of what Millar labelled diplomatically 'the Blackpool experience' came the principles that would guide the writing of Thatcher's subsequent 'major' political speeches. Thatcher 'no longer attempted to write her own major speeches without help'.[34] The speechwriting process also began earlier. Mount remembered that serious speechwriting sessions would 'start towards the end of July'.[35] 'During the summer recess', Thatcher recalled:

> I would have a meeting to discuss the general themes I should put across in my Conference Speech. Speech contributions were commissioned from ministers, advisers, friendly journalists, and academics.[36]

Thatcher, John O'Sullivan (author and journalist) recalled, 'would not come to the first round' of writing.[37] Instead, 'different draft speech sections' would be written by various ministers and political appointments.[38] It was only 'the weekend before the conference'[39] that Thatcher would become more fully involved in the work of her 'Home Team'.

Thatcher's 'Home Team' evolved over the years as the influence of various individuals waxed and waned. However, its composition remained diverse. The 'Home Team' comprised men such as Ronnie Millar, John O'Sullivan and Robin Harris, all of whom had enjoyed privileged educational backgrounds.[40] It also included Alfred Sherman, a graduate of Chelsea Polytechnic. Sherman, like Millar, had experienced wartime service. He had served in the British Army and Millar in the Royal Navy. Sherman, however, had joined the Communist Party in 1937 (from which he was expelled in 1948) and fought for the Republican Army in Spain. Millar's professional career was separate from the world of politics. He had lived for some time in Hollywood, where he wrote scripts for Metro-Goldwyn-Mayer (MGM) Studios. Harris and O'Sullivan, on the other hand, were politically serious in a conventional sense. Harris was director of the CRD from 1985–9, where he played a central role in drafting the Conservative Party's 1987 manifesto. John O'Sullivan stood unsuccessfully as a Conservative Party candidate in the 1970 general election before pursuing a career in political journalism. Thus, there was no 'typical' member of Thatcher's 'Home Team'.

It was this eclectic mix of characters who oversaw the final drafting of Thatcher's major party-political speeches. Various draft sections 'would be laid out and put together – literally – along the table in the Great Parlour at Chequers'.[41] Here, adjustments would be made to the existing speech sections. O'Sullivan recalls how Thatcher:

> would sometimes lean back and then say, 'here's what I want to say' and to anyone writing the speech, and it was often me … she would say John go off into a side room and get this down.[42]

The speech would thus start to take shape:

> Linking passages would be written and then the still disjointed and often repetitive first draft would be typed up. Everyone would breathe a sigh of relief when they knew that we at least had a speech of some sort; even though past experience suggested that this might bear little relationship to the final text. Then would come the long hours of refining and polishing until midnight, if we were lucky.[43]

It was in the polishing phase that members of the 'Home Team' who possessed a flair for language, men such as Millar for example, would come to the fore.

It was Millar, O'Sullivan recalls, who made important stylistic contributions to Thatcher's speeches, especially the perorations.[44] These contributions became so regular that they acquired a name: 'Ronnification'.[45] 'Major' speeches then, like 'middling' and 'minor' speeches, were produced by using set processes, but these were not necessarily orderly.

On 1 June 1979 Ken Stowe (principal private secretary to the prime minister, 1974–9) circulated a minute which outlined how the newly elected prime minister's speeches were to be written. Once it had been established what 'kind of speech [… Thatcher] required' a 'draft speech' was prepared. This draft would be written by one of Thatcher's private secretaries into whose remit the subject of the speech fell. Thatcher would be provided with this draft 'one week before the event',[46] although, in reality, it was often two weeks before the speech.[47] With its emphasis on providing Thatcher with a first draft upon which she could work, the process set out by Stowe was, in many ways, a continuation of the speechwriting process she had established in opposition.

There was, however, a change in the kind of person who now wrote Thatcher's words. Thatcher now spoke not only as leader of the Conservative Party, but also as prime minister. As such, she was required to deliver governmental speeches, as well as party-political speeches. Given their political neutrality, civil servants were theoretically barred from writing Thatcher's party-political speeches. Instead, they played a leading role in contributing to Thatcher's governmental utterances. This distinction seems to have been taken seriously. When Thatcher was left without a speaking-script for a party-political speech she was due to deliver in April 1983, Michael Scholar, her private secretary, offered to help. 'No, no, this is not for you', Thatcher replied, 'this is a Party thing'.[48]

However, Scholar, who had joined the Treasury in 1969 after graduating from St John's College, Cambridge, played a central role in the drafting of governmental speeches. Scholar remembers how he would 'write a half page or one page note to the Prime Minister' in preparation for a particular speech and how Thatcher 'would usually ignore it'.[49]

Thatcher's lack of engagement was not, Scholar points out, due to any 'inconsiderateness on her part'.[50] It was a matter of time management. Nevertheless, Scholar, like all private secretaries, was expected to continue drafting the speech:

> About a week before [the speech was due to be delivered], I would go to a distant part of the House and … write … the whole … [speech], and I would put it in her box. It would normally come out with nothing at all [meaning that Thatcher had not read, and so had not commented upon, the speech draft].[51]

22 *Making Speeches*

It was not until 'the eve of the speech'[52] that Thatcher would fully engage in the writing process. 'Then', Scholar recalls, he would:

> go up to the flat in Downing Street ... Once the [10pm] news was over she would say, 'come on we've got to get down to it.' [We would write the speech] more or less ... on the hoof. She would say 'Yes, we need to talk about this.' [Somebody] would say something and [she would say] 'no, no, no' or 'yes.' And so it would go on for ... hours.[53]

Scholar estimates that, at times, 'none' of his initial draft made it into Thatcher's final speech.[54] Yet, on occasions, Thatcher delivered material which did originate from the pens of her private secretaries. Take the speech which Thatcher delivered at the 1982 Golden Book Ceremony in Berlin. As this was a speech to be given abroad, the first draft fell to John Coles (private secretary for Foreign and Defence Affairs, 1981–4).[55] Coles had joined the Diplomatic Service in 1960 and rose to become head of the South Asian Department of the Foreign and Commonwealth Office in 1980. It was this draft which came to shape large sections of the final speech.[56]

The shift in speechwriting personnel that accompanied Thatcher's transition from opposition to government was best seen in the drafting of her parliamentary words. As leader of the opposition, Thatcher was, at times, forced to draft her parliamentary rhetoric moments before delivery. Replying to the budget, Ridley recalled, was 'hair-raising'.[57] Convention dictates that the leader of the opposition has only a limited amount of time to prepare their response to the budget. Thatcher therefore went into the Chamber with 'modules' and 'one or two polished phrases' which, drawing on her training as a barrister, would then be stitched together in the moment.[58]

Thatcher much preferred to spend time drafting her parliamentary words. Being uncomfortable with speaking in parliament, she drew on the seasoned parliamentarians in her Shadow Cabinet for assistance. Angus Maude (MP for Stratford-upon-Avon 1963–83, later Paymaster General, 1979–81) whose contributions, informed by his career as a journalist, 'Thatcher valued', drafted the speech she delivered in the No Confidence Debate in March 1977.[59] Although Alfred Sherman had provided Thatcher with an initial draft for her contribution to the Industrial Relations Debate of January 1979, it was the old Etonian Peter Thorneycroft, a member of parliament since 1938, whose draft was approved by the Steering Committee and which formed the basis of the sixteen pages of notes from which Thatcher spoke.[60] Perhaps Thatcher had caught a 'whiff of crackpot-righty' which others had noticed hung 'about old Alfred Sherman', and realized that this would not play well in the Chamber.[61]

Thatcher turned to the 'Gang of Four' to aid with her preparations for Prime Minister's Questions (PMQs). The title, drawing parallels between the ideological dogmatism of Madam Mao's attempted 1976 coup in China and Thatcher's leadership of the Conservative Party, originated from an article which appeared in *Labour Weekly*, written by Julia Langdon. Such parallels were exaggerated, not least because there were never just four individuals involved in the work. Airey Neave (MP for Abingdon, 1953–79 and architect of Thatcher's successful party leadership campaign of 1975), whom Langdon suggested was a member of the 'Gang of Four', rarely attended Thatcher's PMQ briefing sessions. Geoffrey Pattie, Thatcher's two PPSs and a representative of the CRD (none of whom Langdon cited) would be in regular attendance. The term did, however, characterize the fact that the men to whom Thatcher turned were relatively new MPs and, partly as a result, stood detached from the inner circles of the party. Pattie and Gardiner were elected in 1974, Tebbit in 1970. None of these men were members of the Shadow Cabinet.

This group of 'tacticians' would meet twice a week, on Tuesday and Thursday, in the leader of the opposition's office.[62] The meetings would last up to two hours, and end immediately before PMQs. Plied with sandwiches, the briefing team would work to identify Harold Wilson's, and then James Callaghan's, 'weak spots'[63] and to decide upon the consequential 'line of questioning'.[64] 'Questions', Ridley recalled, 'were formulated through discussions. Supplementaries [supplementary questions] were pre-cooked with alternatives available dependent on the answers.'[65] Together, the team would then work to 'hone down her [Thatcher's] questions to the shortest and sharpest formulation that could be devised'.[66] The parliamentary language that Thatcher deployed from the opposition benches, in both PMQs and parliamentary debates, was thus shaped by a defined process, and staffed by individuals drawn from across the political and social spectrum of the parliamentary party.

Once in government, former members of the Shadow Cabinet became occupied with their own departments. Thatcher's private secretaries came to draft Thatcher's significant parliamentary utterances. Coles, Scholar and Rickett contributed to Thatcher's Debate on the Address of the Queen's Speech in 1982. Charles Powell (private secretary to the prime minister, 1983–91) played a central role in drafting Thatcher's parliamentary speeches concerning the Westland Affair.[67] Post-1979, civil servants also took the lead in preparing Thatcher for PMQs, although political appointments were also on hand to provide the 'latest [information] from parliament'.[68] Having established the likely questions in early Monday or Wednesday meetings and retrieved the

24 *Making Speeches*

necessary information, a private secretary such as Rickett would begin to script, or semi-script, Thatcher's words:

> Whilst it was useful to have the factual background [to each anticipated question] and the departments' suggested line of response it was often completely unusable in the House. So you [Rickett] had to put it into plain English and tailor it to how you thought she [Thatcher] would speak.[69]

These suggested lines would be further worked upon in meetings held on the morning of PMQs. The team, Rickett recalls, would:

> sit there and balance our papers on one knee [...] and we would go through all the briefing and [...] we would chew over what response to make and [...] over what words to use.[70]

Although these meetings did not produce scripts (Thatcher's use of the term 'frit'[71] was not pre-scripted, but the product of an off-the-cuff remark and a nod towards the dialect of her home county of Lincolnshire), it could produce phrases which Thatcher deployed during PMQs. This occurred during an exchange between Michael Foot and Thatcher regarding the proposed strike by British Rail workers in 1982. The prime minister accused the leader of the opposition of having 'become, and remain[ing], the strikers' friend'.[72] This phrase had been pre-scripted. As Rickett recalls:

> The Opposition were [...] calling on the government to intervene and impose a solution on British Rail, and so [...] we came up with [...] 'the strikers' friend' [...] and [Thatcher ...] repeated it several times.[73]

On other occasions, Thatcher did enter the House of Commons with fully scripted answers. When these dealt with government policy, such as her responses to questions relating to GCHQ employees, or the Westland Affair, civil servants such as Robert Armstrong (Cabinet secretary, 1979–87) or Charles Powell, would provide scripted answers.[74] Yet, like Wilson, who was mocked by Iain Macleod (shadow chancellor of the exchequer, 1965–70, and then chancellor of the exchequer, June–July 1970) for his speeches that were 'witty, cogent and polished [pause], and polished [pause], and polished',[75] Thatcher's determination to 'always have the right answer',[76] and to base this upon her detailed briefing notes could lead to a stilted rhetorical performance. Rickett recalls how, on one occasion:

> A member of the opposition stood up and simply said 'could the Prime Minister tell us the current rate of unemployment?' [Thatcher ...] started trying to find the figure in her folder [of briefing notes], literally leafing through her folder.

The opposition [...] started chanting 'she doesn't know, she doesn't care' and they got louder and louder as she desperately tried to find this number [...] Eventually she did find the figure.[77]

Effective or otherwise, the answers that Thatcher provided as prime minister during PMQs were created in the same way as the answers she had previously provided during PMQs, as leader of the opposition. Both relied on a small group meeting twice a week to devise her words. This continuity of process seems to be indicative of Thatcher's approach to speechwriting as a whole. Although speechwriters changed during the period 1975–90, the processes governing their work, which varied according to the type of speech being written, did not.

Yet one should be wary of imposing a neatness on Thatcher's speechwriting process and, in so doing, failing to capture the messiness which was the product of political pragmatism. Given that Thatcher was the leader of the Conservative Party, as well as the prime minister, the distinction between party-political speeches and those concerned with government policy could become blurred. For major party-political speeches, which nonetheless dealt with the government's foreign policy, Powell would read and 'edit'[78] drafts written by political appointments. At times, Powell would write the sections of Thatcher's speeches himself. As John Whittingdale (political secretary to Thatcher, 1988 to 1991) recalls, the section of the Party Conference Speech dealing with foreign policy would be 'ring fenced [...] nobody else had any involvement [...] Charles would work on it with her, he used to present it as a sort of complete section.'[79] This would, however, be carried out 'discreetly.'[80] During the drafting of Thatcher's 1985 Party Conference Speech, for example, Powell provided Stephen Sherbourne (political secretary, 1983–8) with 'additional material.'[81] Although Powell's contributions did not make it into Thatcher's final script word-for-word, they did shape the final draft.[82]

Powell was not the only civil servant who contributed, or at least claimed to have contributed to Thatcher's party-political speeches. Rickett recalls how civil servants working close to Thatcher did not feel 'any scruples about crafting phrases that others might think were political in character.'[83] Such ambiguity reflected the absence of clearly defined civil service guidance relating to the writing of prime ministerial set-piece speeches. 'I don't remember any written guidelines or anything like that' Rickett notes:

> The Private Secretaries would be perfectly well aware of what [the] boundaries were ... She [Thatcher] is the Prime Minister even if she happens to be the leader of the Conservative Party as well. And you're there to serve her.[84]

The 'boundaries' described by Rickett depended upon a clear distinction between the role of the civil servant and the political appointment.[85] Such a distinction was blurred in the case of the head of the Policy Unit. The complicated nature of the role was made clear by Clive Whitmore (principal private secretary to the prime minister, 1979–82) who, when inducting Mount into the position, informed him that, although he would be a member of the civil service, this would only be in a 'temporary' capacity, and that although he would be 'subject to its disciplines, the Official Secrets Act and so on, the appointment would cease at the general election'.[86] Thus, paid from the public purse, yet not acting within the hierarchy of the civil service, the head of the Policy Unit occupied a position which was extremely difficult to define yet played a central role in the drafting of Thatcher's set-piece speeches. The Policy Unit's position reflected the messiness of day-to-day speechwriting. Whilst a process certainly did exist, the realities of government meant that the 'general rule[s]' had, at times, to be bent.[87] 'You would not have lasted very long', Rickett recalled, 'if you were too much of a stickler for procedure and protocol'.[88]

Both contemporary and later accounts of Thatcher's speechmaking process tend to suggest that in reality, 'procedures and protocols' did little to shape the construction of Thatcher's words. In a letter to David Wolfson (chief of staff of the Political Office, 1979–85), T. E. Utley (columnist and then chief assistant editor at *The Daily Telegraph* and then, in 1987, columnist at *The Times*) stated, in 1978, that the way Thatcher's speeches were constructed was pure 'madness'.[89] Despite Thatcher's public claims to the contrary, the process did not improve significantly during her eleven years of premiership. It was only in 1990 that Thatcher commented to Millar that 'the speechwriting process seemed to be easier than in some previous years'.[90] According to Tim Lankester (private secretary for economic affairs, 1978–1981), speechwriting was characterized by 'chaos'.[91] Although Mount suggests that 'it is difficult to convey the full horror [...] of speechwriting sessions' Hoskyns comes pretty close when he complained:[92]

> [E]very fibre in my being fights against the waste of time on this bloody speech [1980 Conference Speech]. Hours and days compared with the inadequate time on thinking policy through.[93]

From the perspective of the speechwriter, denied the broader perspective of the historian, working with the prime minister to create speech drafts could certainly seem chaotic. The fact that all who support such a conclusion share the experience of personally writing with the prime minister, suggests that such chaos emanated from Thatcher herself.

Thatcher's contribution to the speechwriting process was characterized by a restless desire to become personally involved in the minutiae of a script. Take Thatcher's speech delivered during her visit to Berlin in 1982. The penultimate draft is covered in annotations made in her usual blue felt-tip pen. These annotations shaped the final speech. The first line of the speech: 'Mr. Mayor, this afternoon, for the first time in my life, I saw the wall. I am repelled' was altered by Thatcher to read, 'Mr. Mayor, this afternoon, for the first time in my life I saw the Wall in all its menacing reality'.[94] The next line is also changed by Thatcher. The original reads: 'It [the Wall] is a grim monument to pitiless oppression and cruelty, but also to futility'.[95] This became: 'It [the Wall] is a grim monument to a cruel and desolate creed. Every stone bears witness to the moral bankruptcy of the society it encloses'.[96] Thatcher was not exaggerating when she stressed that 'every' word in a speech draft was subjected to her 'criticism'.[97]

For some, such as George Urban (journalist and broadcaster), the prime minister's involvement in the speechwriting process engendered respect:

> I found the Prime Minister's energy most impressive. She would flit from topic to topic in search of an incandescent idea or meaningful phrase.[98]

For others, particularly those who were regularly involved in the final writing-up stage, it appears that her fixation on detail added considerably to the tortuous nature of the process. The frustration oozes from the pages of Hoskyns' *Just in Time*: 'She [Thatcher] approached a text *seriatim,* making her first objections within seconds of starting to read'.[99] Denis Thatcher, who had 'heard every possible whinge [… that could be made] about a speech over the years' acted to counter such a tendency.[100] 'Look love, it'll be fine', he told his wife whilst she was re-writing, *again*, the speech she was due to deliver in Birmingham in May 1983.[101] However, all too often it seems that his plea to 'Just read it first, dear!'[102] went unheeded as Thatcher went 'straight into nitpicking detail about specific words'.[103] This led Thatcher to 'unfailingly seek to discard the best bits, while rhapsodising over embarrassingly purple passages'.[104]

This obsessive approach to speechwriting was not unique to Thatcher. Meisel has shown that Churchill too would spend hours agonizing over his speeches. A parliamentary speech lasting forty-five minutes could take up to eighteen hours to prepare.[105] Like Churchill, Thatcher could provide phrases over which she would obsess. Scholar recalls:

> The worst moment [of the speechwriting process] came … when we got to the peroration … [Thatcher] would say, 'I've got to say something really inspirational.' And that is the moment she would reach … for Kipling [or] …

> Longfellow ... she would ... then spend a long time looking through a book. We [the speechwriters] were all sitting there, desperate to go home to bed. And then she would find a poem and you would think 'God, we can't use that.'[106]

This relentless approach to speechwriting could transform the process from a 'social' affair to an endurance test, one that the prime minister, despite her 'Iron Lady' persona, could herself fail.[107] Scholar remembers that the speechwriting process never:

> lasted less than two or three hours ... and she [Thatcher] sometimes would drop off to sleep ... midway through sentences ... We [the speechwriters] would write up the next bit or the last bit quietly then she'd wake up and fire away. If you went to sleep, which I did once, she said 'You've gone to sleep Michael [Scholar]' 'Are you sleeping? Are you tired?'[108]

This intense involvement could be seen as an indication of Thatcher's confidence in the speechmaking process, and of her astute understanding of words and phrases. Thatcher was aware of the political significance of her words, and the way that they could be marshalled to shape the government's policy-agenda (see Chapter 2). Thatcher's attention to detail and phrasing was also the result of her desire not to deliver any points which were factually incorrect and which, under the scrutiny of the news media, could be proved wrong. In 1948 Harold Wilson (then president of the Board of Trade) claimed that 'half the children in my [primary school] class never had boots and shoes on their feet'.[109] This claim was checked, and found to be untrue. The press had a field day and afforded him the epithet 'Barefoot Boy'. This nickname stuck with Wilson for decades. Thatcher, with her eye for detail, was careful not to fall into such a trap. Take, for example, Thatcher's speech to the 1980 Conservative Party Conference. When discussing the 'more than 2 million unemployed', and proving why the figure was misleading, Thatcher had been due to say: 'You can add that today many more married women go to work and their jobs appear in the figures [of the unemployed].'[110] Thatcher was uncomfortable with such a claim, which could quite easily be checked and questioned by the news media. As a result, Thatcher made a last-minute adjustment to the sentence: 'You can add that today many more married women go to work ~~and their jobs appear in the figures~~'.[111] It was this amended wording that Thatcher delivered to the Conference. Thatcher's immersion in the speechwriting process was thus partly a result of her realization that her words would be subject to intense scrutiny and partly a result of her appreciation that her words were able to set the policy-agenda.

Yet an understanding of the potential power of a speech does not automatically equate to an ability to write an effective script, and Thatcher was aware of this. Thatcher's involvement was not a reflection of confidence in her writing ability, or as with Churchill, of an astute, practical knowledge of how language works, but resulted from her lack of confidence in speechwriting. Although Thatcher regularly demonstrated great panache when speaking off-the-cuff and was keen for her speechwriters to include 'clap lines', she showed little confidence in her own abilities when it came to creating set-piece speeches. 'It [speechwriting] wasn't her talent' one speechwriter recalled. 'It wasn't her skill. She really couldn't write very well.'[112] As a result, 'It would be very rare for her to write something. And if she did, it would be pretty hopeless.'[113] Hoskyns too, recalled that 'set piece speeches were not her forte. She had little feel for language.'[114] Thatcher herself admitted, to George Urban, the deep-seated unease she felt about the creation of set-piece speeches. 'When it comes to writing down a speech, I don't like doing it. I find it awkward and rather difficult.'[115] However, 'once a speech has been written for me', she told Urban:

> I've got something to sink my teeth into; I can recast it, I can reorganise it. I can throw out a paragraph, bring a bit from someone else's draft, rephrase the language and taste the words I'm going to use [...] Once I've got that, I revivify the argument [...] But I must have a text in front of me.[116]

This lack of confidence ensured that Thatcher occupied a position where, as she admitted to Urban, she was in 'need [of] help'.[117] Mount noticed this vulnerability and the result it provoked; she felt 'isolated and longed to see a fresh face who could tell her something different'.[118] Thatcher then strove to bring an 'independent outside view' into the process.[119] Such a determination to consult a range of opinion added an element of instability into the writing process.

In opposition, in addition to the usual speechwriters, Patten, Ridley and Millar, were other figures who would 'flit' in and out of the speechwriting process uninvited, yet largely unhindered.[120] Although 'interlopers gained entry only with the authority of her [Thatcher's] beady-eyed secretaries outside, who distinguished between the favoured and the unfavoured', individuals would still 'push into the room [in which a speech was being written]', ostensibly to offer their drafting skills, but in reality as an act of 'self-promotion'.[121] Access to the physical space in which a major speech was being written was the only way in which some could guarantee recognition. Unsolicited draft material would be carefully managed by those close to Thatcher. If the material originated from a respected source, then it stood a chance of influencing the final draft. Ridley, for example, recalls how, in opposition, he would read the contributions of Jock Bruce-Gardyne (author and MP for Knutsford, 1979–83) and would inform Thatcher of any noteworthy phrases that she may want to incorporate into the speech. If the contribution originated from an unfavoured source such as Sherman, then Thatcher's secretaries would be instructed to 'put it straight in the bin'.[122]

This continued into government. Mount recalls how Thatcher's writing sessions were characterized by various contributors who 'would flit in and out of the meetings, offering a page or two, perhaps no more than a paragraph'.[123] The actions of David Hart (businessman and 'wordsmith') illustrate this point. Hart, 'would turn up at odd hours claiming to have a personal message which he must deliver personally to the Prime Minister', no doubt the product of his 'squad of West Indians on roller skates whom at a moment's notice could be dispatched [...] to find out what the word on the street was'.[124] Despite excluding Hart from the writing of the 1983 Conference Speech, on returning from lunch, Mount discovered that 'he had come [back] in and rewritten part of the text'.[125] It is no surprise that Hart came to be seen as a 'fucking nuisance'.[126] It was for this reason that, by the late 1980s, Hart was reduced to sending 'short speeches and thoughts for speeches' through to Thatcher, and 'accepting that lesser, closer courtiers would keep them from her until from time to time he broke through'.[127] On receiving regular calls from David Hart during the 1987 General Election campaign, David Young realized that 'the PM is making me the contact point for all the people she occasionally likes to hear from but not the whole of the time'.[128] For many who occupied the political world, but were not seated at its centre, the 'principal purpose' of entering speechwriting sessions was 'to remind her [Thatcher] of [... one's] existence rather than to contribute anything useful: "I think the main theme of your speech this year, Margaret, should be to remind the country of the amazing things your leadership has achieved for every single one of us" etc. etc'.[129] Such interventions were made possible due to Thatcher's unease at speechwriting and thus her willingness to turn to a 'fresh face'.[130]

At first glance, the informality governing the contributions of men such as Hart also characterized the contributions of those who existed further from the centre. Men such as George Urban were invited to participate informally. On one occasion, Thatcher, 'in parting', wondered whether Urban could suggest 'some ideas for her Party Conference Speech and then for the Lord Mayor's Dinner in the Guildhall'.[131] In the case of the speech Thatcher gave to the Winston Churchill Foundation Award Dinner (1983), Urban was recruited into the speechwriting team through an informal request, a result of Thatcher telling 'Charlie Douglas-Home [Editor of *The Times*, 1982–5] that she was looking for fresh ideas for two important speeches she was about to make'.[132] Apparently:

> [A] broadly shared political platform and the right personal chemistry were enough to induce her to entrust her unceasing search for fresh thoughts to a small number of private sympathisers.[133]

However, although peripheral figures were approached in an informal manner, the approach was always initiated from the centre. Preparing for a speech Thatcher was due to give to the Finance House Association in January 1979, Ridley was told to 'get hold of Nicholas Goodison [chairman of the London Stock Exchange, 1976–86] and see if he might contribute'.[134] Ridley did, but was disappointed. 'The results of his labours', he informed Thatcher, 'were, to be candid, disappointing'.[135] Mount recalled how, in government during the writing of the 1983 Conference Speech, Thatcher 'implore[d that] Matthew Parris [...] be pressed into service'.[136] It was not Parris who initiated his own contribution. Urban's account reveals a similar story. Shortly before leaving on a family holiday, he received a telephone call from Charles Powell, who informed him that the prime minister had had a draft for her United States Congress Speech (1985) provided by the FCO, but that she 'didn't like [it] much. It was too matter-of-fact and too pedestrian. She thought that I [Urban] might supply some inspiration and "poetry"'.[137] Powell wondered whether Urban 'would [...] like to send us [Number 10] anything that you think would be relevant to the occasion and would lift the speech above our immediate concerns'.[138] Urban was included on the whim of Number 10 and, just as easily, rejected. Despite having cooperated with the prime minister's wishes, Urban realized, on failing to secure an invitation to a further writing session, that 'the [speechwriting] circle was widening. I was being left out. This was disappointing but not unexpected.'[139]

The same control from the centre, governing which peripheral figures would, or would not be permitted to contribute to Thatcher's speeches was also evident in the creation of speeches dealing with government policy. Here, private secretaries played the role of gatekeeper. Laurens van der Post, an author and expert on Southern Africa, wrote to Michael Alexander (Thatcher's diplomatic private secretary, 1979–82) with a suggestion for Thatcher's speech to the Franco-British Council in 1980. Alexander wrote back to inform van der Post that 'the Prime Minister did not use a great deal of your material'.[140] In an effort to soften the blow, Alexander speculated on van der Post's prospects in relation to Thatcher's upcoming Guildhall Speech. Although he 'had not yet discussed this [the speech] in any detail yet' he would try to:

> persuade her [Thatcher] that there should be a paragraph or so about the situation in Southern Africa [...] Obviously [...] I cannot guarantee that your suggestions would be accepted.[141]

Thus, peripheral figures were controlled from the centre. Those who attempted to involve themselves, uninvited, in Thatcher's speechwriting, struggled to make their contributions count. Nevertheless, Thatcher's vulnerability when it came to writing set-piece speeches, her 'uncertainty about how to judge the quality of a draft'[142] led to Thatcher 'bringing in dozens of other cooks etc.'[143] which, from Hoskyns' point of view, ruined the broth.

Recalling Thatcher's approach to preparing for PMQs during the period 1975–9, one aide recalled that although the process 'did not function that well it didn't seem to change over time'.[144] This observation could be applied just as well to the processes used by Thatcher to construct all her speeches from 1975–90. Thatcher's political speeches, in opposition and in government, were scripted by political appointments in accordance with the speeches' status. 'Minor' speeches were delivered from notes, whereas 'major' speeches followed the tortuous scripting process, established after the writing of Thatcher's 1976 Conference Speech. In opposition, Thatcher's parliamentary language was drafted by individuals drawn from across the parliamentary party. In government, civil servants came to dominate the construction of such speeches, as well as set-piece speeches dealing with governmental themes. Thus, process seems to have guided the construction of Thatcher's public language.

Viewed from the perspective of the speechwriter however, it appears that Thatcher's speechwriting was indeed chaotic. Instability stemmed not only from the indistinct boundaries between speechwriters, but from Thatcher herself. Contrary to the popular perception of Thatcher being self-assured and, at times, presidential in her leadership style, the prime minister, rightly, doubted her ability to draft speeches.[145] This gave rise to her tendency to fixate upon words, phrases and half-remembered quotes, keeping her speechwriters from their beds and slowing the speechwriting process. Millar's re-writing of the words of W. S. Gilbert neatly sums up the experience of speechwriting for Thatcher:

> A wand'ring wordsmith, I.
> A thing of shredd-ed speeches
> Of seaside towns and beaches
> And when are we going to bed?[146]

Thatcher's insecurity in speechwriting drove her to reach out to a great number of contributors. Contributions from peripheral figures were centrally managed either by her private secretaries or by her political private secretary. However, such control was not evident for those closer to the centre. The writing of significant party-political speeches could be seriously destabilized as the 'Home Team' were constantly interrupted by, and forced to respond to, unsolicited contributions offered by individuals operating outside the central writing team.

An analysis of these individuals calls into question the definition of Thatcher's inner circle as being composed of men who existed 'on the margins' of the establishment, men who were not 'public schoolboys, Anglican, or from the south of England'.[147] Such a reductionist definition, based as it is on the nebulous term 'establishment', is of limited use when analysing Thatcher's 'wordsmiths'. Whilst Sherman conformed completely to such a definition, most did not. The men called upon to write Thatcher's speeches cannot be characterized by generalities. Social background mattered little when writing for Thatcher. All were forced to work into the early hours of the morning, to fend off unwanted speech contributions and to prompt Thatcher to abandon her fixation upon a particular phrase. Millar was correct to suggest that the birth of a Thatcher speech was a 'complex and mysterious process'.[148] Yet, as this chapter has demonstrated, it does not follow that Thatcher's speechwriting 'defies analysis'.[149]

2

'Policy hostages'. Speechmaking and the policy-agenda*

Thatcher occasionally drafted her own speeches, but usually employed speechwriters.[1] As a prime minister, she was not unique in this respect. Stanley Baldwin was perhaps the first prime minister to regularly use speechwriters, the most notable of whom was the deputy secretary to the Cabinet, Tom Jones. Baldwin, like Thatcher, found speechwriting difficult. Writing to Jones, Baldwin admitted that 'I have never acquired the art of continuous composition', although he noted that 'I do the occasional good patch amidst yards of bilge'.[2] This practice raised questions over the authenticity of Baldwin's pronouncements. Neville Chamberlain could not think 'how S.B. [Stanley Baldwin] can bear to read out other people's speeches'.[3]

Given the similarity between Thatcher's and Baldwin's approach to speechwriting, it seems legitimate to question the authenticity of Thatcher's public, political statements. To do so raises questions over the way in which Thatcher's speechmaking is perceived. Throughout her memoirs, Thatcher suggests that she used her public speeches to shape the policy-agenda. Public utterances were used to 'push reluctant colleagues further than they would otherwise have gone', a point with which her colleagues, reluctantly or otherwise, agree.[4] Commentators concur with this interpretation. Anthony King for example, suggests that Thatcher's leadership should be understood as an example of 'declarative leadership'; 'the declaration of the ends first, the means to follow'.[5] This supports the suggestion that 'Thatcherism' was defined by 'Mrs Thatcher's views, prejudices and style'.[6] Yet, if Thatcher's words were drafted by others, and did not necessarily correspond with her own political ambitions, then any suggestion that she used her speeches to imprint her 'views' upon the party and on government becomes difficult to sustain.

36 *Making Speeches*

Thatcher understood that her public, political language was part of the process of setting the policy-agenda, not simply an expression of it. On occasion, Thatcher used silence as a means of affecting policy. Lawson's decision to cut interest rates to 7.5 per cent in 1988 was the result of Thatcher's refusal to declare her support for her chancellor's decision to allow the pound to rise.[7] More often she used 'public statements' to 'advance the argument'.[8] In her discussion of the Great Education Reform Bill (1987), Thatcher used her set-piece speeches as a means of opening another front in the policy-battles taking place behind closed doors. Baker (education secretary, 1986–9) was concerned about the logistical feasibility of any rush towards schools deserting the support provided by local authorities. Consequently, Baker refused to predict publicly how many schools would opt out of local authority control, and by when. Thatcher did not agree with such a cautious approach. To force the pace, she declared, 'I think [...] most schools will opt out'.[9] This line was reinforced in her 1987 Conservative Party Conference Speech. Addressing her audience, Thatcher declared her intention to 'create a new kind of school funded by the State, alongside the present state schools and the independent private schools. These new schools', she continued, 'will be independent state schools. They will bring a better education to many children because the school will be in the hands of those who care most for it and for its future'.[10] '"Independent state schools" was just a phrase', O'Sullivan remembers, 'but the fact that it was fought over so bitterly [during the speechwriting process] suggests that [... this] phrase [... was] very important'.[11] Against the wishes of the Department of Education and Science, and of Baker, both of whom were concerned that the phrase's association with fee-paying independent schools could fuel criticism, and that its use would accelerate unhelpfully the implementation of the reforms, Thatcher 'insisted' on using the phrase.[12] In so doing, 'Margaret', Baker recalled, 'rather strayed from the script'.[13] This was not an isolated event. By 1990, members of Thatcher's Cabinet were growing tired of her tendency to fire 'off [...] policy commitments [in public] without any consultation whatsoever'.[14]

In opposition Thatcher would use public statements to shape the party's policy platform. 'Margaret', Howe recalled, 'became increasingly adept at using unheralded public utterances as the means of signalling a policy shift'.[15] On 30 January 1978 during an interview with *World in Action*'s Gordon Burns, Thatcher declared: 'people are really rather afraid that this country might be rather swamped by people with a different culture'. 'Therefore', she continued, 'we have got to [... hold] out the prospect of an end to immigration'.[16] Thatcher claimed that her utterances represented a continuation of 'what Willie Whitelaw said at the Conservative Party Conference in Brighton [in 1976]'.[17] Whitelaw had actually stated that the party must 'follow a policy which is clearly designed to work towards the end of immigration *as we have seen it in these post-war years*' [author's italics].[18] That a copy of Whitelaw's speech had been included in the pre-interview briefing pack, and that Thatcher had read and marked the transcript, suggests that she knew full well that her remarks were not in line with the party. Her statement was designed to undermine the influence that Andrew Rowe's policy position (director of community affairs at Conservative Central Office) was achieving in the vacuum created by Whitelaw's unhurried approach to policy formation.[19] Rowe understood the immigration 'problem' as being the product of those with an 'irrational fear' of 'strangers in our midst'.[20] Consequently, his *The Way Ahead*, published in January 1978, cautioned against employing populist language. He warned against phrases such as 'stemming the flood'.[21] That Thatcher proposed a policy platform based upon a very different conceptualization of immigration and did so using exactly this type of populist language, 'swung the argument her way'.[22] As 'a direct result' of Thatcher's words, Howe recalled, 'Willie [Whitelaw] was obliged to tighten our policy' on immigration.[23]

Thatcher's declaration of a particular policy position did not guarantee that 'she got her way'.[24] This was evident in Thatcher's attempts, during late 1978, to shift the party's position on incomes policy. Unlike debates around immigration and race, debates concerned with incomes policy were a central issue for the party, and one which generated significant differences. Many, including Heath, felt an incomes policy to be unpalatable, but an unavoidable mechanism for controlling inflation. Thatcher however, but not necessarily those considered to be 'Thatcherites', believed that controlling the supply of money would reduce the level of inflation. An incomes policy was therefore not only unpalatable, but unnecessary. On 10 October 1978 Thatcher told ITN's Julian Haviland: 'If we're really going as a result of incomes policies to expect an extra x per cent every year for no extra output, then we're going to have inflation forever'.[25] This attempt to reorientate the party on the issue of incomes policies was immediately countered by Heath. Reinforcing the point that he had made from the floor of the Party Conference, Heath appeared on the BBC's *News at Ten* and declared that '[f]ree collective bargaining' would lead to nothing but 'massive inflation'.[26] Thatcher did not give ground. In her Conference Speech, delivered on 13 October, she made clear that, if elected, her government would return to wage bargaining 'free from government interference'.[27] Thatcher had declared her favoured position and, despite opposition from within the party, stuck by it.

Yet, unlike her pronouncements on immigration, it failed to make an immediate impact upon the party's policy-agenda. The *Conservative Campaign Guide Supplement* (1978) raised the failures of Labour's incomes policies, but little detail was offered about the Conservative Party's suggested response. It vaguely suggested that a future Conservative government would encourage 'better methods of collective bargaining'.[28] This was not only the product of a strategic decision on Thatcher's part, but also of the context in which she operated. The late 1970s were marked by 'a constant feeling that the [Labour] government might fall off the rails'.[29] In such a climate, Thatcher's words were required to fulfil two, often competing, functions: to reorientate the party's policy-agenda and to ensure that this agenda was well-received by the electorate. She was denied the luxury afforded to the prime minister who, at the beginning or mid-point of the electoral cycle, could disregard the 'electoral difficulties'[30] caused by unpopular policy statements. Thatcher led an ideologically divided Shadow Cabinet who would only acquiesce to policy shifts if they were seen to be electorally advantageous. Objections to Thatcher's declarations on immigration policy were mitigated by the eleven-point poll lead that validated her position. In contrast, the electorate appeared to reject Thatcher's position on incomes policy. By the end of October, the Conservative Party's lead in the polls had vanished and Labour took a 5.5 percentage lead. In November a NOP poll showed that if Heath was to return to lead the party, then the Conservatives would establish a 14 percentage point lead over Labour. Thatcher may well have declared her favoured 'ends' but, operating within the constraints imposed upon the leader of the opposition, this did not guarantee that the 'means' immediately followed.

But, in many cases, follow they did, albeit over the longer term. In January 1979 Thatcher was interviewed by Brian Walden. When pushed by Walden to clarify how a future Conservative government would go about 'curbing the unions' negotiating powers', Thatcher responded by taking Walden through a series of proposals, one of which included the possibility of introducing a strike ballot.[31] Social security support would be withheld, Thatcher suggested, from strikers whose action had not been mandated by a ballot. This contradicted the party's position. The previous day, Jim Prior (shadow secretary of state for employment, 1975–9) had stated that compulsory strike ballots were 'not something that you can make compulsory in any way'.[32] Thatcher recalled how the interview marked the moment that she 'had broken ranks' with her Shadow Cabinet's position on trade unions.[33] Yet, despite proposing some potentially 'radical' policy options, Thatcher avoided making any firm policy commitments.[34] She told Walden how she was 'flinching from legislation'.[35] Commentators have come to attach less significance to the interview than Thatcher did.[36] After all, the 1979 election manifesto did not commit the Conservative Party to statutory strike ballots. Her suggestion of holding a referendum on the unions' power never materialized.[37] Some of Thatcher's oppositional language then made little immediate impact upon the party's policy platform. It should perhaps be viewed as 'mere rhetoric', evidence of the pragmatism and caution that scholars have identified in Thatcher's oppositional actions, which appear to undermine the triumphal accounts of Thatcherism.[38] As one commentator put it, Thatcher's early 'rhetoric was radical [...] but from the start her deeds have shown [an...] instinctive caution'.[39]

However, for Thatcher, it was her use of radical rhetoric that gave the interview significance. Early in the interview, Thatcher informed Walden that she, if elected as prime minister, would 'grasp ... [the] nettle' of trade union power.[40] Walden assumed Thatcher's phrase referred to the proposal of new policy 'possibilities'.[41] This was a misunderstanding. For Thatcher, 'grasp[ing] ... [the] nettle' meant that she, as party leader, was now willing to discuss the issue in public, something that the party had been 'afraid' to do 'for [the past] four years'.[42]

It was this change in tone, rather than the declaration of a specific policy that, for Thatcher, marked her breaking of rank, and which shaped the party's policy-agenda in the longer term. Whilst the Shadow Cabinet agreed that the unions' power needed to be curbed, few felt that it was wise to articulate this in public. The party adopted 'a note of moderation and quietness' when discussing the issue.[43] 'The official line', John Hoskyns recalled, 'seemed to be say and do nothing that might jeopardise election prospects'.[44] This, he suggested, led to 'paralysis' in policy-making.[45] Thatcher's abandonment of 'moderation and quietness' acted to validate policy options which previously had remained unspeakable, quite literally. Although Thatcher informed Walden that she was 'reluctant to impose' strike ballots, she caveated this statement with the words, 'at the moment'.[46]

The suggestion of mandatory ballots was rejected by Prior the following day and was not included in the Employment Act of 1980. But Thatcher's words had broken the 'paralysis'. Private discussions surrounding the formulation of the 1980 Act acknowledged that strike ballots were 'the only thing that mattered in the long-term'.[47] Tebbit, who replaced Prior as secretary of state for employment in 1981, avoided including legislation designed to democratize the unions in his 1982 Employment Act as he felt this to be a 'bridge too far'.[48] But he did go on to advocate compulsory ballots in 1983.[49] These suggestions were subsequently included in the party's 1983 manifesto, and realized in the Employment Act of 1984.[50]

Of course, the legislation of 1984 was not a direct result of the words uttered by Thatcher in January 1979. Nevertheless, Thatcher's abandonment of 'moderation and quietness' over the issue of strike ballots revealed her trait, identified by O'Sullivan, of 'provoking the discussion of things that had hitherto simply been ignored'.[51] Thatcher's oppositional rhetoric, at times appearing nothing more than radical rhetoric, could affect the policy-agenda not immediately, but in the longer term.

O'Sullivan is correct to suggest that 'sometimes policy had to reflect [... Thatcher's] rhetoric'.[52] Consequently, after Thatcher's election victory in 1979, the drafting of government speeches became a means by which Number 10 could assert its dominance over the fiefdoms of government departments. Thatcher told her private secretaries that, when making contributions to speeches, they were expected 'to do my [Thatcher's] bidding'.[53] A 'tussle'[54] between Whitehall and Number 10 took place during the construction of the Bruges Speech, and its articulation of Britain's relationship with Europe. It had been envisaged that the acceptance of the College of Europe's invitation for Thatcher to deliver a speech would offer an opportunity for the prime minister 'to spell out her own vision of the future development of Europe, rather than leaving the field clear to others who chose to propagate the myth that her attitude was an entirely negative one'.[55] It was towards this end that the initial FCO-inspired draft worked. Despite John Kerr (assistant under secretary at the Foreign and Commonwealth Office, 1987–90) realizing that the 'No.10 market for constructive language on the Community may still be poor' there was still the assumption that a 'constructive outcome' could be achieved.[56]

However, on reading the draft prepared by Number 10, 'the Secretary of State's overall comment was that there are some plain and fundamental errors in the draft'.[57] There then ensued a form of speech ping-pong as drafts were sent back and forth between Number 10 and various government departments. So seriously was this process taken that 'victory' was precisely judged. Howe remembered that a note attached to the second draft sent back to Number 10 asserted that Powell had bought '80 per cent' of earlier FCO suggestions and thus the fresh objective of the FCO was to 'secure another 10 per cent'.[58] Although Howe had removed any mention of 'the United States of Europe'[59] from the text, he remembered that the final speech 'contained a number of sections where the original Powell draft had actually been strengthened', and with it, the policy

Speechmaking and the Policy-Agenda

direction favoured by Number 10.[60] The 'gloss' that Bernard Ingham had given the speech when briefing the press strengthened Thatcher's desired policy position still further.[61] Howe recalls the long-term impact of the Bruges Speech:

> Where Margaret had drawn the first bucket of Euro-scepticism at Bruges; others were all too ready to follow. Margaret herself began to return, again and again, to the well which she had reopened. She began readopting arguments which she and I had had no difficulty in rebutting in debates over the Single European Act only a couple of years before.[62]

The prime minister's adoption of euro-sceptic language afforded the associated policy-agenda 'new respectability'.[63] This was perhaps best seen in Thatcher's performance in the House of Commons on 30 October 1990. 'The President of the Commission, Mr. Delors', began Thatcher:

> said at a press conference the other day that he wanted the European Parliament to be the democratic body of the Community, he wanted the Commission to be the Executive and he wanted the Council of Ministers to be the Senate. No. No. No.[64]

In response to this, 'Anti-Europeans on the back benches', Howe recalled:

> were cheering loudly by now and beginning to infect their neighbours with enthusiasm. It could hardly be 'unsound', they began to think, to respond positively to such strong signals from one's own Prime Minister.[65]

The effect of the prime minister's legitimatization of the euro-sceptic position came to have significant political ramifications. Although Thatcher's language, first used publicly at Bruges, did not lead to any one specific policy, it did signal a rejection of the pro-monetary union position agreed in a series of meetings between Thatcher, Howe and Lawson in June 1989.

Equally, speechmaking offered departments the opportunity to resist the policy-agenda championed by Number 10. The British government's support for German unification rested not upon what Thatcher said, but upon what she did not say. Sir Patrick Wright (permanent under-secretary at the Foreign Office, 1986–91) wrote to Stephen Wall (private secretary to the foreign secretary, 1988–91) concerned that 'on at least three occasions recently, the Prime Minister has [privately] aired her misgivings about German reunification in very stark terms'.[66] 'There is no doubt', Wright continues, 'that the Prime Minister's views, if they became known, would raise eyebrows (at least) both in Germany and in the United States'.[67] So desperate was the FCO to expunge Thatcher's private language that Wright 'arranged for her remarks on this subject to be removed from the record produced by the Commonwealth Secretariat'.[68] With the exception of her interview with the *Wall Street Journal* in January 1990 (where she was quite clear in her opposition to unification) it appears that the FCO were successful in tempering the public language used by Thatcher to discuss German reunification. Douglas Hurd recalled how, when Chancellor Kohl visited London in March 1990 'the Prime Minister exerted herself to make sure the visit was a success'.[69] A crucial part of this was the way Thatcher discussed the German Question in public. She asserted that 'all of us [are] taking part in that great unification process and bringing it to fruition'.[70] The FCO, like all of those involved in the machinery of government, were aware of the potential impact of the *public* language the prime minister used, or did not use, especially in the context of prepared set-piece speeches and the effect it could have on the perception (and therefore direction) of policy.

What Thatcher chose not to say in her speeches was also politically significant. This is best illustrated in her interaction with Nigel Lawson during the storm around her inability to 'bring herself to indicate that she agreed with her Chancellor' over his interventionist policies intended to stabilize sterling during 1988.[71] During PMQs on 12 May, Thatcher failed to supply a positive reply to Neil Kinnock's question, 'Does the Right Hon. Lady agree with the point that the Chancellor made [that the pound could not be allowed to continue to rise]?'[72] In an attempt to rectify the situation, Lawson and Thatcher set about a 'prolonged drafting session' in which was written the reply to Kinnock's inevitable repetition of the question the following week.[73] According to Lawson, he wrote the first draft which, characteristically, Thatcher rejected, taking 'up her pen and a piece of paper and embarking on a fresh draft of her own'.[74] Lawson recollects how Thatcher suggested that 'the best way to strengthen the effect of the proposed reply to Kinnock [...] was not to alter the draft but to accompany it by half a point cut in interest rates'.[75] To his 'eternal regret', Lawson wrote, 'I accepted'.[76] As a result the interest rate cut did accompany the agreed reply given to Kinnock the following week, in which Thatcher publicly declared that 'it would be a great mistake to think at any time that sterling was a one-way bet'.[77] 'Our back-benchers were delighted', remembered Lawson, although 'if only she [Thatcher] had been able to utter that single monosyllable [yes] five days earlier, there would have been no need for the prepared answer on 17th May'.[78] Whether this would have also mitigated the need for the interest rate cut to 7.5 per cent, a decision reversed a fortnight later, is a moot point. Yet it is clear that the drafting of Thatcher's words (whether said or unsaid) and the setting of the policy-agenda were closely related.

Consequently, those involved in speechwriting were endowed with significant political influence. When preparing for her first major public statement on foreign policy, delivered in Chelsea in July 1975, Thatcher turned not to Reginald Maudling, but instead to Robert Conquest. Tellingly, O'Sullivan, quoting lines from the speech years later, noted that 'these are his [Conquest's] words'.[79] Conquest, viewed by Maudling as a 'fanatic', was 'politically close' to Thatcher (he dedicated *Present Danger* to her, a book on which she drew heavily during speechwriting sessions) and thus bolstered her views.[80]

This was not always the case. There were several moments during the period 1975–9 when Thatcher professed to feeling unease, even anger, when delivering statements which did not align with her own personal stance.[81] On 17 January 1979 viewers watched Thatcher deliver a Party Political Broadcast (PPB) in which she declared that the '[Labour] government and [the] opposition should make common cause on this one issue [of trade union reform]'.[82] In private Thatcher felt uneasy with such a position. She feared that she was being forced to promote a 'one nation Tory message' and, as a result, scolded the script's author, Ronnie Millar.[83] 'No' she told him, 'You don't join hands with a government you are trying to overthrow except in wartime'.[84]

The discrepancy between Thatcher's personal belief and her stated position continued into government. The 1983 Party Conference Speech was drafted in large part by John Gummer. It articulated what some perceived to be his 'wet' line of thinking. It was Gummer who suggested that Thatcher declare: 'the National Health Service is safe with us'.[85] 'It was immediately clear', Mount remembers, 'that it was not what she wished to say' and, as a result, 'it was impossible to make her say it as if she really meant it […] it came out in the listless drone of a hostage reading a statement prepared by her captors – which is what it was'.[86] And it was the 'captors' policy-agenda that was realized. Rickett recalls how he 'would give her [Thatcher] figures which showed how expenditure on the National Health Service had increased in real terms under her government'. These figures were then used 'quite a lot'.[87] Thatcher would 'go on about how … [spending on the NHS] had gone up … as evidence of the NHS being safe with her'. 'After a while', having repeated the phrase, and the statistics to validate it, Thatcher began to 'run out of room for manoeuvre'.[88] Thatcher's speechwriters had the ability to 'put words in Mrs Thatcher's mouth',[89] words that did not always chime with her personal position, but which could nonetheless affect the policy-agenda.

The Times was right to suggest that to become one of Thatcher's trusted speechwriters was to acquire a 'position of influence'.[90] This bred intense competition. Millar, Peter Stothard (journalist and friend of Ronnie Millar) recalls, was 'jealous of her [Thatcher's] attention [won via speechwriting]. He deplored rivals and knew how to make her deplore them too'.[91] He 'would never', for example, 'let David [Hart]' have access to the 'Home Team'.[92] Stothard's recollections relate to the mid-1980s. But it was during the early 1980s, when the party was in government and fraught with ideological strife, when Thatcher's words carried such political weight that the competition between 'wordsmiths' was at its height. Alfred Sherman had recognized early on the political influence provided by speechwriting and made efforts to involve himself in the process. In 1977 Sherman wrote to Thatcher outlining what he considered to be the six 'disparate capabilities'[93] he felt a speechwriter should possess. With characteristic Shermanite modesty he informed her that 'within this framework, I think I might be able to do more than help'.[94] Sherman took the crafting of prime ministerial speeches very seriously indeed, noting that 'we [the speechwriting team] fought over every word'.[95] Sherman remembers how during early speechwriting sessions 'doctrinal disputes' would rage as:[96]

[Chris] Patten and Adam Ridley of the CRD fought to keep the speech as far as possible within pre-Thatcherite parameters. John Hoskyns and I fought to keep it as Thatcherite as possible, generally supported by David (now Lord) Wolfson.[97]

It is interesting that, in describing the scene, Sherman portrays an 'us and them' mentality. Patten and Ridley are discussed almost as one person, both used as personifications of the CRD and the policy direction it proclaimed. The same can be said for his description of himself, Hoskyns and David Wolfson (Thatcher's chief of staff, 1979–85), all of whom are grouped together and used to personify the 'Thatcherite' element within the party. The act of speechwriting then provided a forum in which these opposing political wings of the party could fight over the position, shape and content of the politically significant prime minister's speech. Sherman was therefore unwilling to compromise. This ultimately led to his exclusion from the speechwriting team. By the later years of Thatcher's first government and the pragmatism which came with office, Sherman 'would only last a session or two before denouncing the proposed text as trivial and banal and annoying Mrs Thatcher so much that he was told not to come back'.[98]

The twin struggle of personal ambition and political advancement, so evident in Sherman's behaviour, is exemplified in John Hoskyns, who became increasingly protective of his position within the 'Home Team'. Hoskyns became alert to the threat posed by other 'people [being] anxious to be part of it all [the speechwriting process], and thus *threatening* [author's italics] to help'.[99] Indeed, Hoskyns' recollections of the speechwriting process are peppered with concerns about individuals manoeuvring themselves into the speechwriting team. That Hoskyns recalls, with a degree of cattiness, the supposed pettiness of others, indicates that Hoskyns, like the speechwriters he writes about, was prone to the same insecurity and politically motivated jealousy. In 1979 for example, Hoskyns noted:

> Adam [Ridley was] anxious to be involved in the night-time [speechwriting] session, saying that he'd have to make his economics comments personally so they could be settled, rather than let me [Hoskyns] have them in writing. I wish I didn't have to get involved with such time-wasting charades with people who worry so much about these small things.[100]

Hoskyns was again forced to jockey for position two years later when writing Thatcher's 1981 Party Conference Speech. Days before the speech was due to be delivered Heath stated that the only alternative to a reversal in the government's economic policy would be 'to drag on down the dreary path of ever-deepening recession'.[101] Hoskyns reacted by declaring that 'we may really have to destroy him [Heath] in the [Conference] speech'.[102] This positioning of the speech was, however, contested by John Gummer who was certainly no advocate of the 'Thatcherite' policy-agenda promoted by the Policy Unit. His presence concerned Hoskyns. Gummer, Hoskyns recorded in his diary, was continually 'trying to take control of events'.[103] Even though Hoskyns' and Millar's 'Thatcherite' speech draft had been 'largely agreed', Gummer, utilizing the pragmatic caution expressed by Clive Whitmore, was able to persuade Thatcher to reject it.[104] 'The result', remembered Millar, 'was far reaching. Much of the draft was discarded and a new one written, not by us [but by Gummer].'[105]

The change in political emphasis brought about by Thatcher's decision to reject Hoskyns' draft in favour of Gummer's was picked up on by commentators. The *Daily Express* reported that after 'delivering her prepared speech to the conference Mrs Thatcher promptly left the hall to deliver a second, unprepared script to an overflow crowd'.[106] It was in this second speech which, being unprepared and thus free of any words penned by Gummer, and perhaps the pragmatic concerns aired by the ideologically detached Whitmore, that Thatcher was thought to have 'displayed the real, the genuine Thatcher, throwing the caution of her speechwriters to the wind'.[107]

Gummer, like Sherman and Hoskyns, saw the drafting of the 1981 Conference Speech as a means by which he could advance his own political agenda. It was for this reason that he saw Millar as a potential threat. Although Millar was understood to have little interest in politics, by being so close personally to the prime minister, he occupied a 'unique' position.[108] Thatcher listened to his 'sound political instinct' and 'wise council'.[109] It was Millar, along with Hoskyns, who penned the line 'You turn if you want to, the lady's not for turning' which, in the context of the fractious 1980 Party Conference, had significant political resonance.[110] Francis Pym realized the full political magnitude of the phrase: 'why the hell does she keep on saying that she's not for turning, etc. etc.?'[111] Such language, he realized, 'cut off so many [policy] possibilities'.[112] It was because of Millar's potential political influence that 'Ronnie and John [Gummer] ... developed a strong, though mostly cloaked, mutual dislike'.[113] This led to Gummer's successful lobbying of Thatcher to exclude Millar because his 'thespian interruptions' were hindering the speechwriting process.[114] However, as would be expected of any half-decent courtier, Millar was determined not to become marginalized:

> Ronnie turned up [to the speechwriting session] all the same ... The Prime Minister shot behind the sofa, crouching slightly so she could not be seen, beckoning me to follow her. Ronnie put his head round the door but, seeing nobody in the study, withdrew.[115]

Although the accuracy of this anecdote is questionable, it nonetheless serves to illustrate that the speechwriting process was understood as a factional affair. For example, the 1981 Conference Speech, *The Guardian* reported, 'had been drafted by ... a deeply divided committee', split between 'the hard-liners and the advocates of old-fashioned Tory compassion'.[116] To view the speechwriting process through such a prism is to misunderstand the near apolitical nature of men such as Millar. However, the comment is indicative of the way many, including some of the speechwriters themselves, viewed Thatcher's speechwriting process. In making common cause with Hoskyns, Millar, in the eyes of those such as Gummer and Mount, was part of the 'opposition' and thus a potential obstacle to desired policy direction. Prime ministerial speeches then were not simply benign 'add-ons' to government but were, at times, integral and influential factors in conveying and defining various policy-agendas. For men such as Hoskyns, Gummer and Sherman, ideological concerns came to shape the speechwriting process and, they hoped, the resultant policy-agenda.

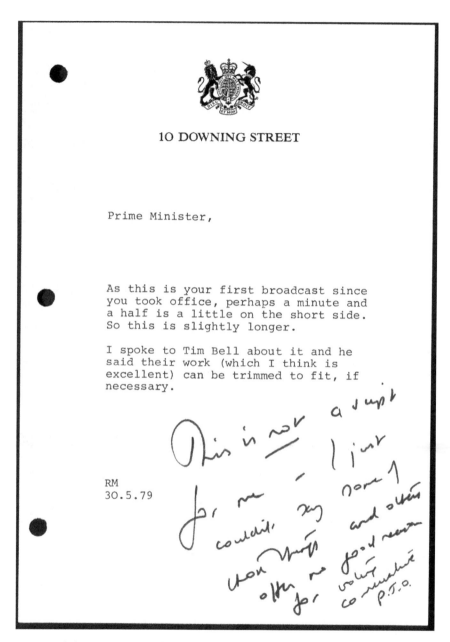

Figure 2 'This is not a script for me'. Although Thatcher employed speechwriters, she would never have words placed in her mouth by others. MTF, 112202, Ronnie Millar draft Party Election Broadcast, 30th May 1979.

This raises questions over the authenticity of Thatcher's words, and the policy-agenda which they shaped. After all, as Ridley recalls, 'If you [a speechwriter] could get a phrase in [to one of Thatcher's speeches] you could make a policy or kill a policy'.[117] However, the relationship between Thatcher and her speechwriters was not that of playwright and actor. Words were not simply placed in her mouth. Having spent hours writing the text for Thatcher's 1975 Conference Speech Millar, Patten and Ridley 'thought that our peroration, if not a masterpiece, was better than routine'. This sense of satisfaction was short-lived. Having read the proposed text Thatcher declared 'Oh no! No, that won't do at all'.[118] On enquiring the reason for her disapproval Millar was simply told: 'It's just not me, dear'.[119] This, Millar recalls, 'was the first time I heard that phrase which was to be a marker buoy for the next sixteen years'.[120] 'The script just won't do for me'[121] or simply 'NO'[122] would become familiar additions to the margins of Thatcher's speech drafts.

Although Thatcher could make statements that aligned with the political position of her wordsmiths, but not with her own, she did so consciously. Whilst Thatcher did not agree with the principle of cross-party cooperation articulated in Millar's PPB draft in January 1979 (she had initially intended to adopt a 'hard-hitting' approach) she nonetheless recognized the tactical advantage of such a stance.[123] 'By agreeing to offer cooperation to the Government on selected measures', Thatcher recalled, 'Jim Prior and his supporters would find it impossible to refuse support to those same measures if and when a Conservative Government introduced them'.[124] Similarly, Thatcher's decision to deliver

Figure 3 The 'wet' John Gummer contributed to Thatcher's speeches, proving that the 'Home Team' was not the exclusive preserve of 'Thatcherites'. (Photo by Keystone/Hulton Archive/Getty Images)

Gummer's line, that 'the National Health Service is safe with us' in 1982 was based on pragmatic politics.[125] The CPRS report on the long-term options for funding education, social security and health had been circulated to Cabinet on 7 September 1982 ready for discussion two days later. The report suggested, amongst other things, that a charge should be introduced for state schooling. Ministers, recognizing the potential toxicity of the arguments contained within the report, insisted that its discussion should not be minuted. Despite the fact that Thatcher required no decision, the Cabinet was shaken. The report was leaked and covered in *The Economist* on 18 September 1982. This created an environment in which Thatcher was forced to publicly respond. Thatcher may not have liked the arguments scripted by Gummer or Millar and was aware that they had the potential to act as 'policy hostage[s]'.[126] But any sense of 'unease',[127] which may have been heightened by hindsight, was overcome by her knowing that politically, she had to utter the phrases, and did so willingly.

That Mount interpreted Thatcher's pronouncement on the NHS as being the product of 'her [wet] captors'[128] is telling. It demonstrates the way in which Thatcher used rhetorical inauthenticity. She had previously used this device to great effect in her 1976 Conference Speech. The speech itself was banal. It did not represent Thatcher's political preferences, but the 'fudge'[129] articulated in *The Right Approach*. This was due in part to the fact that Thatcher spoke against the backdrop of a financial crisis. Interest rates were raised to 15 per cent the day before Thatcher spoke and, as a result, she was 'neurotically conscious of the need for responsibility and caution'.[130] It was also because elements of the speech were written by leading 'wet' voices in the Shadow Cabinet. Reggie Maudling, removed from the Shadow Cabinet the following month, wrote much of the economic section of the speech. Yet, despite the speech 'balancing Right and Left of the party', it was interpreted by Frank Johnson of *The Telegraph*, not as a representation of the views of 'the real Mrs Thatcher'[131] but those of 'bad speech writers'.[132] Thatcher's use of rhetorical inauthenticity or, in the case of her 1976 and 1982 Conference Speeches, other people's assumption of her inauthenticity, was a means of saying one thing whilst simultaneously distancing herself from it.

Thatcher deployed this tactic throughout her career, at times supplementing it with leaked speech drafts. Drafting her 1979 Conference Speech, Thatcher consciously avoided making 'policy hostages'.[133] As a result, she removed sections of her speech:

> I give my pledge that, ~~however often we may be rebuffed~~, my colleagues and I
> will continue to talk to them [Trade Unions], ~~to give these views due weight in~~

~~shaping national policy~~, so long as it is understood that national policy is, ~~in the last resort~~, the ~~sole~~ responsibility of Government and Parliament.[134]

The political significance of Thatcher's decision to delete certain words, and thus avoid her words acting to constrain her movements at a later point, was not lost on contemporary commentators. The *Daily Mirror* noted:

> Parts of her prepared speech were deleted. Especially significant were the deletions of some phrases in the final bit which I read as a serious attempt to open peace talks with the TUC leaders. One sentence in particular promised to give the unions' views 'due weight in shaping national policy'. Mrs Thatcher, the Party Leader, rather than the Prime Minister, omitted that. By oversight? Second thoughts? Considered political judgement? Or just plain error? We don't know. All I know is that it was in the original text.[135]

Such a comment raises the question of how the *Daily Mirror* had gained access to the prime minister's earlier draft. The answer to this is unclear. Yet the leak afforded Thatcher a degree of political capital. She was able to distance herself from, and implicitly question, her public words and thus satisfy a broad range of opinions within the Conservative Party.

Moments before taking to the platform to deliver her 1990 Conference Speech Thatcher began to worry. Her script included a riff on *Monty Python's* 'Parrot sketch'. The Liberal Democrats' new logo, Thatcher was due to tell her audience, is:

> an ex-parrot. It is not merely stunned. It has ceased to be, expired and gone to meet its maker. It is a parrot no more. It has run down the curtain and joined the choir invisible. This is a late parrot.[136]

Thatcher was unsure. She had watched the sketch during the writing process and had not found it amusing. Turning to Whittingdale she sought last-minute reassurance: 'John, Monty Python – are you sure he's one of us?'[137] Whittingdale paused. 'Absolutely, Prime Minister'.[138]

In some ways Thatcher's question is not surprising. That humour was not Thatcher's strong point is well documented. However, in terms of speechmaking, she was not an 'ideologically paranoid person', a phrase used by O'Sullivan to suggest that Thatcher's speechwriters did not necessarily have to believe in a 'Thatcherite' policy-agenda'.[139] When applied to the speechwriting process '"One of Us" was quite an elastic phrase', O'Sullivan recalls, 'it wasn't a narrow group of ideologues'.[140] Even supposedly politically neutral civil servants who supported the drafting of Thatcher's governmental speeches were known to question

Thatcher's position. 'I wasn't "One of Us"' remembered Caroline Slocock (Number 10's first female private secretary, 1989–91), a fact of which Thatcher became aware.[141] Thatcher's speechwriting showed little concern for the 'party of ideological doctrine' identified by commentators.[142]

This is not to say that ideological concerns were absent from Thatcher's speechwriting process. Many of Thatcher's 'wordsmiths' were driven, at least in part, by ideological ambitions. Thatcher used her public words (and silences) to 'achieve what I [Thatcher] wanted', both in the short and longer term.[143] But the ability to write, rather than any ideological allegiance, acted as the overriding qualification for admittance into her speechwriting circle. Nicholas Ridley, Robin Harris recalls, contributed to speechwriting chiefly because he was 'not a bad draughtsman'.[144] John Gummer too was described as being 'good at drafting' and so was included in Thatcher's team.[145] Gummer's recruitment was perhaps more surprising than Ridley's because Gummer was suspected by the Whips of being the author of Julian Critchley's letter, published in *The Observer* in early 1980, in which Thatcher was accused, amongst other things, of being 'didactic, tart and obstinate'.[146] Chris Patten recalls how he and Millar were passed down from Ted Heath like 'baubles', retained by the new leader not for their ideological allegiance, but for their 'ability to write'.[147] Some of the most 'Thatcherite' speeches, delivered by Thatcher both pre- and post-1979, were the products, at least in part, of Patten's pen.[148] As Thatcher later told Ferdinand Mount, 'We always need fresh ideas, but you're such a wordsmith'.[149] The word 'but' being key.[150] Thatcher saw speechwriters as 'nearer to being a dental technician than a nuclear physicist', much to the disappointment of many of her 'wordsmiths'.[151]

This pragmatism, combined with the political weight carried by Thatcher's public words, attracted men from across the political spectrum of the party, such as Conquest, Gummer, Sherman and Hoskyns, who aspired to positions of political influence. This transformed the act of speechwriting into a process in which speechwriters (both political and governmental) fought over competing policy-agendas. Although not a member of the 'Home Team', George Walden's recollections of speechwriting are telling. He 'saw it [speechwriting] as a chance to get some of my ideas on to the agenda'.[152] This raises questions over the authenticity of Thatcher's words. Did Thatcher's speeches articulate what Thatcher 'wanted', or did they, at times, articulate the political wants of her speechwriters?

According to Thatcher's memoirs, at times, her speechwriters did force words into her mouth. Her public appeals for cooperation, made in 1979, advocated by those such as Thorneycroft and Millar, made her feel 'uneasy'.[153] Whilst such statements do not sit comfortably alongside the triumphalist account, promoted by Thatcher post-1990, they do reflect the pragmatism that characterized her speechmaking process. By stating positions seemingly at odds with her own preferences, Thatcher was able to position herself in relation to, and comment upon, the policy-agenda being pursued by her own government and party. She was able to invest multiple meanings within her public utterances, calling for the NHS to be protected or signalling a hardening in approach to trade union reform, whilst at the same time distancing herself from such a stance. This ambiguity, often driven by immediate, tactical concerns, allowed her to appeal to a diverse range of opinion.

Yet this should not be taken as a sign of Thatcher's words being somehow inauthentic. Thatcher, Millar recalls, was 'involved personally in all major speeches from the beginning at virtually every stage of their development'.[154] Speechwriters' efforts were constantly questioned. Unlike her predecessor Heath, whose unwillingness to engage in the speechwriting process led to him advocating positions with which he did not wholly agree, Thatcher was deeply immersed in the speechwriting process.[155] Words, phrases and entire arguments could be scrapped. She may not have written the words she delivered in public, or even personally agreed with the political position they articulated, but they were unmistakeably *her* words.

3

'We are playing to our geographical strengths'. Thatcher's electioneering platform*

Scholars have long interpreted the development of the political platform within the context of the development of democracy. The platform's 'controlling function' in British politics starts, according to Henry Jephson, with the passing of the Great Reform Act of 1832 and many accounts of the platform begin, in one way or another, with Jephson.[1] Jephson's *The Platform*, published in 1892, presents a Whiggish account. By the time of writing, he argued, 'Parliament has been becoming every year more and more the executive of the Platform'.[2] It is perhaps not surprising that Jephson held such views. He surveyed the history of the platform from the perspective of the 1890s. The memory of Gladstone's Midlothian campaign (1879) would have been fresh in his and his readers' minds. The average contemporary parliamentary candidate spoke at more than one hundred meetings during a constituency campaign.[3] Jephson's work describes, and is, a product of what has come to be seen as the 'Golden Age' of speechmaking.

Jephson's account has been used as a reference point by later scholars. Some, like Luke Blaxill, have extended the 'rise and progress' of the platform beyond the 1890s through to the early twentieth century. Others, such as Jon Lawrence, extend the study into the age of electronic broadcasting and, in so doing, trace the decline of the platform during the late twentieth century.[4] It is logical then to begin a study of Thatcher's platform from the perspective of her electioneering platform, its effect on her speechmaking and its relationship to the current narrative of the platform's place within British political history.

There is no doubt that the radio and television studio offered an alternative space where 'high' and 'low' politics could interact. During the 1983 general election campaign for example, Thatcher appeared on the BBC's *Nationwide*

54 *Making Speeches*

programme, hosted by Sue Lawley. Diana Gould, a retired geography teacher had, a year earlier, been shocked not only by the sinking of the Argentine ship the *Belgrano*, and the resultant loss of 360 Argentine lives, but also by the fact that the attack had, she felt, put paid to the peace proposal put forward by Peru. On 24 May 1983 Gould appeared on the programme to question the prime minister. 'Mrs. Thatcher', Ms Gould began:

> why, when the *Belgrano*, the Argentine battleship, was outside the exclusion zone and actually sailing away from the Falklands, why did you give the orders to sink it?[5]

Thatcher, unaware of Gould's detailed knowledge (she had previously been a meteorological officer in the Royal Navy) and the tenacity of her questioning, tried to bat the question away: 'But it was not sailing away from the Falklands. It was in an area which was a danger to our ships and to our people on them.' This did not deflect Gould. 'Mrs. Thatcher', she continued:

> you started your answer by saying it was not sailing away from the Falklands. It was on a bearing of 280 and it was already west of the Falklands, so I'm sorry but I cannot see how you can say it was not sailing away from the Falklands when it was sunk.[6]

Perturbed, Thatcher repeated her position: 'When it was sunk it was a danger to our ships.' Gould, becoming frustrated with Thatcher's prevarication, shifted in her seat and leant towards the camera. She continued: 'No, but you have just said at the beginning of your answer that it was not sailing away from the Falklands, and I'm asking you to correct that statement.'

Thatcher, realizing that she had met her match, faltered: 'Mrs. Gould, when orders were given to sink it and when it was sunk it was in an area which was a danger to our ships. Now, you accept that, do you?' 'No, I don't', retorted Gould. Seeming to accept that she was unable to convince Gould of the soundness of her position, Thatcher stated that 'one day, in about thirty years' time, all the facts will be published and … ' Gould, unwilling to be side-lined, interrupted, 'That is not good enough Mrs Thatcher'. Thatcher, half closing her eyes and trying to stay calm, attempted to continue. 'I am just trying to … ' Gould continued to make herself heard, and at this point Thatcher struggled to stay calm. 'Would you please let me answer?' she said firmly; 'would you please let me answer?' she repeated. Thatcher then, in her best schoolmarm tones set forth: 'I answered the question giving the facts – not anyone's opinions, but the facts and', she continued, 'I am going to finish [my answer uninterrupted]'.[7] To this Gould rolled her eyes and sighed. The prime minister then proceeded to deliver her point at Mrs Gould, providing little opportunity for interruption.

Thatcher was initially content with the programme but, upon reflection, became furious that the BBC had selected a member of the public to question her, during an election campaign, on the sinking of the *Belgrano*. Though the interview has since reached legendary status (the *Radio Times* voted it the ninth-best interview of all time), received widespread coverage in the media and ensured that Sue Lawley was never again granted an interview with Thatcher, it had little effect on Thatcher's polling.[8] The Conservatives went on to win a convincing victory in the 1983 general election and did so, in part, due to the Labour Party being viewed by large sections of the electorate as 'unpatriotic', a view seemingly bolstered by Kinnock's ill-judged comments to a Television South audience in June 1983. 'At least Mrs Thatcher had guts', shouted a member of the audience, 'And it is a pity that people had to leave theirs on the ground at Goose Green to prove it', replied Kinnock.[9] The public's reaction was immediate. The audience began to jeer, and, by the following day, the media was criticizing Kinnock for making such a comment.

Gould's encounter with Thatcher can be seen as emblematic of the current understanding of the set-piece speech's place within the landscape of late-twentieth-century British elections. Although politicians continued to crave interaction with the public, political communication in the television age did not revolve around the platform but instead, the television studio or the staged 'walkabout'. Following the election campaign Lawley wrote to Thatcher and, although she expressed regret that Thatcher had been 'unhappy about how the programme went' continued:

> I have to say that I am still of the opinion that it was successful in so far as the format allows: that is to say, viewers were able to question and, indeed, cross-question the Prime Minister on matters which, representatively, they considered important.[10]

The interaction of 'high' and 'low' politics had migrated from the platform to the television studio – in this case, the *Nationwide* studio.

But such a narrative is perhaps more complicated than it first appears. Thatcher's electioneering speeches could be broadcast across the nation, and beyond, from any location. Unlike orators of the 'Golden Age', who spoke in a world before mass, electronic media, Thatcher did not need to travel to broadcast a particular message widely.[11] A well-deployed phrase articulating a nationally relevant point, delivered to a bank of television cameras – and a small, and at times bemused local audience – could, within a matter of minutes, reach a national audience. Yet, over the decades leading politicians have increased the number of speeches they deliver during election campaigns, and the variety of locations from which they are delivered.[12]

In explaining such seemingly contradictory behaviour this chapter will first look at the reason why Thatcher, like her peers, felt the need to increase, during general elections, the number of speeches she made, and to increase the range of locations from which she delivered them. In so doing the physical act of speechmaking, and the platform from which the speech was delivered, will be shown to have been central to Thatcher's electioneering. It will be shown also that general election campaigns had a marked impact upon the content of Thatcher's public language, though little allowance was made for the local context in which the speech was delivered.

In the third week of the 1979 general election Thatcher decided to call off her planned visit to Fulham to work on her upcoming speech to Conservative Trade Unionists. The cancellation caused a media stir. David Holmes of the BBC noted how 'journalists', travelling on the campaign trail with the leader of the opposition, 'got it into their heads that the reason [for her decision to cancel her visit to Fulham] was perhaps that Mrs Thatcher was losing her voice'.[13] Thatcher used her morning press conference of 27 April to set the record straight. Shouting, she told the assembled journalists how she would 'give [...] a demonstration' of her voice. Once the laughter had died down, she underlined her point. 'There's no problem with my voice. All right, OK.'[14]

The merriment hid a serious point. In 1984 *Time* magazine published an article entitled 'The Fatigue Factor'. The article dwelt upon the way candidates attacked the campaign trail 'at ferocious pace, running an electoral marathon at sprinters' speeds'.[15] Such a line could just as easily have been applied to Thatcher's approach to electioneering. Operating in a media landscape in which candidates' words could be shared nationally (and internationally) they still felt the need to travel the length and breadth of the country to address the electorate. This is because the delivery of party messages was not the sole objective of the candidate's itinerary. The physical effort of the campaign trail tested and hardened presidential and prime ministerial hopefuls. Candidates were required to prove that they had what it took. It is for this reason that, as Roderick Hart has shown, presidential candidates spoke and travelled more during campaigns, and why *Time* tracked candidates' ages, blood pressure, and cholesterol counts.[16] Any sign of weakness counted against the candidate.

As the first female leader of the Conservative Party, indeed the first female leader of any political party in the Western world, Thatcher was perhaps subjected to a greater degree of scrutiny than her male peers. 'It is when she is tired', one commentator wrote, 'that her frailty, a frailty that calls forth a protective instinct in women as well as men becomes exceptionally apparent'.[17] One cannot imagine such a line being written about a tired Wilson or Heath. As a female orator, Thatcher was susceptible to losing her voice, partly because she was required to speak an octave below where she would usually speak.[18] Tim Bell was often required to produce drinks of warm water, honey and lemon to soothe and relax sore vocal cords. So regularly did Thatcher lose her voice that the manufacturers of Olbas sent her a vast supply of tablets. Such challenges were not unique to Thatcher. In 2017 Theresa May was forced to stop addressing the Conservative Party Conference due to a prolonged period of coughing during which the chancellor was obliged to provide her with a cough sweet. For May, as with Thatcher, such challenges were at least in part caused by there being a media requirement to sound authoritative.

Thatcher's team were aware of the need to protect Thatcher. Thatcher's earlier trip around Scotland and the Borders in 1978, though deemed a success, had raised concerns that, if repeated over the course of an election campaign, would run the risk of 'exhausting our Leader'.[19] The narrative of a 'battle-worn Maggie' losing her voice became politically dangerous, especially when set in the context of polls suggesting that the Conservative Party's lead was shrinking.[20] Playing up to her persona as the 'Iron Lady' Thatcher herself became determined to prevent any public sign of physical weakness. She successfully kept her toothache from the media during the 1987 election campaign. In fact, having been kept awake most of the night by the pain – 'Crawfie' (Cynthia Crawford, Thatcher's personal assistant) had provided pain killers in the early hours of the morning – Thatcher demanded that she lead the following morning's press conference. No questions could be raised about Thatcher's physical ability whilst on the campaign trail.

As it turned out Thatcher was more than up to the physical demands of the campaigns in 1979, and in 1983 and 1987. Yet a quantitative assessment of Thatcher's speechmaking during general election years does not reveal a simple correlation between rhetorical output and the election cycle. In 1978 she delivered sixty-nine speeches (not including statements delivered in the House). In 1979 Thatcher delivered ninety-eight speeches. In the non-election year of 1982, Thatcher delivered a total of eighty-nine speeches. In the election year of 1983, this rose to 122 speeches. In 1984, the total number of speeches fell to eighty-eight. However, this pattern was not repeated during the 1987 general election. In 1986, Thatcher delivered a total of 105 speeches. In 1987, this total fell, with her giving ninety-eight speeches. In fact, Thatcher delivered more speeches in 1988, speaking on 143 occasions. The relationship between Thatcher's rhetorical output and the electoral cycle then, was not as clear-cut as might be assumed.[21]

Thatcher's early inexperience in the sphere of foreign affairs has been well documented.[22] Much of the detailed policy work was left to Lord Carrington. Partly as a result, the elder statesmen of Europe, men such as Helmut Schmidt and Valéry Giscard d'Estaing tended to treat Thatcher with condescension and disdain. The latter compared Thatcher to his English nanny.[23] By 1987 however, Thatcher had become the elder statesperson of the European scene and played a prominent role in the rapidly changing international landscape of the late 1980s. This development in Thatcher's status as a world leader was reflected in the location of her speeches. The years 1982–4 saw Thatcher deliver a relatively consistent number of speeches abroad. In 1982 she gave sixteen speeches, which dropped to eleven during the election year of 1983, before rising again to sixteen in 1984. However, by 1986 Thatcher was making thirty speeches abroad. This dropped to seventeen during the election year of 1987, and then rose dramatically to fifty-nine during 1988. It is this sudden rise in speechmaking abroad which masks the fact that, in terms of domestic speechmaking, 1987 saw a rise, from seventy-five in 1986, to eighty-one in 1987. Although it is still true to say that Thatcher spoke more often from a domestic platform in 1988 compared with 1987, the difference is relatively small, eighty-one compared with eighty-five.

The increase in rhetorical output in 1988 was part of a wider trend. Thatcher's last three years in Number 10 saw a steady increase in her speechmaking. 1989 saw Thatcher make a total of 136 speeches and in 1990, although she did not complete the year as prime minister, she gave a total of 127. Even if the thirty-eight speeches Thatcher delivered abroad (more than double the total number of speeches she gave in the years 1982 and 1984) are subtracted from the total, she still spoke more than she did in 1988, in a shorter period of time. One must therefore be cautious when comparing Thatcher's total rhetorical output of 1987 with 1988. The latter marks the beginning of a general increase in her speechmaking, limiting its use as a marker against which one can discern the impact of election years on the frequency of her speechmaking. In general, Thatcher's domestic speechmaking increased during election years (and her speeches abroad decreased), though this became less pronounced as her premiership continued (and thus her status as an elder statesperson developed) and her total annual rhetorical output increased.

Electioneering affected the location, as well as the frequency of Thatcher's speechmaking. London, the political centre of British politics and home to Thatcher's Finchley constituency was, unsurprisingly, the location for many of her speeches in both election and non-election years. However, Thatcher spoke more in the capital during election years than during non-election years.[24] In 1977 Thatcher spoke in London eighteen times. In 1979 this rose to thirty-one times. Even considering the increase in speechmaking that accompanied Thatcher's elevation to Number 10, this still represented an increase in speechmaking. She spoke thirty-four times in the capital in 1983, twenty-two times in 1982 and twenty-nine times in 1984. This pattern was repeated, albeit to a lesser degree, in the election year of 1987, with Thatcher making twenty-two speeches in the capital, compared with nineteen speeches in 1986.

This increase in speechmaking was repeated outside the capital, but to a greater extent. Thatcher delivered two speeches in Scotland in 1982 and one speech in 1984. However, she gave four speeches in Scotland in 1983. The same pattern emerges in the election year of 1987. During 1986, Thatcher delivered one speech in Scotland. In the East of England, Thatcher spoke four times in 1983, having never spoken in the region in 1982 or 1981 and only once in 1984. In the East of England, she spoke four times in 1987, having spoken twice in 1986 and once in 1988.[25] In the West Midlands, Thatcher spoke three times in 1983, having delivered no speeches there in 1982 or 1984. In the West Midlands, Thatcher repeated the totals seen in the earlier 1983 election year, speaking three times yet having delivered no speeches in 1986 or 1988.

The pattern of speaking in locations which, whilst not ignored, were undervalued by Thatcher in non-election years, is best demonstrated by Thatcher's speaking engagements in Wales. Thatcher spoke here a total of nine times during her premiership. However, only twice did Thatcher address audiences which were not annual conferences, either the CBI or the Welsh Conservative Conference. Both of these non-Conference Speeches, one in Cardiff (1983) and one in Newport (1987) took place during election years. It seems that Thatcher's electioneering speechmaking conformed to the 'love-'em-and-leave-'em' approach undertaken by modern US presidents.[26]

But Thatcher's decision to 'love' particular locations was not, as with presidential candidates, driven by a desire to speak in politically neutral constituencies. Cardiff played host to the first major election rally of the 1979 campaign. The location was an 'appropriate place to start', Thatcher recalled, as it sat in 'the heart of enemy territory'.[27] Cardiff South East was Callaghan's constituency. Targeting the Labour Party's strongholds was not, however, a criterion that was used to select the location from which Thatcher would speak. In typical fashion, Thatcher fixated upon the practicalities of the campaign (the 1979 election saw the introduction of the 'Battle Bus') rather than the strategy that underpinned it. On 31 January 1979 Richard Ryder wrote a note for Thatcher. The secret document, entitled 'Election strategy' began, rather ironically, 'We need an agreed strategy'.[28]

Over the course of the 1980s two principles evolved that came to dictate where Thatcher spoke. The first was logistical. Thatcher was particularly keen during election campaigns, to chair the daily press-conference, which began at 9.30 every morning. As a result, Thatcher's tours would be 'arranged ... so that I, [Thatcher] spent very few nights away from London'.[29] Cecil Parkinson, appointed by Thatcher to manage the 1983 campaign, ensured that she 'was back [from campaigning] in Number 10 by 8.30 most evenings to work on her Prime Ministerial papers and her next speeches'.[30] It was for this reason that, in planning for the 1983 election campaign, the 'draft outline programme' for a 'sample day when touring away from London' assumed that the prime minister arrived at Central Office at 8.15am and, having spent the entire day campaigning, would 'return to Number 10 no later than 11.00pm'.[31] This limited the time she could spend speaking in regions such as the North East or South West. It is no coincidence then that the locations of Thatcher's electioneering speeches decreased the further they were from, and thus the longer it took to get back to, London.

The second factor was political. Roderick Hart has shown that the location of US presidential speechmaking favoured politically 'neutral' states.[32] Although it is questionable whether presidential candidates addressed neutral crowds, given that speeches were directed towards politically favourable audiences, Hart's work indicates that presidential candidates wanted to be seen to address crowds, and thus win votes, in neutral locations. Thatcher seems to have pursued a different strategy during the 1983 election campaign. Defending her landslide majority, Thatcher's 'objective' was to 'hold our vote and seats'.[33] These seats, of which there were eighty-eight during the 1983 campaign, were categorized as 'critical'.[34] Although, as A.S. Garner (Conservative Party director of Organization and Community Affairs, 1976–88) made clear, some of these seats were, in fact, 'highly marginal', they were 'mainly seats which additional help should enable us [the Conservative Party] to hold or win'.[35] The media attention stimulated by a prime ministerial speech was, according to Thatcher, key in supporting 'our candidates'.[36] As a result, Thatcher asserted, 'my task was to concentrate on campaigning in Conservative-held seats'.[37] Thus Thatcher tended to speak in regions that were expected to return, and often did return, a high proportion of Conservative seats. In 1983 for example, the Conservative Party won fifty-six seats in London, an area which had the highest number of 'critical seats' (twelve).[38] Thatcher spoke there ten times. In the East Midlands (which contained ten 'critical seats') the Conservative Party won thirty-four seats, whilst in the West Midlands (which contained eleven 'critical seats') the Conservative Party won thirty-six seats. Thatcher spoke three times in each region. In Scotland, where Thatcher delivered two speeches, the Conservatives won twenty-one seats. In Wales, where the Conservative Party won just fourteen seats, Thatcher spoke only once, though the area contained a relatively high number of nine 'critical seats'. Although there exists no list of 'critical seats' for the 1987 general election campaign, a similar correlation can be identified between seats won and the frequency of Thatcher's speechmaking. London recorded the highest number of Conservative seats and was again the location in which Thatcher spoke most often. The East of England returned nineteen Conservative seats and Thatcher spoke in the region six times. The North West returned eight Conservative seats and Thatcher spoke in the region three times. The fact that Thatcher tended to speak in the same regions in 1987 as she had in 1983 would suggest that she had continued to pursue a policy of 'concentrat[ing her] campaigning [and thus her speechmaking] in Conservative-held seats'.[39] A statistical analysis of Thatcher's speechmaking during both the 1983 and 1987 election campaigns confirms the opinion expressed by Anthony Shrimsley (journalist and Conservative Party press director, 1983 general election) that 'we [the prime ministerial team] are playing to our geographical strengths'.[40]

However, there were exceptions. The South West, for example, returned forty-four seats in the 1987 election, yet Thatcher spoke only twice in the region. This was a repeat of the 1983 election where the region returned forty-four seats yet hosted only two prime ministerial speeches. Such an anomaly was perhaps the consequence of the time it took to reach the South West from London. It may also have been the result of Thatcher's determination to visit as many regions as possible. 'Nothing is more devastating', Thatcher asserted, 'to candidates and Party workers than to think they have been written off'.[41] This meant that Thatcher's time was precious. No one region (except perhaps London) could be allowed to dominate the prime minister's electioneering schedule, regardless of its political leanings.

Election years affected not only where Thatcher spoke, but also what she said. Unsurprisingly, during election years Thatcher's rhetoric became more concerned with domestic themes. In 1986 for example, Thatcher used the term 'European' 123 times, using the word 'Europe' ninety-eight times. This was a consequence of her tendency, during non-election election years, to discuss certain policies, such as defence policy, in international terms, especially when speaking abroad which, as discussed above, was more prevalent during non-election years. 'We need to promote collaboration [in defence]', Thatcher told an audience in Florence, 'with Europe and the United States'.[42] Similarly, Thatcher tended to set Britain's economic policy in a European context. To the Conservative Central Council, for example, Thatcher declared that 'in this favourable [economic] climate more jobs are coming, more than in any other country in Europe'.[43] This rhetorical trend changed during election years. In 1987 the word 'European' ceased to appear amongst Thatcher's ten most frequently used words. Instead, new words appeared, such as 'party' (used 212 times) and 'Labour' (her most frequently used word, appearing 392 times). In 1988, 'Labour' and 'election' were no longer amongst Thatcher's seven most frequently used words and 'Europe', used 280 times and 'European', used 167 times, reappeared.

It is difficult to assess the impact of the 1983 election on Thatcher's public language, given the unique situation in which her government found itself during the Falklands War in 1982. The words 'Argentine' and 'Security' feature prominently in Thatcher's set-piece speeches in 1982, the former being used 152 times and the latter 157 times. However, the domestic focus discernible in the 1987 election is again evident in the 1983 election campaign. 'Labour', which was not one of Thatcher's ten most frequently used words in 1982, appeared 316 times in 1983. Other words focused upon domestic politics were regularly used. 'party' was used 190 times and 'industry', 187 times. 'Jobs' was used 250 times. Although the word 'jobs' was prominent again in 1984, being used 134 times, 'Labour' fell out of her top ten words and was replaced by words such as 'world' (used 236 times) and 'Europe' (used 196 times). The content of Thatcher's public language predictably followed the electoral cycle.

There is some evidence to suggest that during an election campaign, contrary to her usual approach to speechmaking, Thatcher deployed regionally specific language. During the 1979 election campaign it was agreed that Howell and Millar 'would assist [Thatcher] with speech writing, and would travel with the Leader on those days when she was due to make a major speech'.[44] 'David Howell', it was decreed, 'will do Leader's Speeches, and travel to revise and add topicality'.[45] Addressing a rally in Wales during the 1983 election campaign for example, Thatcher made direct reference to the locality. 'Llanwern and Port

Talbot', Thatcher told her audience, 'are symbols of that new sense of pride – breaking production records week after week; securing their future by making themselves among the best in Europe'.[46] Similar, regionally specific language is evident when Thatcher visited an Essex farm during the 1987 general election campaign. Thatcher noted:

> Unfortunately there was, a fortnight ago, a very, very cold, bad high wind, which I am afraid took some of the flowers off, the blossoms off, so they reckon that their blackcurrant crop is down by twenty percent.[47]

Yet such local references were never more than superficial asides, bolted onto national messages. Thatcher tended to focus on overarching themes. 'Our main aim', Thatcher recalled when discussing the 1983 election campaign, 'was to deal with the difficult question of unemployment by showing that we were prepared to take it head on and prove that our policies were the best to provide jobs in the future'.[48] Thatcher made this clear when addressing Conservative Party candidates at the start of the election campaign at Westminster. 'We are in the battle for more jobs', she said. 'Our policies will produce jobs in the future.'[49] Although in Wales, where Thatcher did note the regional situation, the main message she delivered was again tailored to articulate the 'main aim[s]' of the national campaign.[50] Dealing with the 'difficult question … [of] unemployment',[51] Thatcher told her audience:

> We are going to train the young people to ensure that they have the skills which the new jobs will require. This autumn, we are starting the biggest and most exciting training programme for young people in our history. That means a year of training for 450,000 young people.[52]

A similar message was articulated in Harrogate:

> Everyone understands the feelings of a man who sees his skills suddenly become redundant. Everyone understands the frustrations of a school-leaver looking for his first job. And I know what it must be like for his family too. But concern is not enough. There must be action. Practical, effective action to tackle the root causes of unemployment. And this Government is taking action.[53]

During the 1987 election, Thatcher again tackled national themes. She used her speech in London, to Conservative Party candidates, as an opportunity to stress that the National Health Service was 'safe only in our [the Conservative Party's] hands'.[54] 'That done', Thatcher recalled, 'I devoted the rest of the campaign to stressing our strong points', specifically on 'defence'.[55] In Scotland, Thatcher attacked the Labour Party and their 'eerie silence' on their defence policy.[56] In London, the same message was articulated. 'The defence of Britain is only safe in Conservative hands.'[57] In Wales, Thatcher again repeated the message: 'the defence of the country would not be safe with Labour'.[58] In recalling the speech she delivered in Wales during the 1983 campaign, Thatcher's comments are telling. 'It was a long speech', she noted, 'I covered all the main election issues – jobs, health, pensions, defence'.[59] These issues were understood by Thatcher as 'election' issues, not regional issues, although of course the two were not always mutually exclusive. Already, as the 1979 campaign was nearing its close, Thatcher was 'becoming tired of the standard speech I was making to audiences around the country'[60] in which 'the same message' was 'repeated insistently'.[61]

The fact that Thatcher failed to modify her language depending on the geographical location of her speeches is reflected in the speechwriting process during general election campaigns. Like the 'middling'[62] speeches of non-election periods, Thatcher's scripts would be drafted by one author. In the build-up to the 1979 general election, it was agreed that Angus Maude (deputy chairman of the Conservative Party and chairman of the Conservative Research Department) should 'draft speeches on main subjects, which the Leader might look at and amend during August [1978]'.[63] Once in government the head of the Policy Unit usually drafted significant sections of Thatcher's campaign speeches. During the 1983 campaign Ferdinand Mount headed up the Policy Unit. Much of Mount's work was completed before the campaign. 'There is a lot to be said', Mount informed Thatcher:

> for having one basic speech into which we insert ... a chunk of 500–700 words on the issue of the day for the media to pick up. This is a tried and proven technique. Callaghan and Reagan both used it to considerable success. If the speech hits the right note, it is worth repeating. And where it is off-key, we change it as we go along.[64]

The danger, Mount foresaw, was:

> [P]eople covering the campaign might begin to feel that the material is a bit thin. 'It's the same old speech; why doesn't he/she ever really get down to discussing X or Y?' The best way to counter this is to use the run-up to the Election, as Wilson did in 1963–64, to build up a solid impression by a series of major speeches focussed on specific issues. Those who want to ask about X or Y can then be referred back to the 'Cardiff speech' or the 'Sheffield lecture'. I suggest, therefore, that we should try and target your speeches over the next 6 months or so more on specific issues than we have done in the past.[65]

Thatcher did not entirely follow Mount's suggestion of drafting before the campaign speeches which would articulate a particular policy-agenda. Although Mount's suggestion of using Thatcher's forthcoming speech in Glasgow as a means of discussing 'Industrial Recovery and the depressed regions' was acted upon, other suggestions were not.[66] Thatcher did not speak at the Women's Conference, which Mount had selected as a platform from which Thatcher could 'concentrate on the Family and the Individual' and she chose to make defence, and not law and order, the focus of her speech to the Young Conservatives.[67]

A similar picture emerges with regard to Mount's suggestion of creating a speech template which could be used throughout the campaign. Although Robin Harris remembers that, in relation to the 1983 and 1987 campaigns, it is 'quite correct' to suggest that template speeches, or 'modules' were pre-prepared, it is difficult to assess the extent to which they were used because few speaking scripts remain.[68] However, it does seem likely that pre-prepared scripts which took little account of the region in which Thatcher spoke were used. Recalling the speechwriting process of the 1983 general election campaign, Thatcher noted that Mount 'prepared about half a dozen speech drafts on different topics before the campaign'.[69] John Gummer, Ronnie Millar and Alfred Sherman would then provide 'additional' material before the speech was delivered.[70] This process was pre-planned. In preparation for the 1983 election campaign, it was noted that Thatcher would require a 'separate speech writing team'.[71] The team, it was suggested, would not travel 'directly with the Prime Minister on all occasions', but would meet 'the Prime Minister's Party on location'[72] presumably to make last minute, regionally specific additions to the pre-written script. One is not able to ascertain with any certainty, whether Thatcher did, or did not, use 'modules' for the majority of her speeches during election campaigns. However, the fact that these were discussed and that their creation was accommodated within the pre-election planning, would suggest that Thatcher's speechwriting process employed during election campaigns, was unconcerned with creating speeches tailored to the specific locations from which she spoke.

Reflecting upon the role that geographical location played in her campaign speechmaking Thatcher noted: 'as the importance of television and the "photo-opportunity" increases, the leader's physical location on a particular day is rather less important than it once was'.[73] It could be suggested then, that during a general election campaign, the location from which Thatcher spoke was of little significance. Although election years, and election months, saw an increase in Thatcher's rhetorical output, and a focus upon domestic as opposed to international issues, there was little variation in the language she used from one region to another. Although Thatcher did, at times, devote small sections of her speeches to local issues, these were often little more than asides, minor deviations from the main, national messages she hoped to communicate, irrespective of geographical location.

Yet, although Thatcher did not deliver language tailored, in any meaningful way, to the regions in which she spoke, her electoral behaviour puts into doubt her suggestion that 'physical location ... [became less] important than it once was'.[74] Election years and election months saw an increased diversity in the locations from which Thatcher delivered her set-piece speeches. Regions in which Thatcher had not delivered a speech for several years, such as the North West, suddenly hosted several prime ministerial speeches. Thatcher did value the physical location, and value it for a range of reasons. A prime ministerial speech, and thus a prime ministerial visit and the media attention which went with it, was an integral part of the Conservative Party's election tactic of holding seats. Additionally, Thatcher was conscious that she should travel to areas in which the Conservative Party struggled. Such visits, although less frequent than those to regions with a higher number of safer seats, were used as a means by which Thatcher could show local party workers and Conservative Party candidates that they had not 'been written off'.[75] Perhaps most importantly, as the West's first female political leader, the sheer physical effort that it took to travel from platform to platform became symbolically important during periods of electioneering. It proved Thatcher's mettle, and her fitness to lead. Thus, although Thatcher's language was not regionally specific, there is no doubt that the location from which she delivered her national message remained significant. Though commentators noted the importance of television in every election that Thatcher fought between 1979 and 1987 – and were not wrong to do so – the platform continued to be an important feature of electioneering.

4

'The trip itself is the message'. Thatcher's platform*

Despite the prevalence of the electronic news media the platform remained a significant feature of Thatcher's three general election campaigns. This raises questions over the supposed side-lining of the platform in the post-1945 British political landscape, and in turn raises questions over the position of Thatcher's platform in non-election years. At first glance it would seem that the supposed decline of the platform is applicable only in non-election years. Thatcher herself seemed to express such a view. Shortly after being elected leader of the Conservative Party, she declared that 'oratory', by which she meant the art of speaking to the immediate audience from the platform, was only used by 'old politicians – and Quintin [Hailsham]'.[1]

This conclusion has two, albeit implicit, consequences for the relationship between Thatcher's speeches and the platform from which they were delivered. If the interaction between politicians and the public now took place chiefly within television studios or on radio phone-in shows, their output being intended for national consumption, then it is legitimate to suggest that political communication had become detached from the geographical location of the platform. This being so, then it follows that the traditional set-piece speech grew less concerned with, directed towards, or shaped by the immediate audience.

Yet, it should be borne in mind that any perception of 'decline' is relative. The political platform of the post-1918, and particularly post-1945 British political landscape appears to have 'declined' when compared with the interaction between 'high and low' politics that occurred around the platforms of Gladstone and Disraeli. An assessment of Thatcher's platform supports such an interpretation by illustrating the way in which the platform *evolved* in response to the broadcasting age of the twentieth century.

Figure 4 When speaking from the platform Thatcher was often required to address both the immediate, and the national audience. (Photo by Georges De Keerle/Getty Images)

By widening the scope of the study of the platform beyond the usual confines of general elections, it will be suggested that although interaction between 'high' and 'low' politics took place within television studios – either between members of the public or with 'expert television interviewers' – interaction between speaker and audience still took place around the platform. Because the immediate audience was not separate from, but part of the broadcast media's coverage of Thatcher's set-piece speeches, such interaction (positive and negative) became significant in framing the manner in which speeches were broadcast to a national audience. It was for this reason that Thatcher and her wordsmiths paid keen attention to rhetorical devices and to the design and location of the platform. All of these elements were utilized to elicit positive reactions from the audience.

Whilst Thatcher's platform did not resemble those of the 'Golden Age' of speechmaking, it does not mean that the platform was in decline – although it had certainly evolved. The immediate audience, and thus the platform, will thus be placed back into the political landscape of the 1970s and 1980s and consequently, back into the assessment of Thatcher's set-piece speeches.

Thatcher's public language remained geographically consistent throughout her leadership of the Conservative Party. As leader of the opposition, for example, Thatcher used the word 'jobs' fifty-three times in the South East, the same number of times as she did in the North West.[2] As prime minister, addressing audiences in the North West of England, she made use of the word 'jobs' eighty-two times. 'Jobs' was Thatcher's seventieth most frequently used word in the North West. Addressing audiences in the South East of England Thatcher used the word 'jobs' eighty times, her sixty-eighth most frequently used word in the region. Addressing a national, rather than a regional audience in a speech, regardless of the location of the platform, was typical of Thatcher's approach both in opposition and in government. 'The Prime Minister', *The Guardian* reported in October 1980, 'rattled the grisly bones of last week's Labour Party Conference at her Conservative faithful yesterday as the ultimate justification for backing her government'[3] This, a central element of Thatcher's Conference Speech, 'was a message addressed beyond the crowded conference hall in Brighton to her vast television audience'.[4]

It was not only the topic, but the political message associated with it, which remained consistent, regardless of location. In opposition Thatcher's discussion of 'jobs' was often used as a vehicle to deliver a wider attack on the government who, she suggested, 'put shackles on some of those who create our wealth'. It was for this reason, she told an audience in Edinburgh, that the Labour Party 'cannot [...] be the Party of jobs'.[5] The Conservative Party, on the other hand, would 'throw the shackles off'.[6] This message had been repeated from Oxfordshire in 1977 to Wales in 1978.[7]

Being in government necessitated a change in the message conveyed by Thatcher's discussion of 'jobs'. Opening the new ICI plant in Runcorn in 1980, she reminded her audience that the creation of jobs was built upon keeping down costs. 'Lower pay settlements now will mean lower unemployment later.'[8] A similar message was repeated four years later. Addressing the Small Business Bureau in Surrey, Thatcher told her audience about a small pattern-making company that was able to create jobs in a way that larger competitors could not. This was achieved, she informed her audience, because the small firm kept 'overheads low'.[9]

Thatcher's message when discussing 'jobs' may have changed with her accession to Number 10, but its geographical consistency did not. The South East experienced a similar pattern of unemployment to the North West, rising during the mid-1980s before falling away from 1987 onwards. However, the percentage of the region's population affected was lower than in the North West. At its height in 1986, 8.4 per cent of the South East's population was out of work compared with 14.2 per cent in the North West.[10] Regardless of the local levels of unemployment Thatcher's message around jobs remained the same.

This apparent focus on the national rather than the local audience was reflected in the speechwriting process. Michael Scholar recalls that perorations for governmental speeches were, at times, based upon a common template:

> I found a speech that she'd given which had had the peroration written by John [Vereker] ... which I knew ... [had] got roars from the audience and [which] she liked ... very much. [The peroration had a] certain rhetorical pattern to it. 'We will not do this, we will do that'. ... what I did ... was subtly change it. I kept changing it just a bit.[11]

Thatcher's attachment to particular rhetorical patterns was not restricted to the constructing of her governmental speeches. It was also evident in the drafting of her political speeches. Preparing the Conservative Central Council Speech in 1982, Ian Gow wrote to Ferdinand Mount noting that 'pages' had been cut from the speech which Thatcher had previously delivered to the Institute of Directors because she did not 'have too long [to deliver the speech]'.[12] 'But', Gow continued, 'the PM liked them and wanted them saved ... for the Central Council Speech'.[13] As a result, Mount wrote to Thatcher to inform her that not only had he completed 'a rough attempt to put together some of the points you wished to make [in the Conservative Central Council Speech]' but also that he had 'included the passage you wanted kept over from the IoD [Institute of Directors] speech'.[14] Such re-working of a speech draft, whilst uncommon, was not unheard of. In 1982 Thatcher addressed an audience in New York, with passages on British defence policy taken from an older speech, albeit 'in a re-worked form'.[15] In opposition, Geoffrey Howe sent Thatcher a copy of a speech on trade unionism which he had planned but declined to deliver. He did so on the assumption that Thatcher would take his 'thoughts on board'.[16] Caroline Slocock recalls how, when asked to 'say a few words', Thatcher would combine brief speaking notes with 'her own recycled material that she had used many times before'.[17]

As Harvey Thomas recalled, Thatcher's speeches may have been 'regionalised with some of [their] emphasis, [but] the basic message[s] would always be the same'.[18] That Thatcher dismissed Hoskyns' suggestion to record her PPB in, and make reference to, Liverpool when addressing the 1981 Toxteth riots, seems to support Thomas' recollections.

Yet the fact that Hoskyns suggested that Thatcher should record her PPB in Liverpool demonstrates that, in some instances, the geographical location of her platform was important. Thatcher only seems to have rejected the suggestion due to security fears. In a hand-written annotation, Hoskyns tried to persuade Thatcher by drawing on her previous selection of geographical locations. 'Your [Thatcher's] decisions to visit Northern Ireland … have always been 100% vindicated by their public impact.'[19] The relationship between the platform and Thatcher's speechmaking existed beyond the uniqueness of a Northern Irish platform.[20] Even for Thatcher's most parochial speeches, such as the one she delivered in Swale (1976), location was important. This point was made clear by the *Faversham News*:

> It was not what she said – most of the contents of a swiftly-delivered speech would already be familiar to followers of the 'Iron Lady' – but that she was in Swale to say it, which pleased guests.[21]

This was particularly true when Thatcher spoke abroad. The location of the platform was used to underline the political message she wished to communicate. In 1984 Thatcher, concerned about Reagan's Strategic Defence Initiative (SDI) and fresh from her meeting with Gorbachev, was, as Robert McFarlane (Reagan's national security adviser, 1983–5) noted, 'eager'[22] to meet with the president and address the public from Camp David itself. In the opening line of her statement following the meeting, Thatcher stressed that she and the president had physically met to discuss the issue of SDI. 'As you know', Thatcher told the assembled media, 'we [the British delegation] have had talks with the President this morning'.[23] Such eagerness was manifest in Thatcher's decision to travel for approximately fifty-five hours in order to deliver her message from Camp David, emphasizing 'the whole tenor' of Thatcher's message, one of outward 'unity and agreement on arms controls',[24] or, as Thatcher put it, 'Wedge-driving [by the Soviet Union] is just not on!'[25] The importance which Thatcher attached to location was fully understood by her hosts. Preparing for Thatcher's impending visit to the United States in 1983 the US ambassador in London wrote to the secretary of state and explained:

> The U.S. link is central to her [Thatcher's] foreign policy, and the trip is designed in part to make that point as her second term begins. As her Cabinet Office Foreign Policy Adviser told us: to an extent, the trip itself is the message.[26]

The location of the platform could also shape the content of Thatcher's speeches. It was no coincidence that Thatcher launched her first salvo against 'Butskellism' during her tour of the United States in 1975. Locations were carefully selected to ensure that she addressed sympathetic audiences presenting 'fewer constraints'[27] than a British audience.[28] By contrast, hostile crowds had the potential to silence Thatcher. The proposed idea of a two-day regional visit to the West Country, an event which would require Thatcher to give at least a short piece of public oratory, was turned down because a local bacon factory had just made 450 workers redundant. 'We can't go there!' Thatcher scribbled in the margin of a note proposing the trip.[29] A similar situation occurred the following month. 'Are you prepared to go to Hull', Mike Pattison (Home Affairs private secretary, 1979–81) asked Thatcher, 'in the face of the tremendous problems of the area …?'[30] Unlike her proposed trip to the West Country, Thatcher did visit the area, but avoided any set-piece speechmaking, preferring instead controlled meetings with the local mayor, newspaper editors and local party workers.[31]

Of course, Thatcher was not always able to avoid heckling. Her audience at St Lawrence Jewry Church in 1981 included members of the Young Communist League who chanted 'Jobs not words' and 'Thatcher out'.[32] Thatcher's response was shaped by the location in which she was speaking. In response to the 'lefties' who heckled Thatcher, the *Express* recorded that she replied: 'You see why I fight these people?'[33] This was met with applause. Recalling the event, she noted how the location of the speech limited her response. 'I felt a little constrained … if I had not been in a church it would have been "Wham!"'[34] Thatcher made clear that, in another setting, she would have rhetorically attacked the protesters. Location then could silence, accentuate or liberate Thatcher's words.

This sits uncomfortably with conclusions derived from corpus analysis which as discussed, suggest that location was of little relevance to Thatcher's speechmaking. This contradiction is the result of Thatcher's localized oratory being largely ignored by commentators. In total, forty-seven prime ministerial speeches went unreported. When she was in opposition nineteen of Thatcher's speeches went unreported or, where reports did not include direct quotes her unreported speeches tended to be directed towards local audiences and, as a result, held little interest for national media outlets. Few people in 1976 would have tuned in to the evening news, or hurried to buy a newspaper, to learn what Thatcher had said to the National Playing Fields Association. Eighteen unreported prime ministerial speeches were given to local Conservative Clubs, and another two to local Conservative Councillor Conferences. 'There were', O'Sullivan recalls, 'speeches where she is just speaking to the people in front of her.'[35] These parochial speeches often went unreported and as a result, are unrepresented in any conclusions drawn from corpus analysis.

But the media, particularly television, paid close attention to how an immediate audience reacted to Thatcher's significant speeches. The audience was used, as Max Atkinson points out, as a 'barometer of … approval'.[36] ITN's coverage of Thatcher's speech to the Young Conservatives in February 1979 closed with footage of Thatcher receiving sustained applause from the audience. Michael Brunson noted that 'the young Tory audience approved [… of Thatcher's speech] and showed it'.[37] Brunson's words accompanied twenty seconds of footage (of the one minute forty-two-second report) showing the audience applauding Thatcher. Such coverage was typical. The BBC, reporting on Thatcher's speech to the Young Conservatives four years later, noted how the 'Young Conservative audience loved it [Thatcher's speech]'.[38] Even when live footage was not available, such as in John Cole's report of Thatcher's speech to the 1922 Committee in 1984 (all meetings of the 1922 Committee are held behind closed doors), reference was still made to the audience's reaction. 'The Prime Minister's twenty-four-minute speech', Cole told the audience of the BBC's *Nine O'Clock News*, 'received the usual standing ovation'.[39] 'It is very hard', O'Sullivan recalled, 'to make a distinction between different [televisual or immediate] audiences'.[40]

Because of this, Thomas recalls, 'The reaction of the immediate audience', was 'extremely important',[41] and had to be managed. The set from which Thatcher spoke offered an opportunity to do so. 'Under Harvey Thomas' supervision', Thatcher recalled, Conservative Party 'rallies … moved into the twentieth century with a vengeance'.[42] In 1981 Thomas secured permission from the party chairman to erect two screens above and behind the platform from which Thatcher addressed the Party Conference. By the time of the 1987 general election, Thatcher's arrival on the stage would be accompanied by dry-ice, lasers and a video of her various international visits. Celebrity endorsements from the likes of Bob Monkhouse and Jimmy Tarbuck were used to prepare the audience to respond to Thatcher's words in the required fashion.[43] Music too was used to create a sense of occasion. In 1979 the song 'Hello Maggie' was sung at election rallies, much to Lord Thorneycroft's disapproval. In the late 1980s, audiences at larger speeches, such as the Party Conference, were encouraged to sing 'Land of Hope and Glory' and to wave the 2,000 Union Flags which Thomas and his team laid on their seats. 'It worked',[44] recalled Thomas. Television cameras lapped up the pictures.[45]

Eliciting barometric displays of approval from the audience required more than dry-ice, flags and a sing-song. It also relied upon Thatcher's deployment of a range of rhetorical devices, such as humour. In opposition Thatcher collected speech-material which she filed under the heading: 'Ideas. Funny'.[46]

This pragmatic approach to scripting the humorous passages of her speeches does little to counteract the idea that Thatcher 'distrusted frivolity'.[47] It is perhaps telling that this folder contained the grand total of just four sheets of paper. Unsurprisingly, some of Thatcher's self-scripted attempts at comedy did not work. In the final hours of the 1979 election campaign the soon-to-be prime minister seemed to confuse rhyme with humour when she was reported as 'joking':

> We never count our chickens before they are hatched, and we don't count No.10 Downing Street before it is thatched.[48]

Bemusement rather than laughter greeted the 'joke'. This is not to say that Thatcher was unable to script and deliver humorous lines. Thatcher announced her resignation as prime minister on 22 November 1990. Despite this, she was still able to deliver a masterful performance on the floor of the House of Commons, responding to Denis Skinner's interjections and provoking sustained laughter and applause.[49] Such skill was evident at the start of her career too. In 1975 Thatcher read in *The British Genius*, a report published by the Institute of Directors, that 'the production of our industry is actually lower than it was in

Figure 5 Although Thatcher was not known for her sense of humour, she regularly used scripted jokes to elicit positive reactions from an audience. Here Thatcher used humour to stress the common bond between the United States and the United Kingdom.
(Photo by Peter Jordan/Popperfoto via Getty Images)

the middle of the three-day week.[50] The absurdity of this situation was utilized for comic purposes. 'The Labour government', she wrote, had 'caused a level of production that was just below that of the 3-day week in 1974. It seems that we have a 3-day week now only it is taking 5 days to do it in.[51] This line made it into her 1975 Party Conference Speech, albeit in a polished form:

> And it's the Labour Government that have brought the level of production below that of the 3-day week in 1974. We've really got a 3-day week now, only it takes five days to do it.[52]

The line, deploying humour as a means of undermining the credibility of the government, and advancing her pathos-driven style of oracy, elicited the desired response from the audience which was subsequently reported by ITN. This technique was used again in Thatcher's speech at the British Residence in Washington in 1985. Set against a backdrop of Anglo-American tensions surrounding the SDI programme, Thatcher was careful to give 'strong *public* [author's italics] support' for the United States, and did so using humour.[53] Having declared her respect and support for the president, she concluded by stressing the common bond between the two English-speaking countries: 'And alas I cannot imitate this wonderful English-American accent; You ain't seen nothing yet!'[54] The audience erupted in laughter, a positive reaction which was captured by the news cameras, showing six seconds of first Reagan, then Denis Thatcher, laughing at the joke. Laughter then, underlined the comradeship between the two leaders at a time of private, and diplomatic, tensions.[55]

Humour was just one of an array of rhetorical devices deployed by Thatcher. Take, for example, her speech to the 1988 Conservative Party Conference. When discussing the preceding Labour Party Conference, Thatcher employed *erotema* (the use of a rhetorical question) to elicit a positive response from the audience: 'Was Labour about to shake off its union shackles and go it alone? Not on your tod'.[56] This rhetorical question, using a play on Ron Todd's name (leader of the TGWU, 1985–92 and, in 1988, a staunch opponent of Kinnock's modernization programme) generated laughter and applause, captured by the television cameras. Later in the speech, Thatcher moved on to rebut the charge that Conservative policies had created a 'selfish society' by drawing the audience's attention to the increase in charity donation.[57] Thatcher used *erotema* to underline her point: 'Is this materialism?' Yet she followed this with another two rhetorical questions: 'Is this the selfish society? Are these the hallmarks of greed?'[58] In so doing, Thatcher employed *epiplexis* (the use of a pointed series of rhetorical questions to express indignation) as a means of underlining her point. Unusually this did not mark a 'completion point' which would have

76 *Making Speeches*

prompted applause.[59] Instead, Thatcher went on to use *antithesis*: 'The fact is that prosperity has created not the selfish society, but the generous society.'[60] This provoked nine seconds of applause, footage of which was included in the evening's news reports.[61] By deploying rhetorical devices, Thatcher was able to elicit the desired reaction from her immediate audience which, she hoped, would be used by the news media to frame the reporting of her speeches to the wider, national audience.

But it should not be assumed that Thatcher's speechwriting process drew explicitly upon classical rhetoric. Ronnie Millar understood classical rhetoric. He studied Classics at King's College, Cambridge, and was fascinated by Seneca. Perhaps he saw a parallel between himself and the Roman playwright who wrote speeches for Emperor Nero. His bookshelf contained a collection of Cicero's speeches. However, the fact that he studied Latin verbs in The Old Rose, a now derelict pub in Wapping, suggests that his knowledge of rhetoric was that of a keen amateur. Adam Ridley, recalling the scripting of Thatcher's words in opposition, noted that 'we [the speechwriting team] did not go back to Demosthenes, or whoever'.[62] Even Michael Scholar, who had a background in Classical Studies, knew little of formal rhetoric: 'I've never studied Quintilian [a Roman rhetorician]. I couldn't write an essay on rhetoric.'[63] Robin Harris recalled that 'the only phrase used frequently [during speechwriting sessions] was "clap lines"'.[64] He was unaware of the rhetorical devices discussed above: 'They are all Greek to me.'[65]

Unaware of the techniques of classical rhetoric, Thatcher and her speechwriters tried to emulate men whom they *thought* to be classical rhetoricians. Harris remembers how, 'as a young man [I was] much impressed by the speeches of Enoch Powell which were of course very classical ... and sometimes [I wrote] ... in that way myself'.[66] Thatcher was personally inspired by the oratory of Winston Churchill and was not afraid to quote him in her speeches, much to the annoyance of Reggie Maudling.[67] Yet neither Powell nor Churchill had studied classical rhetoric.[68] Nevertheless, the rhetorical devices identified in Thatcher's speeches were intentional. After all, one does not have to know the definition of *anaphora* to use *anaphora*. There was, Scholar recalls, 'no question' of speechwriters using an 'academic template'. 'In my case', he continued, 'it was simply using a flow of speech which was in fact a rhetorical figure. I bet there's a name for it. I've never been bothered to look up what the name is.'[69]

The deployment of rhetorical devices, whether or not they were understood as such, did not guarantee that the audience reacted in the desired way. Thatcher was plagued by the fear that her 'speech would fall flat' and that 'she would lose her

Thatcher's Platform 77

audience'.[70] These fears were not misplaced. Addressing the Young Conservatives in 1979 Thatcher made it clear that, if she were in government, she would give official support for volunteers to replace striking workers: 'It would be the duty of government to harness this spirited reserve to the service of our people. Wouldn't you in this room volunteer if called upon to do so?' Thatcher's use of *erotema* to create a crescendo did not elicit the desired response. Instead of full-throated applause there was a muted reaction. The Young Conservatives were not keen on the prospect of exchanging their Barbour jackets for donkey jackets. 'Come on', Thatcher continued, a little deflated and sounding more 'panto' than 'Iron Lady', 'I want a bigger yes than that!'[71]

The threat of losing her audience did not disappear with Thatcher's ascent to Number 10. In 1981, Thatcher addressed a Gala Lunch in Bonn, where she delivered a speech which included numerous name-checks of distinguished guests in the audience.[72] Unfortunately for the prime minister, the guest list had been changed and, as it became apparent that the individuals being referred to in the speech were not in fact in the audience, the crowd descended into laughter. So angry was the prime minister that Sir Michael Palliser (permanent under-secretary and head of the Diplomatic Service, 1975–82) felt compelled to write a letter of apology. 'I want you to know how deeply I regret that … Diplomatic Service incompetence should have landed you in such an embarrassing position'.[73]

However good the script, however well choreographed the set, the audience's reaction relied, in large part, upon Thatcher's delivery. Of this she was aware. Throughout her career Thatcher would 'mark up the text [of a speech] with my own special code, noting pauses, stresses and where to have my voice rise or fall'.[74] For her first Conference Speech Thatcher added notes. 'Relax', she wrote on the top of the first page.[75] Before the 1984 Conference Speech, Thomas recalls working with Thatcher and an autocue 'adapting the speech [which was never delivered], right up to eleven o'clock' when Thatcher informed Thomas that she had 'to go and visit the parties' and advised him 'to go to sleep for a while', but with the caveat, 'I may call you again at 2.30 in the morning to do some more'.[76] So concerned was Thatcher about her delivery that, on occasions, she videotaped herself delivering the speech. This allowed her to watch the tape back and adjust the text and delivery accordingly.[77]

Thatcher thus strove to ensure that she could 'say things [in] the best way'.[78] To do so enabled Thatcher to guide her audience's reactions. In her penultimate Conference Speech, Thatcher told her audience that 'today inflation is 7.6 per cent. For a Conservative government that is far too high. We must get it down again, and we will.'[79] The applause provoked by this line did not so much rely on her use of the pronoun 'we', but on the nature of its delivery. Her breaking of eye contact with the audience, combined with the drop in tone when delivering the word 'will', signalled that a 'completion point' had been reached and that applause was expected.

Mis-delivery of her lines could lead to the audience reacting in unexpected ways. In *A View from the Wings* Millar recalls the 'clap line' delivered by Thatcher during her Conference Speech of 1980:

> To those waiting with bated breath for that favourite media catch phrase, the U-turn, I've only one thing to say. "You turn if you want to. The lady's not for turning."[80]

He also recalls his surprise that the media 'latched onto ... the *second* [author's italics] sentence'.[81] Millar's recollection is based upon the line that Thatcher delivered, not the line which Millar himself had composed, which read:

> To those waiting with bated breath for that favourite media catch-phrase the U-turn, I have only one thing to say. **You** turn if you want to: the Lady is NOT for Turning.[82]

The final line comprises *one* sentence, split into two clauses by a colon, not, as Millar (and Thatcher) later recalled, two separate sentences.[83] This discrepancy is a result of Thatcher's delivery. Having told her audience 'You turn if you want to', Thatcher dropped her tone and her head, breaking eye contact with the audience.[84] Both actions indicated to the audience that Thatcher had reached a 'point of completion', encouraging the audience to applaud. This applause continued for eight and a half seconds. This was not planned. The script only allowed for a brief pause, indicated by the use of a colon which, in the earlier line ('But I believe that certain lessons have been learned from the experience: that we are coming slowly, painfully, to an Autumn of Understanding') was afforded a one second pause.[85] Indeed, one second was the average time given to the pause Thatcher assigned to colons in the entire speech. It is only after Thatcher had delivered the second clause of the sentence, where she stressed the word 'lady', as well as the word 'NOT' whilst, at the same time dropping her tone and bowing her head to signal a completion point, that the audience broke into seventeen and half seconds of applause. Thus, the audience's reaction to Thatcher's delivery of her words re-shaped the initial script and, in so doing, created perhaps Thatcher's most iconic lines.[86]

Heckling was commonly used by an immediate audience to express disapproval during Thatcher's speeches despite suggestions by some commentators that by the 1970s and 1980s, it had 'disappeared from British political life'.[87] But hecklers' ability to shape Thatcher's words should not be written out of an account of her speechmaking. 'High' and 'low' politics could, and did, collide around Thatcher's platform. 'In the last election [1983]', Thatcher told *Woman's Hour's* Sonia Beesley, 'I said [presumably to party officials] let's speak from the back of a lorry in the marketplace, and back came the heckling, back came the shouting'.[88] Indeed, during the 1983 general election, assessed by pundits to have been devoid of heckling, hecklers interrupted several of Thatcher's speeches, forcing her to depart from her script. When Thatcher told a crowd that 'the National Health Service was safe with the Conservatives' an audience member shouted, 'Oh yeah?'[89] Thatcher was forced to respond to the heckler by *ad libbing*. 'Maggie will [ensure that the NHS is safe with the Conservatives]'.[90] She continued, 'Don't get excited, dear boy, you have a bit more to hear yet, you are going to hear the facts'.[91] Nor was heckling restricted to periods of electioneering. During the 1980 Conference Speech, Thatcher was forced to respond to heckles from the floor by *ad libbing*:

> Never mind, it is wet outside. I expect that they wanted to come in. You cannot blame them; it is always better where the Tories are. And you – and perhaps they – will be looking to me this afternoon for an indication of how the Government see the task before us and why we are tackling it the way we are.[92]

However, exchanges between 'high' and 'low' politics, between the prime minister and the heckler, were never prolonged. Thatcher's recollection of her interaction with hecklers as representing 'verbal combat' seems a little exaggerated.[93] Only on the rarest of occasions were hecklers able to seriously disrupt Thatcher's set-piece speeches, such as the speech she attempted to give in Finchley after being re-elected in the 1987 general election.[94] Most hecklers were bundled away from the platform by Thatcher's security before they could shout more than a brief slogan or personal insult. Such a fate befell a heckler during Thatcher's 1980 Conservative Party Conference Speech. Nevertheless, negative audience reactions added another dimension to Thatcher's speechwriting process, forcing her to adjust, supplement or revise her intended speech mid-delivery.

Commentators have tended to view the world of television and the set-piece public speech as occupying two separate and distinct spaces. Yet, televised news reports of Thatcher's speeches were in fact composed of a relatively high proportion of footage depicting the audience's reaction. This was often commented upon by the reporter and used as a means of contextualizing the speech. It was for this reason that Bernard Ingham recalled, if Thatcher did not pay attention to 'the audience that … [she was] giving the speech to', then the speech would naturally 'fail'.[95] This chapter has placed the immediate audience, and thus the platform, back into the political landscape of the 1970s and 1980s and consequently, back into the assessment of Thatcher's set-piece speeches.

This is not to say that modern British politics had not witnessed what might be described as 'the decline of the platform'.[96] A quantitative analysis of Thatcher's words indicates little regional variation in her public language. The speechwriting process made little allowance for the location from which Thatcher delivered her words. This did not necessarily mean that location was no longer important. Not only could a location amplify the significance of Thatcher's words but, on other occasions, it could prevent a speech from taking place. It should also be borne in mind that the quantitative analysis indicating Thatcher's use of a national, as opposed to a regional language relies upon a corpus formed of existing speeches. Whilst the record of Thatcher's set-piece speeches represents perhaps the most complete record of any British prime minister, it is still incomplete. The speeches which went unreported, or were not reported in detail, tended to be those which held little interest for the mass media, speeches which were directed to a small, local audience, tending to discuss specific issues. Thus, whilst the conclusions derived from corpus analysis may not be wrong, they are not comprehensive.

Although Thatcher did encounter heckling, it no longer had the intensity it once had, although it could still disrupt pre-planned scripts, extending the speechwriting process into the act of delivery. Nevertheless, this did not result in Thatcher disregarding her immediate audience when constructing her own set-piece speeches. Although, as in the case of the 1980 Conference Speech, the audience's reaction could shape the speech itself, Thatcher deployed a range of rhetorical and non-verbal communication devices to ensure that her speeches did not 'fall flat'.[97] The set too, complete with music and celebrity appearances, was created in such a way as to encourage a positive audience reaction, captured by television cameras and broadcast across the nation.

The relationship between Thatcher's set-piece speeches and the platform in non-election years, like those in election years, had changed since the political orators operating in the 'Golden Age' of public speechmaking. But the significance of the platform had not necessarily declined. The immediate audience still figured prominently in the creation of Thatcher's set-piece speeches, both before and during delivery.

5

'We have issued a speech text which does not relate to the one spoken by the Prime Minister, in every respect.' The press and post-delivery speechmaking*

On 28 April 1978 Peter Thorneycroft, chairman of the Conservative Party, sent a letter to the party's frontbench spokesmen. He reminded them that 'most popular [Saturday] newspapers have eight pages of television and are heavily sports orientated'. This, combined with the deluge of speeches sent by members to the press on a Friday afternoon (Thorneycroft estimated that this totalled an average of 15,000 pages every Friday) meant that 'our press releases for Saturday go straight into the waste paper basket'. 'Make important statements on any other day than a Friday', Thorneycroft begged. 'Speeches are not necessary', he continued, 'a mere statement will do'.[1]

The origins of the Saturday newspapers' style, described by Thorneycroft, lay in the half-penny dailies which emerged around 1900. They prided themselves on 'reduc[ing] … the speeches of politicians to their right proportions in the daily prints'.[2] Nearly eight decades later this approach had taken its toll on political speechmaking. Now 'mere statements' would suffice. Drawing attention to the Saturday press' lack of serious political comment, Thorneycroft's letter also correlates with the assumption that it was television, and not the press, that set the political news-agenda. 'The British press of the post-war [1945] age', one commentator noted, 'if not exactly tame, no longer functioned as a beast of prey'.[3] Yet, when studied in relation to Thatcher's speechmaking, it is evident that the press continued to exercise a significant, though not exclusive, degree of influence over the political and media landscape.

82   *Making Speeches*

In 1855 one issue of *The Times* could contain 60,000 words of reportage on parliamentary speeches. By the early 1990s this had dropped to an average of just 100 lines.[4] This brevity was replicated in the reporting of Thatcher's speeches outside the Commons. Less than 30 per cent of Fred Emery's article on Thatcher's 1978 Conference Speech is dedicated to direct quotations.[5] This is more than Robin Oakley's report on Thatcher's 1986 Conference Speech, where only 16 per cent of the article is devoted to quotations.[6] The bulk of the article consists of commentary, where Oakley explains the speech, and its significance, to the reader. *The Times'* report of the Bruges Speech, crucial in setting-out Thatcher's thinking regarding future European policy, consists of 951 words, 275 of which are devoted to quoting Thatcher's 3,519-word speech.[7]

A lack of verbatim reporting was not the exclusive preserve of the broadsheets. Joe Haines, writing for the *Daily Mirror* and reporting, like Oakley, on the 1986 Conference Speech, used no direct quotes from the speech. This was symptomatic of the tabloids' move, during the 1970s and 1980s, to a 'magazine' style, where dense pages of text were replaced by short stories interspersed with visual stimulus. The *Daily Express,* for example, chose to intersperse its report of Thatcher's 1979 Conference Speech with references to her 'moist forehead' which, it suggested, 'show[ed] the effect[s] of the blazing heat of the platform'.[8] The text of the speech Thatcher delivered to the Sri Lankan Parliament in May 1985 received substantially less attention (across both television and press) than her need for a drink of water halfway through. Although such frivolous detail tended not to be replicated in the broadsheets, whose commentary more often set speeches within wider political stories, both categories of newspaper mediated, through comment, the readers' direct access to Thatcher's complete speech.

This stylistic development coincided with, and was possibly the result of, the changing social composition of British political journalists. Bernard Ingham remembers that the 1970s and 1980s witnessed the growth of press journalists' 'own self-esteem [and] arrogance' which resulted, he suggests, in a 'lack of reverence' for the politicians they reported upon.[9] This could be read as representing nothing more than a by-product of Ingham's past relationship with the press. Yet others seem to agree, though in slightly less blunt terms. Riddell identifies (and personifies) the rise of what he calls 'the celebrity journalist' who 'share[d] the educational and social backgrounds of the politicians they cover[ed]'.[10] Peter Jay, friend of Dr David Owen and son-in-law (until 1986) of James Callaghan, spent ten years as *The Times'* economics editor, as well as being appointed ambassador to the United States in 1977. It was widely expected that he would enter the world of party politics. Although this made Jay a unique figure in the journalistic and political world of the 1970s and 1980s, his Oxbridge background (he graduated from Christ Church, Oxford) was similar to many of his contemporaries. Ian Aiken entered journalism, having graduated from Lincoln College, Oxford and the LSE, before moving to *The Guardian* in 1964. Alan Watkins too spent time at the LSE, working as a research assistant, having graduated from Queens' College, Cambridge before accepting a job at the *Sunday Express*. Watkins attended Cambridge alongside John Morris (later secretary of state for Wales, and attorney-general), John Biffen and Douglas Hurd. Simon Hoggart was a product of Cambridge and, having written for *Varsity* was, in 1968, one of only two graduates to be taken on by *The Guardian*. In the period when the National Union of Journalists (NUJ) stipulated that trainees could not be trained in the central offices of national newspapers (Hugo Young, having graduated from Balliol, Oxford, worked for two years on the *Yorkshire Post*) such an entry into national journalism was rare and raised suspicion. Peter Preston (editor of *The Guardian*, 1975 to 1995) was 'sceptical about graduate entrants' and 'their lack of regional experience'.[11] Such a practice did, however, become more common as the 1970s wore on. Peter Jenkins shared Hoggart's elite educational background and resultant by-passing of regional reporting experience. Having graduated from Trinity Hall, Cambridge he joined the *Financial Times* in 1958, before moving to *The Guardian* two years later. At the *Financial Times,* Jenkins joined several other young journalists including Nigel Lawson, William Rees-Mogg, Sam Brittan and Shirley Williams, who took advantage of the newspaper's willingness to recruit straight from university. Watkins is right to note that, at Cambridge at least, whilst the 'political haul of the 1950s was sparse … the journalistic catch was bigger'.[12] This, Watkins asserts, marked a 'decisive shift in terms of trade between politics and journalism',[13] a shift that would be felt by the 1970s and 1980s.

This marked a contrast with the previous generation of journalists. 'I didn't go to university' recalled Bill Deedes. 'I passed my matriculation and spent six months learning shorthand and typing then, through an uncle, I got a job on the *Morning Post* in 1931.'[14] Mary Kenny (*Telegraph* and *Daily Mail*) also remembered how 'Fleet Street was my university. I was expelled from school when I was sixteen and didn't have any formal education after that.'[15] Bernard Ingham, on being offered a position on the *Hebden Bridge Times*, agreed to 'learn shorthand and typing at night school'.[16] Yet this point should not be pushed too far. Deedes, whilst not possessing a university education, was certainly not viewed as a social inferior by the politicians he reported upon. Like Nigel Lawson

84   *Making Speeches*

and Shirley Williams, Deedes was able to move from a career in journalism, to become a government minister.[17]

The fact that Geoffrey Goodman wrote, as part of Terence Lancaster's obituary, that he 'was [...] carved in the traditional mould of Fleet Street journalism in that he did not go to university but travelled the route of local and regional papers before stepping into the big time' demonstrates that the journalists of the 1970s and 1980s did not necessarily represent a distinct break with the past.[18] Yet the very fact that Lancaster was classed as coming from the 'traditional mould' suggests that there was a sense that the world of journalism was changing.[19] Established political journalists of the 1980s, men such as Watkins and Jay, were distinct from preceding generations of journalists in that they viewed the politicians on whom they reported as equals and were, as a result, 'never content to report [rather than comment on] what ... [they found] going on around ... [them, including Thatcher's speeches]'.[20]

Journalists' desire to comment on Thatcher's speeches led to newspaper readers being presented with speeches which, at times, bore little resemblance to those she had delivered. Take Hoggart's report on Thatcher's 1983 Young Conservative Conference Speech. Whilst the speech revolved around an attack on the Labour Party's defence policies, it was also used as 'an opportunity for the achievements of the Government to be outlined to the YCs [Young Conservatives] and [the] public at large'.[21] Thatcher therefore not only celebrated the government's economic record, but also spent considerable time on the government's education policy, claiming that children were 'well-taught' and that the government was pursuing a 'positive approach – the right approach'.[22] Readers of *The Guardian*, however, read a very different speech, distorted by Hoggart's interpretation, and coloured by his personal, political view which understood Thatcher as being 'increasingly mad'.[23] The interpretation of the speech presented to his readers ignored Thatcher's outlining of the government's achievements. It focused instead on just 289 of Thatcher's actual words, selected by Hoggart, which related to defence. This was a favourite topic of criticism for some on the Left. Hoggart also used his article to comment upon wider political stories which related, however tenuously, to the topics Thatcher discussed. Particular attention was paid to the disagreement within the government regarding the economy. To report these wider stories, Hoggart included ninety-six words from the speeches of other politicians. He chose to end his piece by quoting, at length, Jim Prior's criticism of government policies that were 'in grave danger of creating two nations'.[24] Thatcher's objective of outlining 'the achievements of the Government' was thus undermined.[25]

The fact that readers of newspapers accessed Thatcher's words through the interpretations of journalists meant that readers of different titles could be left with widely different impressions of the same speech. In the reporting of the 1982 Conference Speech Terence Lancaster, writing for the *Daily Mirror*, noted that 'Mrs Thatcher dwelt on the Falklands triumph'.[26] He went on to assert that 'this was the bull-point of the Conference. She was into the Falklands within 38 seconds of her standing up'.[27] The *Daily Express*, however, took a different and more accurate line. Whilst acknowledging that 'Mrs Thatcher got her speech off to an uncompromising start by invoking the spirit of the South Atlantic' the article goes on to report that 'the real substance of Mrs Thatcher's speech was her high confidence that she will overcome all the economic difficulties now in her way'.[28] A similar example can be seen in the Conference Speech the previous year, when *The Times* claimed that 'the Prime Minister wasted little time on her political opponents', whilst the *Daily Mirror* told its readers that Thatcher's 'main ammunition was reserved for the policies adopted at last week's Labour Conference – abandoning nuclear weapons and leaving the Common Market'.[29] It was surely then, with tongue planted firmly in cheek, that Thatcher told the Birmingham Press Club how much she owed to the press as it was they who 'help us as politicians ... get across our message to the people'.[30] Newspaper journalists did not act as conduits, but took an active part in the creation of Thatcher's speeches, albeit after they had been delivered.

The post-war period saw several newspapers switching their support from one party to another. This, it has been suggested, demonstrates the primacy of commercial rather than ideological proprietorial interests.[31] But during the period 1979 to 1990 the press remained relatively consistent in their support for one party or another. In 1979 *The Times* (which had supported a Conservative-Liberal coalition in 1974) and the *Sun* (which, when launched as a tabloid in 1969, had been on the Left of party politics) had joined the *Daily Express*, the *Daily Mail*, the *Daily Telegraph* and later *Today*, in supporting the Conservative Party. All would remain supporters for the whole of Thatcher's premiership.

Motivation for such consistency was not driven solely by commercial interests. The political position of a title was often related to the commercial interests of its owner. Nowhere is this better illustrated than on the seemingly innocuous night of 19 January 1986. Disappointed at not being offered a cigar, Woodrow Wyatt had left a social gathering at Chequers with a fellow guest, Rupert Murdoch. On the way home Murdoch gave Wyatt a tour of his unopened printing plant in Wapping. During the tour the two continued to discuss the theme that had dominated their conversation over lunch – Westland. The subject clearly played on Murdoch's mind. Later, at 10.30pm, Murdoch called Wyatt and informed him of his idea to encourage United Technologies (the owner of Sikorsky, of whom Murdoch was a director) to buy 15 per cent in Westland and, in the process, save Thatcher politically.[32] Murdoch's planned move to Wapping relied upon Thatcher's support, so little wonder that in January 1986, he was keen to save her politically. Little wonder too that proprietors such as Murdoch, whose commercial interests benefitted from Thatcher's premiership, supported the Conservative Party throughout the period 1979–90. Jeremy Tunstall, in setting down the key characteristics of the new generations of media moguls such as Murdoch, who came to prominence during the 1960s, eclipsing the press barons of the previous decades, noted that the former believed in exploiting 'political support for future regulatory favours'.[33] Newspaper proprietors then increasingly interested themselves in the editorial policy of their newspapers precisely because of their business interests.

Harold Evans (editor of *The Sunday Times*, 1967–81 and *The Times*, 1981 to 1982) recalled his relationship with Murdoch whilst editing *The Times*:

> The pressures to change it [*The Times*' line taken towards the government] developed perceptibly as Mrs Thatcher's standing in the opinion polls failed to revive and the Social Democrats gained ground [...]. He [Murdoch] did this by persistent derision of them [the Social Democratic Party] at our meetings, and on the telephone, by sending me articles marked 'worth reading!' which espoused right-wing views, by jabbing a finger at headlines which he thought could have been more supportive of Margaret Thatcher – 'You are always getting at her.'[34]

At first glance this would seem to indicate that Evans' initial editorial approach towards the government, one of 'support with vigilance and chastisement' crumbled under Murdoch's proprietorship.[35] Murdoch went on to dismiss Evans in 1981, appointing Charles Douglas-Home in his place. 'Heroic Charlie'[36] had, upon taking up his position, assured Ian Gow by telephone that 'he was determined to reverse the increasingly hostile tone of recent Editorials' so far as the government's economic strategy was concerned.[37]

This partisanship seems to have set the context in which Thatcher's speeches were reported. Take, for example, the way Murdoch's *The Times* and Maxwell's *Daily Mirror* reported Thatcher's 1986 Conservative Party Conference Speech. *The Times* provided a favourable reception for Thatcher's key messages, applauding her for 'the most successful conference in years'.[38] The piece begins with the words 'Mrs Thatcher yesterday launched the Conservatives' bid for a third successive election victory by pledging a crusade for popular capitalism'.[39]

Within the first twenty words of the report Thatcher's 'single most important' theme had been relayed to the readers of *The Times*.[40] It was continued on page four with the article 'Thatcher crusades for popular capitalism'.[41] The piece returned to this theme in the third column, quoting Thatcher: 'Popular capitalism is nothing less than a crusade to enfranchise the many ... that is the way to one nation, one people'.[42]

The *Daily Mirror* however, presents a very different interpretation to its readers. The newspaper's main article, 'Thatcher fires a nuclear missile'[43] focuses almost exclusively on Thatcher's attack on the Labour Party's policy of unilateral disarmament, a popular stance for some on the Left. 'Margaret Thatcher launched an all-out attack on Labour's non-nuclear defence policy yesterday in a bid to wreck its election hopes.'[44] 'Mrs Thatcher', the article continues 'clearly believes [...] [that] defence will be a big vote-winner for the Tories'.[45] Unlike the speech's coverage in *The Times*, there is next to no mention of the 'single most important' theme of the speech, Thatcher's discussion of 'popular capitalism'. The article continues to undermine Thatcher's intended political message, concluding by juxtaposing the third and final direct quotation 'we're in our prime' with the comment, 'the tired looking Prime Minister laughed off claims that her Government had run out of steam'.[46]

Yet the fact that Murdoch felt it necessary to send Evans articles, to criticize completed headlines and to demand greater support for Thatcher's government suggests that Evans *continued* his policy of 'support with vigilance and chastisement', even if this became increasingly difficult.[47] Indeed, Alan Walters was dismayed by *The Times'* coverage of Thatcher's monetarist policies. Writing to Ian Gow, he noted how 'The standard of *The Times'* economics is far below that of the ... *The Guardian*. That is a statement one could never have made when Peter Jay was the Economics Editor'.[48] Similarly, it should not be assumed that Douglas-Home transformed *The Times* into an uncritical supporter of Thatcher's government. This is evident in the way *The Times* covered Thatcher's three Washington speeches of 1983. Thatcher approached the speeches under the shadow of the KAL flight disaster (when, on 1 September 1983, a South Korean airliner was shot down by a Soviet missile) and was consequently keen to use the speeches to communicate internationally the message 'that long-term stability is unattainable unless the Soviet Union is convinced of our collective strength of will and the adequacy of our collective defences'.[49] Thatcher did just that by delivering a fiercely anti-Soviet line. David Watt, writing in *The Times*, raised doubts over such an approach. It was 'absurd', he suggested, that 'some tough talking by a British Prime Minister would have some effect on Soviet behaviour'.[50] The speeches were simply dismissed as an 'extraordinary outburst'.[51] Though no direct link existed between a proprietor's business, and so political bias, and the political line articulated in the titles they owned, party-political interests and business interests could, and did, combine to shape the editorial context in which journalists interpreted and reported Thatcher's words.

It is not surprising then that the press, rather than Thatcher's set-piece speeches, appear to have regularly set the news-agenda and, in so doing, undermined Thatcher's set-piece speeches as an effective tool of political communication. Take for example the BBC's coverage of Thatcher's speech to the Young Conservatives at Wembley in 1983. The BBC carried reports of the speech and, whilst the BBC included a clip of Kenny Everett telling the audience 'Let's bomb Russia. Let's kick Michael Foot's stick away' it did so in the context of reporting on the humour being used in Thatcher's main speech.[52] 'The Premier got a laugh too', Nicholas Witchell told his viewers, 'She claimed that Labour even wanted to control the division of work between husband and wife'.[53] However, this initial line was altered when reported in the press. Although the *Sun* ran with the headline 'Superstar Maggie is a wow at Wembley',[54] *The Times*, and other titles, took a less positive view, stressing that 'there may be embarrassment over the cheers that he [Everett] received [...] protests were made last night after the episode was shown on television'.[55] By reporting Everett's joke, and the complaints it generated, rather than Thatcher's speech, the press diluted both the political message of the speech and news-agenda initially set by television. The press' reporting of Thatcher's Young Conservatives Speech seems to underline the point made by Jeremy Tunstall: 'Typically it is the newspaper which first spills the politician's blood'.[56]

The press' ability to set the news-agenda, and thus wider interpretations of Thatcher's speeches, was not based upon originality. The press relied upon past news stories as a means of interpreting 'the news'. Ingham was aware of this phenomenon. Writing to Thatcher in 1982, he noted that 'the media finds it much easier to run on the tracks formed by clichés rather than reporting fact'.[57] Some of these 'tracks' were laid by Thatcher pre-1979. On 24 January 1976 the *Red Star*, reporting on the speech Thatcher delivered to an audience at Kensington Town Hall five days earlier, branded her the 'Iron Lady', a sobriquet about which Thatcher and her team were 'ecstatic'.[58] Thatcher began her speech in Finchley in late January 1976 by asserting: 'Yes I am an Iron Lady if that's how they wish to interpret my defence of values and freedoms fundamental to our way of life'.[59] Thatcher took the intended insult and wore it as a badge of honour, using it to portray herself as a 'cold war warrior'.[60] In so doing, Thatcher transformed the label into an interpretive reference point by which her later discussion of the Cold War would be understood.[61]

Reporting on a speech that Thatcher delivered during her visit to the United States in 1983, Nicholas Ashford, writing in *The Times*, noted that 'Mrs Margaret Thatcher, living up to her reputation as the "Iron Lady", yesterday delivered a blistering attack on the Soviet Union'.[62] This echoed earlier reports of Thatcher's speeches during her trip.[63] Whilst Thatcher did indeed use her trip to North America to attack 'Soviet tyranny', she also stressed the need for dialogue. 'We have to deal with the Soviet Union', she reminded an audience in Washington, 'we live on the same planet and we have to go on sharing it. We stand ready therefore [...] to talk to the Soviet leadership'.[64] Caught in the interpretive 'tracks' formed by the phrase the 'Iron Lady' 'many of the papers', complained Thatcher, failed to take 'any notice' of her assertion that a dialogue should be initiated.[65]

Further interpretive 'tracks' were established once Thatcher was in government. 'You turn if you want to, the Lady is not for turning' first uttered in 1980, was perhaps the most significant of these. In 1981, Ingham noted that the press 'has not [...] abandoned its search for the great U-turn, though increasingly it expresses the question in different terms'.[66] The term served as the basis for several of the press reports of Thatcher's 1981 Conference Speech. The *Daily Mirror*'s Terence Lancaster reported:

> Thatcher has made some bad speeches before at conferences when she was only party leader. But this was the worst she has made as Prime Minister [...] it seemed that she had nothing new to say, and didn't say it very well.[67]

By relying on the interpretive 'tracks'[68] formed by the coverage of the previous year's Conference Speech, the *Daily Mirror* was guilty of the very charge it levelled against Thatcher, namely that it had 'nothing new to say'.[69] In 1980, the newspaper had declared that 'The lady is not for learning'.[70] A year later it interpreted Thatcher's message in the same way and only slightly adapted the article's title: 'the Lady's NOT for changing'.[71]

Interpretative 'tracks' could thus undermine the effectiveness of Thatcher's speeches, becoming, as the BBC's Michael Cole put it, 'one of the screens of filtration between [Thatcher] and the public at large'.[72] These 'tracks' could also, as in the case of Thatcher's use of the term 'Iron Lady', enhance Thatcher's chosen message.

The lobby system, rooted in Number 10, but speaking with a non-attributable voice, was harnessed as a less haphazard means by which the journalistic interpretative environment could be moulded to promote the desired message(s) of Thatcher's speeches. Thatcher was not unique in this approach.[73] However,

Figure 6 Bernard Ingham, chief press secretary, 1979–1990. Ingham played a key role in managing the media's coverage of Thatcher's speeches. (Photo by Bryn Colton/Getty Images)

under Ingham's direction, and coinciding with a period when the majority of British newspaper titles were sympathizing with the Right, the Lobby became more dominant than ever before.[74] This was best demonstrated in the press' reporting of Thatcher's response to Francis Pym's declaration that 'we have to find ways of coping with higher levels of unemployment than we have been used to … Let nobody think it is going to be easy'.[75] Pym's speech, coming just days after the chancellor had made a speech emphasizing the growing evidence of an economic recovery, was not well received by Thatcher. Nonetheless, she responded with nothing but praise for Pym: 'My Rt. Hon. Friend made an excellent speech last night, so good that I wish to quote from it.'[76] She went further: 'The speech is so good that I might have written it myself.'[77] However, the following day's reports did not reflect Thatcher's apparent warmth for Pym. *The Daily Telegraph* noted that 'The Prime Minister was dismayed by some of Mr Pym's phraseology' whilst the *Sun* declared that 'Maggie sends grim Pym to the doghouse' and the *Daily Express* noted that 'Maggie' was 'cross at Pym's gloomy view'.[78] The press universally interpreted the meaning of the speech, its 'newsworthiness', in a way completely at odds with Thatcher's actual words. The reason for this is hinted at in *The Times*' report:

> It was admitted openly in Government quarters that Mr Pym's main sin, in the eyes of Mrs Thatcher, was that he approved the release by Conservative Central Office of extracts of his speech which made little of the good news and much of the bad.[79]

The phrase 'Government quarters' stood as an opaque reference to Ingham's Lobby briefing sessions which, in providing journalists with 'facts', created or at least shaped the interpretative framework with which they approached, and understood, Thatcher's words. The fact that Ingham had used the Lobby briefing session to set Thatcher's apparently warm words in 'context' created an interpretative framework which ensured that the intended message was reported by the press to the wider audience. So effective was this approach that, as in the case of Thatcher's response to Pym, a prime ministerial speech did not have to literally state its intended meaning.[80]

The controversy surrounding the interpretation of Thatcher's reaction to Pym's speech not only highlights Number 10's use of the Lobby as a means of controlling the post-delivery creation of Thatcher's speeches, but also draws attention to the use of press releases as a means of directing press reportage. After all, Pym's sin was not simply his utterances, but it was that extracts of his speech were then released by Conservative Central Office.

Release of Thatcher's speeches to the media was initially rather haphazard. The formal channel of the Lobby was used at times; 'If the Central Council speech is going to be regarded as a key-note speech', Patten wrote to Thatcher in 1975, 'I imagine you will want to have it "trailed" at Thursday's lobby'.[81] At other times it was left to those close to Thatcher to exploit their social network to ensure that her speeches, and the messages they conveyed, found their way into 'the hands of key commentators'.[82] Adam Ridley ensured that his 'old friend' Sam Brittan (economic correspondent for the *Financial Times*) was provided with the key speeches that Thatcher delivered during her visit to the United States.[83] It was only by doing so that Thatcher would be assured of coverage in the *Financial Times*.

Informal networks continued to be utilized in government. 'I would be talking to [journalists]' Whittingdale remembers, telling them, 'this is a major announcement, this is a new policy, this is a changed position, this is a theme for the manifesto'.[84] This provided the press with 'an idea of ... one or two of the themes' Thatcher wanted to be highlighted in her speeches, and thus directed the journalists' interpretation of the forthcoming speech. However, as Thatcher became more confident, she involved herself in the minutiae of how her words were relayed to the press via formal press releases. In 1981 for example, David Boddy (political press secretary, 1979–83) decided to release only an extract of the speech that Thatcher delivered to the Women's Conservative Conference. This decision ensured the speech's communicative success. Derek Howe (press adviser to the paymaster general, 1979–81) noted that even though 'some press were there', the majority of newspapers took the lead from the section of the speech given out by Number 10, which directed the press' attention towards Thatcher warning television and the press not to provide terrorist groups with vital publicity.[85] However, Boddy's decision also led to Ingham receiving 'some flak at the Lobby' as Lobby journalists wanted to 'make ... [their] own judgement[s] about the news value of the Prime Minister's speeches'.[86] This triggered an internal squabble between Howe and Ingham. The latter demanded that 'full texts of ... [Thatcher's] major speeches should be issued when they are made in public with the press present'.[87] Given the success of the partial press release in directing press attention towards key political messages contained within her speech, it is not surprising that Thatcher intervened on the side of Howe. She made it clear that in 'future there will not [the word "not" is underlined twice in blue felt-tip pen] be a full text [of a speech released to the press]'.[88] Despite Ingham's reticence in 1981, he endorsed the use of the partial press release throughout the remaining years of Thatcher's premiership. John Whittingdale remembers that after the text of a governmental speech had been completed, Ingham would call him and 'say "when can I get a copy?"' so that he could show 'selected journalists *one or two passages* [author's italics]'.[89]

The formal, and informal, release of speeches not only allowed Thatcher to shape how they were reported, but also extended the speechwriting process itself. The speech Thatcher was due to deliver to the Institute of Socio-Economic Studies in New York (1975) was, for example, the product of a 'frenzied last-minute re-write'.[90] At the last moment Thatcher, on Gordon Reece's (head of publicity at Conservative Central Office, 1978–1980) advice, decided to transform it from a low-key address into a 'block buster' speech. In the chaos Thatcher and her 'wordsmiths' failed to spot the potentially explosive passage where Thatcher questioned the assumption 'that the state must provide and service artificial kidney machines to all those who need them' without also acknowledging 'the limited resources available'.[91] It was Reece who, on reading a copy of the speech issued by Conservative Central Office, understood the implications of Thatcher's proposed words. The well-connected Reece swung into action. Newspaper editors were informed that the passage would not be used by Thatcher and, as a result, should not be reported. Reece had acted just in time. The *Sun* had already prepared their front page: 'Let 'em Die, Says Maggie'.[92] Although Reece was unable to prevent kidney machines from developing into a popular means of criticizing the government's spending priorities (Paul Weller sang 'You'll see kidney machines replaced by rockets and guns') his last-minute adjustment to the press release did prevent Thatcher's ill thought-through comment from distorting subsequent reports of her speech. 'The main message of the speech', Thatcher recalled, 'was given maximum attention on both sides of the Atlantic'.[93]

Six years later Thatcher was again completing a speech in a state of panic, this time for the Export Group for the Construction Industries. Again, the press release was used as a means of extending the speechwriting process, buying Thatcher more time, and thus settling her nerves. In an attempt to calm the prime minister, Ingham wrote to her, suggesting that she did not 'waste too much time this weekend worrying about this speech from a media point of view'.[94] 'If, after due reflection over the weekend and on Monday morning, you have any particular message you would like to get over [with the set-piece speech], let us know and we could [...] tip off radio and TV about the point to cover [... and] highlight this passage to the writing press.'[95]

Ingham's nonchalance indicates the frequency with which such a situation occurred. When addressing an audience in Cardiff during the 1983 general election for example, Thatcher attacked the Labour Party, specifically the supposed threat it posed to people's savings. She stated, 'put your savings in your socks and they'd [the Labour Party] nationalise socks'.[96] This line was omitted from the final press release. In Scotland, two years later, the press release following her address to the Scottish Conservative Party has been found to have been 'subject to extensive revision to improve the flow and to introduce a few lighter touches'. Indeed, 'scarcely a sentence of the press release was left unchanged'.[97] In 1981, the original script for the Women's Conservative Conference Speech, minus the *ad hoc* changes Thatcher had made during delivery, was released to the press. This resulted in the observation that 'we have issued a speech text which does not relate to the one spoken by the Prime Minister, in every respect'.[98] Thatcher scribbled in the margin of the text 'who issued this text? I did not [underlined twice] agree to it.'[99]

Yet even if there were inconsistencies, Thatcher defended the press release, the final draft. In an interview in *The Times*, Robin Oakley drew Thatcher's attention to the fact that although she had delivered the line 'we are all too young to put our feet up' during the 1986 Conservative Party Conference Speech, she had not uttered the words 'and I hope you will excuse me if I include myself!' Thatcher replied, 'I did say the next line, but the applause came and totally obliterated it

[...], I stand by that line in the text'.[100] The press release thus enabled Thatcher's speechwriting process to transcend prescribed speechwriting sessions, as well as the delivery of the speech itself.

By the 1980s the press had abandoned any significant use of verbatim reporting, in favour of comment-heavy reports. This was, in part, a reflection of the changing nature of journalists themselves, who were often better educated and frequently shared the same social backgrounds as the politicians upon whom they reported. This trend was rooted in the decades before Thatcher won the leadership of the Conservative Party. 'The atmosphere' at the *Financial Times* during the 1950s and 1960s, William Rees-Mogg recalled, 'was that of a senior common room of young dons'.[101] The 'young dons' of the 1960s became the journalistic elite of the 1970s and 1980s and tended towards commenting upon and interpreting, rather than simply reporting. The wider electorate was therefore denied direct access to Thatcher's words and instead accessed speeches in a mediated format. This left the speech, and its intended messages, vulnerable to both the political leanings and interpretations of journalists, and the proprietors for whom they wrote, as well as to previous interpretations of Thatcher's words. As a result, the press were often able to set the news-agenda and, in so doing, distort, edit and at times rewrite Thatcher's set-piece speeches and the political messages they articulated.

Yet, when set alongside the range of apparatus employed to ensure a favourable press reception, the set-piece speech appears still to have acted as a significant form of political communication during the 1970s and 1980s. Informal networks were used in opposition to ensure that Thatcher's extra-parliamentary speeches reached friendly journalists. The lobby system was used prior to 1979 but, once in government, it became a more powerful tool for Thatcher. The Lobby shaped the interpretative context in which journalists encountered, and understood, Thatcher's Parliamentary speeches. In the case of Thatcher's rhetorical response to Pym's assumed pessimism, this could create meaning which was not immediately clear. Press releases directed press coverage towards key messages articulated within Thatcher's speeches. It also extended the speechwriting process beyond scheduled gatherings of 'wordsmiths' and beyond the delivery of the speech itself. Despite comment-heavy reporting altering Thatcher's speeches, Number 10 and the party continued to exert pressure over the post-delivery speechwriting process. This ensured that set-piece speeches continued to act as effective political tools in Thatcher's armoury.

6

'Tight and taut'. Speechmaking and the electronic news media*

Bernard Ingham recalled how 'Television was ... the most persuasive medium, if you got it right'.[1] From the mid-1970s onward, much of Thatcher's media-related activity can be seen as her attempting to 'get it right', and the same can be said of her colleagues. John Nott, up until the very end of his career, devoted a great deal of energy to 'put[ting] up a good performance on television'.[2] Commentators, both then and now, have done little to challenge this view. Why would they? Not only did Thatcher indulge the cameras with 'spontaneous' scenes of her in a variety of 'walkabout' locations – at times, at the expense of a set-piece speech – but she also spent a great deal of time preparing for set-piece interviews. She gave twice as many interviews on television than on radio or in the press. Footage of Thatcher addressing audiences was often limited to only a few seconds.[3] As a result, her advisers warned her against deploying 'detailed discourse' in her set-piece speeches which, it was felt, did not play well on television, or in the living rooms of the viewing public. Such actions, Thatcher hoped, would allow her to harness the persuasive power of the medium.

Yet, in August 1982, Ingham wrote to Thatcher and noted: 'In my view we expect too much of television'.[4] This chapter will show that Ingham's observation is as applicable to modern-day scholars as it was to Thatcher. Radio broadcast remained an important and effective channel of political communication. Thatcher tailored her set-piece speeches for television *and* for radio. She used both, in combination with the press and her set-piece speeches, to set the news-agenda. Number 10, and the Conservative Party, exploited the technical requirements of both media to shape the presentation of her speeches, and the policy-agenda they articulated. Consequently, it is more useful to understand the set-pieces speeches' relationship with the electronic media, rather than

Figure 7 Brian Walden, one of Thatcher's favoured television interviewers until 1989, when their relationship soured. (Photo by Arthur Sidey/Mirrorpix/ Getty Images)

simply with television alone. In so doing, television, it will be suggested, was a 'persuasive medium', but it was not the 'most' persuasive medium, nor did it eclipse the set-piece speech as an effective channel of political communication during the 1970s and 1980s.[5]

Reece had been the first to advise Thatcher of the potential significance of television interviews. His *Some Guidelines on the Media in a General Election* advised Thatcher to take part in 'one on one interview[s]'.[6] In opposition Thatcher's preparation for such interviews was often driven by guess work. On 14 September 1977, four days before Thatcher was due to appear on Brian Walden's *Weekend World*, the CRD assembled, amongst other things, 'a note detailing such straws in the wind as we have on how Walden's mind is working'.[7] The note, bordering on ambivalence, would hardly have filled Thatcher with confidence, nor would the briefing material provided by Sherman. Signs of Thatcher's approval (underlining points in felt-tip) gave way to disapproval as Sherman's document descended into rantings about 'organized child-molesters' and 'university staff' who were 'ready to condone barbarism'.[8] By the penultimate page Thatcher resorted to correcting the author's spelling mistakes. Despite being in opposition, some of Thatcher's advisers recognized the importance of television but others, it seemed, did not.

Ingham echoed Reece's advice once Thatcher entered Number 10. 'Blockbuster interviews', Ingham recalled, were felt to be 'very important' in setting the news-agenda and thus 'influenc[ing] national thinking'.[9] However, unlike in opposition, her preparation for such interviews was now meticulous. Not only was the location carefully arranged by Ingham, but Thatcher also received a substantial briefing the day before the scheduled interview.[10] Gone was the guesswork that characterized briefings in opposition. Prime ministerial briefings were the result of a discussion between Thatcher's staff and the interviewer. Briefings would point towards the key topics upon which questions would be asked.[11] Before Thatcher's interview with Walden in January 1980 for example, Reece informed the prime minister that Walden would be 'determined to pursue you ... [on] policies which lead to greater inequality [and which] are likely to cost you the next Election'.[12] It was thanks to this preparation, combined with the advice offered by Ingham ('most people, in my view, do not object to others getting on if they work hard for it'), that when Walden raised the predicted topic, Thatcher delivered one of her most memorable statements: 'No one would have remembered the Good Samaritan if he'd only had good intentions. He had money as well.'[13]

This was not the first time that Thatcher had publicly used the biblical reference in discussing this political point. During her CPS Lecture in 1968, Thatcher stated: 'The point is that even the Good Samaritan had to have the money to help, otherwise he too would have had to pass on the other side.'[14] The phrase was used again, albeit in a modified form, in 1978, when Thatcher addressed an audience at St Lawrence Jewry Church, London. 'I wonder', she mused, 'whether the state services would have done as much for the man who fell among thieves as the Good Samaritan did for him?'[15] Although both previous occasions received media attention, it was Thatcher's third use of this biblical reference on Walden's *Weekend World* that achieved the greatest resonance. This was because Thatcher's post-1979 words attracted more attention. Perhaps it was also because, as Reece and Ingham suggested, television, by the 1970s and 1980s, had become the dominant channel of political communication.

Television's assumed dominance is evident in the media 'stocktake' undertaken by Ingham in August 1982.[16] An entire section of the eighteen-page document is devoted to 'Radio / Television'.[17] Despite the title, no mention is made of radio. This seems more than a typo. In opposition Thatcher gave a total of 115 television interviews, fifty-four more than she gave on radio. In government Thatcher gave 610 television interviews, 356 more than she gave on radio. Television seemed to be Thatcher's favoured method of communication. This was, in large part, the result of radio's inability to attract significant audience numbers compared with other media. On 14 November 1979 Reece produced a report listing the chief political television programmes and the size of their audiences. Thatcher ranked, by hand, the list of audience figures. Reece also provided a list of radio stations' audience figures. Radio 4's weekly listening figures are listed as 6.6 million.[18] The *Today* programme for example, could only attract two million listeners at 8am. This fell to 1.3 million by 8.05am.[19] Such figures appeared insignificant compared with the nightly audience figures of television programmes. BBC's *Nationwide* could boast an average audience size of 11.2 million. Statistics such as these only reinforced the views expressed by Reece the previous year that radio audiences (apart from those tuning in in the morning) were composed of 'insomniacs and radio freaks'.[20]

By the mid-1980s Reece's conclusion continued to ring true. Only 4 per cent of the British population could cite radio as their main source of political information. For 63 per cent of the electorate television was seen as the most important, with 88 per cent agreeing that television, along with the press, was one of their top two means of acquiring such information. 'Sound broadcasting', Andrew Crisell observed, 'was no longer a preoccupation of the majority'[21] and nor, it seems, was it a preoccupation of Thatcher and her team.

But set against the tiny proportion of those who cited radio as an important source of political information, Thatcher's use of radio is surprising. Thirty-seven per cent of all of Thatcher's prime ministerial interviews (and 32 per cent of those made in opposition) conducted through the electronic news media, were radio interviews. Thatcher appeared on radio a disproportionate number of times given the size of audience it could attract. Clearly, radio continued to function as an effective channel of political communication.

This was, in part, due to the composition, if not size, of its audience. Richard Wade (chief assistant to Ian McIntyre, BBC Radio 4 Controller) boasted an audience demographic which, whilst small compared with rival television channels, was characterized as being of 'higher class' and 'better educated than the norm'.[22] Thatcher herself was an avid listener to the radio. Ingham recalled how Thatcher listened to the World Service from 6.00am, and then 'always switches to *Today* at approx. 6.30am and listens through to 8.45 every day'.[23] As a result, Whitelaw recalled how Thatcher 'came to ... meetings with that day's programme in the forefront of her mind.[24] Thatcher also listened to *Farming Today*, which Charles Powell called 'the bane of my life' because he would be forced to investigate random issues which had pricked the prime minister's interest.[25]

Virginia Bottomley, minister for health, 1989–92, recalled listening to Niall Dickson, the BBC's health correspondent, 1988–9, and thinking how 'he always seemed to have a better briefing than I had myself in the [ministerial] box'.[26] William Waldegrave (amongst other positions, Waldegrave was minister of state at the FCO, 1988–90) too was an avid listener to the *Today* programme which, he recalled, 'was an important way of judging whether a story which may be in the papers is going to run'.[27] This was because 'it is the first time you see whether *other* serious editors and journalists feel the story is a big one'.[28] The programme thus provided the 'first independent commentary of the morning press',[29] a role which attracted an 'a good, intelligent and influential audience'.[30] Richard Wade's assessment of the political significance of radio's audience at this time then, seems entirely valid.

It is of little surprise then that Thatcher used radio interviews to broadcast semi-scripted statements to such an audience in the hope of shaping the news-agenda. Thatcher's answers were not usually crafted word-by-word in advance, but question topics were known beforehand. This allowed her and her team to prepare to address interview 'objectives'.[31] Following his briefing for *The World This Weekend* Ingham concluded his note by informing Thatcher that 'I am at home most of Saturday if you wish to discuss'.[32] Discussions would revolve around potential questions and areas that interviewers would be warned to stay away from. Prior to her interview with Peter Allen in 1982 Ingham warned Allen of the topics that Thatcher was 'unlikely to want to get deeply into'[33] and advised Thatcher that 'Mr Allen intends to deal only with the Falklands'.[34] This, Ingham told Thatcher, gave the prime minister the opportunity to make the point that 'the Argentines fired the first shot and invaded [the Falklands]'.[35] Possible acceptable answers were devised, some of which were scripted. Thatcher used the interview to deploy her premeditated answer and thus achieve her 'objectives'. 'They're [the Argentines] the invader', Thatcher told Allen. 'They're the aggressor [a phrase Thatcher used twice in the interview], we are the aggrieved.'[36] Thatcher's words were reported in the press the following day.[37] As Caroline Thomas noted, Thatcher could use the radio as a means of shaping the news-agenda. Her appearance on radio could receive 'widespread secondary publicity, both on television and in the press'.[38]

100   *Making Speeches*

Given the effort that Thatcher and her advisers devoted to her appearances on
radio and television it is hardly surprising that one contemporary commentator,
surveying the media landscape in 1979, notes how:

> Political rhetoric has virtually lost its standing as a separate technique of political
> communication, and ... oral performance in its surviving manifestations is an
> archaic, subsidiary method in comparison with electronic technology.[39]

This assumption is, to a degree, borne out by the fact that from the 1970s onwards,
a background in formal oratory, particularly the style practised in the House of
Commons, had little impact on a politician's career. In late 1938 Edward Heath
achieved his ambition of becoming president of the Oxford Union. Michael Foot
and Tony Benn would go on to replicate this feat. Margaret Thatcher could not.
It was not until 1963 that women were permitted to join the Oxford Union. It
took a further five years for the Oxford Union to elect its first woman president.
Yet it was Thatcher who was to reach the highest office and occupy it for the
longest period. The importance of the Oxbridge unions should therefore not
be overstated. After all, Iain Macleod spoke only once in the Cambridge Union,
devoting most of his time to bridge. Enoch Powell used the Union as a means
of acquiring a German newspaper and an evening meal. Though the televising
of the House of Commons in November 1989 led to an increase in reports of
Parliamentary proceedings – The *Daily Mirror*, for example, doubled its coverage
of the Commons between 1989 and 1990 – there is little doubt that the form of
speechmaking honed in the unions, or even in debating societies such as Eton's
'PolSoc', seemed to lack the weight it once had in the pre-television age.[40]

Speeches were covered on television as stories in their own right, but their
coverage was often characterized by simplified and truncated reports, which
appeared 'brief and lifeless'.[41] Due to television's aversion to 'talking heads', footage
of Thatcher speaking was often accompanied by snippets of information or
footage showing what was assumed to be visually interesting, but which often had
only tenuous links to the political message communicated in the speech itself.
As part of her visit to the United States in 1977, Thatcher delivered a speech at
the British American Chamber of Commerce. ITN's report lasted for one minute
forty seconds. Viewers witnessed only thirty-four seconds of Thatcher speaking.[42]
Footage deemed to be of visual interest dominates the report. Thirty seconds of the
report is devoted to Thatcher's walking with Andrew Young (US ambassador to the
UN) and to the venue in which she spoke. In early June 1983 the BBC ran a piece on
Thatcher's visit to North London. The report consists of a montage concentrating
on Thatcher eating marzipan, wearing a 'frilly white hat' and rejecting 'nuts which

are not up to standard.[43] Only the last few seconds of the report are devoted to Thatcher's set-piece speech and the political message she wished to broadcast.[44] The presentational demands of the medium seemed to side-line the set-piece speech, undermining it as a significant form of political communication.

But it was not just the presentational demands peculiar to television coverage that prevented extended extracts of Thatcher speaking. Twenty-four seconds of ITN's coverage of Thatcher's British American Chamber of Commerce speech are devoted to the reporter talking to camera, explaining the significance of the speech. That almost the same amount of time was devoted to footage of the reporter's explanation of the speech as to the speech itself reflected the shift taking place within television journalism. In 1975 *The Times* published two articles, the first by John Birt, then head of current affairs at LWT, and the second by Birt and Peter Jay. The articles called for television journalism not only to report, but also to explain and contextualize 'the news'.[45] Such an approach spread throughout television journalism, both at ITN and in the early debates surrounding the creation of Channel 4 News. But it was at the BBC that the impact was to be most keenly felt. 'An old newsroom hand' remembered how the arrival of 'very smart, young men'[46] preaching 'Birtism' had a profound impact upon reporting. News now 'had to "mean something"' and to be placed in 'context'.[47]

Contextualization, however, could lead to distortion. The BBC's *Tonight* programme covered Thatcher's first Conference Speech as leader of the opposition via *The Kinnock Report*. The report lasts four minutes. Only in the last thirty seconds does Kinnock discuss Thatcher's speech. None of Thatcher's words are reported. Instead, the speech is set in the context of the party's perceived ideological splits. The report begins with Kinnock informing the viewer that 'this week, the Tory Party has been in pieces'.[48] This was accurate. Hours before Thatcher stepped onto the platform Heath had refused Whitelaw's attempts to engineer a *rapprochement* between himself and his successor. However, the report did not reflect Thatcher's objective which was to articulate 'an indictment ... of the whole socialist approach' to the management of the country.[49]

Although this is perhaps an extreme example, the media's distortion of Thatcher's intended message was common. In 1988 Thatcher addressed the College of Europe. So great was the difference between the speech Thatcher delivered and the one that was reported, that Harvey Thomas, having watched coverage of the speech on television, called Charles Powell to ask whether a last-minute re-write had taken place.[50] Mount too felt compelled to write an article in the *Spectator* explaining what Thatcher had 'actually' said at the College of

102   *Making Speeches*

Europe, namely that 'our destiny is in Europe, as part of the Community'.[51] 'There were some very pro-European passages in it [the Bruges Speech]' Anthony Parsons (amongst other notable positions, foreign affairs adviser to Thatcher, 1982–3) recalls, but the 'net effect was negative' as a result of the explanatory approach that characterized journalistic coverage of the speech, itself shaped in part by Number 10's 'spin'.[52] The BBC's *News at Nine O'Clock* for example, opened with the line, 'Mrs Thatcher tells Europe that we will stay British; we will not be part of a European super state'.[53] Before the viewer heard Thatcher, Michael Buerk interpreted and explained the meaning of Thatcher's speech in just nineteen words. Even though Buerk went on to note that Thatcher suggested 'that our destiny was in a more united Europe',[54] he also informed the viewer that:

> Mrs Thatcher has drawn the line on how far she will allow Britain to be part of Europe ... She said we could not abolish frontiers nor allow power to be centralised in Brussels. She agreed that our destiny ... [and that of] Britain would stay British and not become what she called an identikit European state.[55]

Thus, the interpretive framework in which the viewer would understand clips of Thatcher's speech is created by Buerk's commentary and supported by the selection of footage showing Thatcher speaking. The first twenty-six second clip of Thatcher speaking focuses on her opening joke, in which she compares herself to Genghis Khan, whilst the second, twenty-eight second clip, focuses on Thatcher's warnings of the dangers posed by a 'European super-state'.[56] This had a significant impact upon the wider interpretation of the speech, and Thatcher's position on Europe more generally. The nuances of Thatcher's argument, identified by Parsons and Mount, were lost in the selection of footage. In a media landscape shaped largely by television, the set-piece speech did seem to have become an archaic form of political communication.

The tendency to explain was less evident in radio's coverage of Thatcher's speeches due to its lack of visual demands. Radio reported more of Thatcher speeches verbatim than did television or the press. Radio reports of Thatcher's speeches devoted an average of 40 per cent of their total length to audio of the prime minister's verbatim words. Radio 4's *Six O'Clock News* report on the 1983 Conference Speech for example, devoted 38 per cent of its content to Thatcher's words,[57] only 4 percentage points less than the same report the previous year.[58] Television news devoted less time to Thatcher's words. BBC television's *Nine O'Clock News*, covering Thatcher's 1980 Conference Speech, devoted 33 per cent

Speechmaking and the Electronic News Media

of its broadcast to footage of Thatcher speaking.[59] This was 9 percentage points less than its radio counterpart's broadcasting of similar audio clips.[60] Again, BBC television's *Nine O'Clock News* used fifty-four seconds of footage of Thatcher delivering the Bruges Speech during a thirteen-minute report dominated by commentary.[61] Thatcher's verbatim words therefore accounted for just 7 per cent of the report.[62] Stephen Jessel's report for BBC Radio 4's *Six O'Clock News* devoted 24 per cent to an extract of Thatcher addressing her audience.[63] Although this represented a relatively low percentage of verbatim words for a radio report on Thatcher's speeches it nonetheless stands as an example of how radio was unconcerned with visual images. It was thus less prone to potential distractions and, consequently, had the potential to act as a more effective channel of political communication, compared with television and the press.

This did not mean however that radio reported Thatcher's speeches, and the messages she wished to articulate, without distortion. Take Radio 4's reporting of Thatcher's 1983 Conference Speech. Whilst a relatively high number of Thatcher's words were relayed to listeners in the main report, the initial commentary chose to make Cecil Parkinson's resignation 'the story', rather than Thatcher's speech. The commentary included only eighteen of Thatcher's own words: 'We thank you all and we do not forget today the man who so brilliantly organised the campaign.'[64] This was the only occasion in the whole speech when Thatcher referred to Parkinson, and she did so without naming him. Thatcher's objective was to divert attention away from Parkinson's resignation which, she felt, had the potential to 'weaken the government'.[65] This brevity only increased the 'newsworthiness' of Parkinson's resignation. 'So', noted the BBC's Brian Curtois:

> the briefest of mentions – thirteen words [it seems that Curtois did not count the first five words of Thatcher's statement as they do not relate directly to Parkinson] – for the man who'd been one of her closest and influential advisers. She'd [Thatcher] given him [Parkinson] his opportunity for political stardom ... but in the end she had no alternative but to accept what must look like the end of his ministerial career.[66]

Here *Today* had fulfilled its *raison d'etre*, defined by Jenny Abramsky (appointed editor of the *Today* programme in 1986), as 'set[ting] the agenda'.[67] This ambition was not new. 'Every set-piece interview', claimed Julian Holland (who replaced Ken Goudie as editor of *Today* in 1981) 'was expected to create what the news team called "news lines"'.[68] *Today*'s coverage of Thatcher's speech to the House of Commons on 27 January 1986 did just that. The statement aimed to quell

104 *Making Speeches*

questions raised over her earlier statement of 23 January regarding the Westland Enquiry.[69] It was intended to deal with:

> first, the circumstances leading up to the letter of 6th January by my Hon. and Learned Friend [Sir Patrick Mayhew] the Solicitor-General; secondly, the reasons for having an inquiry; and, thirdly, the outcome of the inquiry.[70]

This Thatcher did in a narrative, factual fashion, hoping to put an end to the political capital being gained by the Labour Party. Douglas Hurd was then assigned the job of touring various media outlets and reinforcing the message articulated by the prime minister in the House of Commons. Consequently, Hurd was interviewed the following day on the *Today* programme. During the interview Hurd noted that Thatcher 'must not run the Government as a one-woman band'.[71] That day's edition of the *Evening Standard* ran the headline 'Hurd Warns Maggie'[72] whilst *The Times* noted Hurd's musings 'on the need to have better Cabinet discussions'.[73] Radio's coverage of Thatcher's speeches, like television's, had the potential to set the news-agenda, though not in the way that Thatcher had hoped.

However, the broadcast media's ability to set the news-agenda did not automatically make the set-piece speech redundant as a form of political communication. The set-piece speech was not eclipsed by, but existed alongside, the broadcast media. Often Thatcher's speeches operated in combination with reports transmitted by the broadcast media and did so in a way that set the news-agenda on Thatcher's terms. In March 1988 Thatcher delivered a scripted statement at the beginning of a press conference convened to launch 'Action for Cities'. She was clear about the key messages she wished her statement to articulate:

> The point of today's launch [of 'Action for Cities'] is [...] first to intensify the attack [on inner city problems]. Secondly, [to] show [...] our [the Conservative Party's] determination to advance on a broad practical front. And thirdly, our success in winning the increased involvement of the private sector. That is the key to real success because it engages the commitment of people who have a real stake in the inner cities.[74]

These aims, especially the third, were repeated in later radio interviews. The involvement of the private sector in the project to regenerate cities was, Thatcher told Peter Murphy of IRN, 'absolutely vital'.[75] To substantiate the point Thatcher goes on to elaborate with a list of examples:

> Go and look at London Docklands; there is a massive amount of private sector money. Go and look at any big shopping centre, you will find a massive amount

Speechmaking and the Electronic News Media 105

of private sector money. Go and look at Halifax; the great new enterprise there of the old carpet factory taken over by Ernest Hall out of his enterprise [Dean Clough Mills]; not a penny piece of public money.[76]

This interplay between speech and interview was also evident in Thatcher's use of television. In 1990 for example, Thatcher delivered a speech at a dinner hosted by President Mikhail Gorbachev. No country was 'more entitled to assurance, and re-assurance, about the future of Germany than the Soviet Union',[77] she stated, adding that by:

putting Germany's membership of NATO into this much broader context one can see that it is part of a peaceful coming together of the countries of Europe. I believe it will add to stability and be the best guarantee which both our countries can have against any repetition of the tragedies and disasters of the past.[78]

The five television interviews following Thatcher's speech bore a remarkable similarity to each other, and to the speech which had preceded them. 'They [the USSR]', Thatcher told Michael Brunson of ITN:

want some extra reassurance that a united Germany in NATO will not be to their disadvantage and both the United States and ourselves ... will seek to ... give them that reassurance because we do not think it is to their disadvantage at all that Germany goes into NATO.[79]

To David Smith of Channel 4 Thatcher asserted:

They [the USSR] accept that argument [that a united Germany will join NATO], but the fact is that they are still apprehensive about the unification of Germany – not surprising, they lost 27 million people, dead, in that war and they really want some kind of reassurance.[80]

As Kenneth Baker noted, Thatcher used television interviews to 'get across to viewers the simple message she wanted'.[81] In reality however, this objective was achieved by the combined use of television interviews, radio interviews and set-piece speeches.

Thatcher's set-piece speeches could, on occasions, shape the questions asked of her during subsequent interviews. On 23 September 1980 Hurd sent Thatcher a prophetic minute, warning that 'some forecasters see unemployment rising as high as 3 million in 1985'.[82] The period was dominated by tense industrial relations. Steel workers for example, called a strike on 2 January 1980, only ending the action in April. Ingham had identified these areas as topics on which Thatcher needed to speak publicly and make the case for the success of government policies. On 29 September 1980, six days after the minute sent by Hurd, Ingham laid out Thatcher's presentational priorities:

> It will be vital to demonstrate before Christmas that, whatever is happening for the time being to unemployment, inflation is coming down; money supply is under control [...] and public sector pay settlements are generally going to be a lot lower than last time round.[83]

Thatcher tackled the issue head-on in the speech given to the Conservative Trade Union Conference at the start of November:

> From time to time we have taken this prescription of sound money and good financial housekeeping. But we gave up because we didn't like the pain and discomfort that any medicine can cause when it starts to take effect [...]. Today we know that excess money creates the fever of inflation.[84]

Thatcher underlined her point by drawing a parallel between herself and the resolute will of Queen Elizabeth I who, by restoring 'the coinage in 1561' created 'temporary discomfort' to address inflation.[85] The speech shaped the wider context in which Michael Charlton would later interview Thatcher on *Analysis*. Charlton raised the issue of the economy, specifically inflation. He did so by explicitly referencing Thatcher's recent set-piece speech:

> Prime Minister, the other day in a speech about inflation you invoked the memory of the first Queen Elizabeth and her battle with inflation [...] what convincing answer would you like to give [...] to Sir Harold Wilson, who believes that in three years [...] you'll be replaced?[86]

Thatcher used the opportunity to achieve the wider objective, identified earlier by Ingham, to 'get over our economic messages'.[87] 'Mr Charlton', Thatcher began:

> attitudes are changing. Trade Unions and their members are acknowledging that pay increases have to be earned. Exports have done well, despite the pound's strength [...] the number of strikes have fallen [...] we have got inflation right down [...]. Unemployment [...] takes longer to reduce [...] for the simple reason that people can always be more efficient than they are on the number of people they have now.[88]

Thatcher's appearance on *Analysis* seems to have had the desired result. 'Your *Analysis* interview', Ingham reported to Thatcher the following day 'got good coverage in today's daily press. They concentrated on the economic message: we are reaching the trough and things should start to turn up towards the end of next year. In addition', Ingham continued, 'your interview got on to the BBC news bulletins last evening; has been transmitted abroad in the World Service;

and will appear in *The Listener*. Your economic message [...] is at last being widely broadcast.'[89]

Thatcher's appearance on *Analysis*, and other news programmes, set the news-agenda because, in part, it was reported upon by other media channels. The news, in short, became the news; a symptom of the news media's unquenchable thirst for 'news'. This was exploited by Thatcher and her team. The media's access to Thatcher's words was controlled in order to maximize their impact. Before the 1979 election Reece arranged a meeting with Michael Brunson (ITN diplomatic editor, 1978–86) who had just returned from the United States. Discussion revolved around how the Conservative Party's election campaign could better accommodate the broadcast media. Brunson advised Reece that Thatcher needed to shape her schedule 'around the main television news bulletins of the day', a strategy which would not be possible with today's twenty-four-hour news media.[90] Reece acted upon this advice. Thatcher's electoral set-piece speeches were timed to catch the early-evening news programmes. Central Office mapped journey times from locations across the country to processing laboratories and studios. Speeches and walkabouts were staged at times which allowed maximum publicity. The strategy was a success. Michael Brunson, recalling his coverage of the 1979 election, remembered:

> We [television journalists] fell far too easily for the Thatcher-Reece game plan ... offering interesting and different pictures to television news producers is like offering Mars Bars to someone addicted to chocolate.[91]

By the 1980s the 'vast travelling circus of cameras and other equipment'[92] which previously accompanied the coverage of a key prime ministerial speech was replaced with a 'target team' of two cameramen and a reporter.[93] This increased news teams' ability to gather 'the news'. This ability to report upon more 'news' items did not satisfy, but fed, an ever-growing demand for 'news'. This led, one contemporary commentator noted, to 'news production [... becoming] increasingly passive'.[94] News gathering became dominated by 'the diary', a record of forthcoming 'news stories' which eased the gathering of 'news'. Up to 70 per cent of the stories carried on BBC news bulletins during the 1980s derived from 'the diary'. This was exploited by Number 10's media machine as a means of controlling the way Thatcher's speeches were reported to a wider audience. In September 1988 Michael Buerk welcomed viewers of the BBC's *News at One*:

> Good afternoon. Mrs Thatcher has renewed her attack on the idea of a United States of Europe. In Luxembourg she said that a central European government would be a nightmare and an absurdity.[95]

108 *Making Speeches*

Even though Thatcher was still delivering the speech in Luxembourg (she gave the speech in Echternach, between 13.15 and 14.45 local time, so 12.15 to 13.45 British time) Buerk used the past tense to report on Thatcher's speech and the political message it articulated:[96]

> Mrs Thatcher said that European unity must not be achieved at the expense of the customs and traditions of each country. She said we haven't rolled back the frontiers of the state in Britain only to see them re-imposed at a European level.[97]

Thatcher did indeed utter these words, but given that the speech was being delivered more-or-less simultaneously with the news bulletin, and the fact that the bulletin is devoid of any actual footage of the speech, one suspects that such knowledge was provided to the BBC in advance, rather than being reported from the scene.[98] This is made clear when the camera cuts away from Buerk in the studio to a photograph of Thatcher speaking and a quote superimposed above. Buerk's voice-over narrates Thatcher's words: 'Countries like the USSR, which have tried to run everything from the centre [...] are now learning that success depends on dispersing power away from the centre'. Buerk then states, 'Mrs Thatcher says, "It would be absurd for us in Europe to move in the opposite direction".'[99]

The BBC's later *News at Six* repeats the soundbite Thatcher had delivered in Luxembourg hours earlier. However, the later edition dispenses with presenting Thatcher's words as text and instead shows footage of her delivering the lines in person. The footage reveals subtle, yet noticeable differences between the reports:

> Countries like the Soviet Union [not USSR] which have tried to run everything from the centre are now learning that success depends upon dispersing power and decisions ['and decisions' does not appear in the earlier text] away from the centre and it would be absurd for us in Europe to move in the opposite direction.[100]

The discrepancy between the two news bulletins suggests that scripts, or partial scripts, had been provided for the BBC in advance, or at least, whilst the speech was being delivered. The control that the government had exercised over the BBC's access to Thatcher's words – to 'the news' – ensured that the speech was able to communicate Thatcher's intended messages effectively.

'Editors', Ingham noted, were 'inclined to broadcast the "sound bite" in preference to complex lines of argument'.[101] *The Guardian* lamented how 'the headline phrase which will make the bulletins will [...] crowd out old style [...] oratory in the Foot or Powell tradition'.[102] Yet brevity should not be

Speechmaking and the Electronic News Media

equated with insignificance. Ingham recalled how Thatcher 'tailor[ed] speeches for radio [...] and TV',[103] in a way that Foot and Kinnock famously struggled to do. Frank Johnson mocked the latter in articles in *The Times* entitled: 'Kinnock continues windbag tradition.'[104] This brevity, demanded by the broadcast media, was used to full effect when articulating a point.[105] As Ingham made clear, 'you had to have your mind on how you were going to get the ballpoint [of a particular speech] over [to the wider audience, via the media]'.[106] The answer, as Thatcher realized, was to develop a 'different style' of rhetorical communication, one that prioritized pre-constructed soundbites.[107] Whittingdale remembers that Thatcher and her 'wordsmiths' were fully aware that, except for the Party Conference Speech, coverage would be limited to 'a couple of sentences'.[108] Thatcher, Hoskyns remembers, had 'little feel for language'.[109] Consequently, her 'wordsmiths' were expected to 'add a phrase' which could articulate a political message in a concise, media-friendly fashion.[110] In 'earlier centuries', Millar noted, 'there appeared lengthy "rhetorical masterpieces" but the same was not true for the 1980s: "write it tight and taut, I told myself"'.[111] This style conformed to the truncated presentational demands of the news media of the 1980s.

Nowhere was Millar's 'tight and taut' approach better illustrated than in his now-famous soundbite, 'You turn if you want to. The lady's not for turning.'[112] Although Millar suggests that 'a soundbite can't be struck off like a stamp' it appears that he did just that whilst sitting opposite John Hoskyns in Number 10's Policy Unit.[113] Both were aware of the need to write something for the media to 'latch onto', something which 'might fit a headline space [or be short enough to require minimal editing for broadcast news bulletins]. Not too long, not too short, crisp and easily remembered'.[114] It was Millar who fulfilled the brief. 'I scribbled it [the line "the lady's not for turning"] before pushing it across to him [Hoskyns]'.[115] The phrase gained instant traction, despite Thatcher's mis-delivery of the line.[116] The BBC's television news bulletin, presented by John Simpson, stressed the phrase (and thus the political message) to the wider, television audience. 'Thatcher says she has no intention of u-turning – "you turn if you want to, the lady's not for turning"'.[117] This gained traction on the radio too. 'Driving back from Brighton [following Thatcher's 1980 Conservative Party Conference Speech]' Millar recalls how he heard 'the "Turning" line' quoted 'over and over on the car radio'.[118]

The speech itself was judged to have 'definitely worked'.[119] Millar's soundbite was used as a means by which this success could be measured. Hoskyns remembers that the 'line worked perfectly', allowing Thatcher to communicate

110 *Making Speeches*

her 'single most important message [...] that the Thatcher Government would not change course'.[120] Thatcher herself acknowledges this when she remembers that the entire speech had been constructed to convince both her 'colleagues in the government' and 'politicians of other parties' that the government was not 'prepared to alter course under pressure'. 'I made the point', she continued, 'with *a line* [author's italics] provided by Ronnie Millar'.[121] So effective was the phrase at attracting media attention that Ingham 'speaking as a journalist', noted that 'if you hadn't picked that up then you ought to have been shot'.[122] Brevity was no obstacle to effective political communication.

Ironically, the phrase's popularity led to it becoming an interpretive 'track' which came to distort the reporting of Thatcher's later speeches. Yet Ingham was alert to the potential benefits of repetition. He advised Thatcher 'to keep repeating' messages she wished to communicate, exploiting journalists' tendency to construct 'the news' with reference to past stories.[123] Ingham was preaching to the converted. Since her days in opposition, Thatcher had employed repetition as a rhetorical device. She discussed Britain's relationship with Europe in generally positive terms, reaching back to an understanding of Europe borne out of the ruins of the Second World War, and the tensions of Potsdam. This was a 'free but not a standardised Europe', a Europe 'concerned with democracy [and ...] with peace'.[124] Thatcher referenced this vision explicitly in five speeches during her years in opposition and included near identical passages in her speeches to make the point.[125] Little wonder then that the language Thatcher used during her tour of Europe in 1988, on her self-styled 'mission to explain', attacking the idea of further European integration, became increasingly repetitive.[126] In Bruges Thatcher warned of the threat posed by a 'European super-state exercising a new dominance from Brussels'.[127] The following day in Luxembourg, she continued to argue her case by deploying similar language:

> A centralised European Government would be a nightmare and we have not rolled back the frontiers of the state at home, only to see them re-imposed at a European level. Our future must lie in the willing and active cooperation between independent sovereign governments, each answerable to their national parliaments.[128]

The BBC's coverage reflected Thatcher's repetition. Reporting on her speech at the College of Europe, the BBC's *News at Nine* reported: 'Mrs Thatcher tells Europe that we will stay British; we will not be part of a European super-state.'[129] This was continued the following day when the BBC reported that Britain would embrace a 'European identity [...] working in the best interest of trade, finance and defence' but would oppose any perceived 'loss of national identity and any idea of a United States of Europe'.[130] The BBC noted such repetition. It was reported that, on leaving Bruges and arriving in Luxembourg 'the British message will stay the same, both here and in Spain tomorrow'.[131] The BBC went on to introduce their report on her speech in Luxembourg with a reference to the previous day's speech in Bruges: 'Mrs Thatcher has *renewed* [author's italics] her attack on the idea of a United States of Europe'.[132] Although by the late 1980s repetition did not guarantee that particular messages would gain traction, it was widely accepted that 'there existed a "war of repetition" as each party leader delivered public statements with a "paint-by-numbers" feel about them, as old statements are repeated word for word'.[133] In so doing, Thatcher situated her speeches within particular past resonances which, at times, shaped the way journalists interpreted, selected and reported her words.

Sitting in a television studio and being interviewed by Ludovic Kennedy, the former Prime Minister Harold Macmillan explained the supposedly corrosive relationship between television and oratory. 'The art of speaking, which is a very difficult art, [has] now almost gone. For instance, take the last election [1983]', Macmillan told Kennedy, 'it was almost entirely fought on the television'.[134] For all his nostalgia Macmillan, the self-styled 'Edwardian gentleman' had been a keen advocate of television. His third general election victory in 1959 marked the birth of the age of the 'television election'.[135] Macmillan thus articulated and personified the perception, as common now as it was then, that the post-war media landscape was dominated by television.

To an extent this is true. Reece, and then Ingham, saw 'blockbuster' interviews as key in communicating Thatcher's political messages, and understandably so. Thatcher's preparation for these occasions became ever more professional. At times, these interviews eclipsed Thatcher's set-piece speeches. They carried Thatcher's political messages to a far greater audience than radio (or the press) could hope to do. Size, however, is not everything. The quality of radio's audience ensured that it was used by Thatcher surprisingly often given the size of the audience when compared with television. Radio interviews, like television interviews, were used by Thatcher to deploy partially, or fully scripted words that were used to set the news-agenda. Contrary to widely held assumptions, television did not entirely dominate the broadcast media landscape of the 1970s and 1980s.

In some ways Macmillan's point, that the 'art of speaking' had now perished, is valid. The art of speaking, as practised in the Oxbridge unions, came to carry less weight than it had once done. Endless footage of a prime minister's 'talking head' did not generate 'good pictures' and was thus ill-suited for television. Moreover, the Birtist era in electronic broadcasting left little space for speeches to be reported at length. Thatcher's words were now interpreted, rather than reported. Set-piece speeches seemed a hangover from a past political age, at the mercy of the broadcast media (and the press) that distorted Thatcher's intended messages and, in so doing, set the news-agenda.

But Macmillan was too quick in sounding the set-piece speech's death knell. Far from being eclipsed by the broadcast media, it evolved to suit the media landscape of the 1970s and 1980s. It existed alongside broadcast media channels. Radio and television interviews were used to hammer-home positions first articulated in set-piece speeches either by simply repeating, almost verbatim, the same point or by creating a context which would be referred to by interviewers at a later point.

That Thatcher's interviews became 'the news' in themselves, pointed to the electronic news media's need for 'news'. The more technologically developed the broadcast media became, the more it needed to be fed news, and the more it became passive and open to manipulation. This situation was exploited by Thatcher and those around her. By controlling the broadcast media's access to her words – 'the news' – the party and the government were able to ensure that the set-piece speech remained an effective channel of political communication. Similarly, the set-piece speech itself was created in a way to maximize the media landscape in which it existed. 'Wordsmiths' produced phrases that were 'tight and taut',[136] that encapsulated Thatcher's key political messages and that proved irresistible to the brevity demanded of television and, to a slightly lesser extent, of radio reporting. Thatcher's set-piece speeches, far from appearing 'archaic' did in fact evolve to exploit the modern media landscape into which they were deployed.[137]

7

'Changing the climate'? The speechwriter's political influence*

Drafting the speech Thatcher was due to deliver at the memorial to Airey Neave, Hugh Thomas (chairman of the CPS, 1979 to 1991) noted:

> The word 'renewal' is deliberately used throughout as an indication of what we hope [...] this government will do for the country [...] General de Gaulle used the same word 'renouveau' in the volume of his memoirs to describe his actions after 1958.[1]

Although the word 'renewal' did not make it into the final script, the note indicates the precision with which Thomas and 'wordsmiths' like him, selected their words. It also indicates the degree to which he overstated Thatcher's understanding of de Gaulle. It is doubtful whether she possessed sufficient knowledge of de Gaulle's career to be able to relate to his note. It is also questionable whether the wider audience would have understood the significance that Thomas attached to the word. That he makes no allowance for this suggests that both the speechwriter and the speaker overestimated the agency of their words. Whilst Thatcher's speeches played a role in 'changing the climate' it should not be assumed that they were in some way detached from their context.[2] To state a position in public did not guarantee that the wider audience understood the speaker's intended meaning, or that the intended purpose of the speech would be achieved.

'Politicians', Philip Williamson notes, '*are* what they speak'.[3] This is true and, as this chapter will suggest, the impact of what they say (or, importantly, choose not to say) may not correlate with the intended outcomes of such language.[4] Due to the shifting political landscape in which Thatcher spoke, her attempt to cast herself as a 'conviction politician', but not as an ideologue, was only ever partly achieved. Her attempt to prevent others using the term 'Thatcherism' as a means of casting her as an ideologue often met with failure. Conversely, the political context in which Thatcher operated could facilitate, as much as it could undermine, the realization of her rhetorical goals. The much-repeated claim that Thatcher 'was extraordinary lucky in her enemies' will be problematized.[5] The 'enemies' with whom Thatcher engaged rhetorically were often constructions of her own speechmaking. But the extent to which Thatcher was able to benefit electorally from such labels was, in many ways reliant, at least in part, on pre-existing and popular understandings of her political opponents. Her speechwriters may have identified and played to these popular, and politically useful understandings, but they rarely created them. Thatcher then was what she said, but what she said was not always understood in terms of what she meant.

Peter Riddell, articulating a commonly held view,[6] noted that Thatcher's leadership was characterized by 'conviction politics'.[7] Certainly, Thatcher believed herself to be a 'conviction politician'. In late 1978 she made a private New Year's resolution: 'that I should not depart from my convictions by one iota'.[8] In public she declared that her approach to politics was 'born of the convictions which I learned in a small town from a father who had a conviction approach'.[9] This was evident in her speechmaking. When preaching the importance of individual and social improvement in a speech given in March 1978, for example, she used the same biblical extract (Mark 12:17) that she had heard her Methodist father, Alfred Roberts, use three decades earlier, to make the same point.[10] There is nothing then to suppose that Thatcher's convictions, and the way in which she expressed them, were not the product of her childhood.

In the gloomy climate of the mid-to-late 1970s A.J.P. Taylor spoke for many in the middle class when he saw 'no future for this country'.[11] Thatcher's moral convictions sat comfortably alongside those of Mrs Mary Whitehouse and the former's concern at Britain's economic decline was shared by many. It seemed, for some at least, that Thatcher was the right woman for the moment, yet it is equally true to say that the wife of a millionaire, who rarely returned to Grantham, was not. Thatcher's status as a 'conviction politician' was not simply a reflection of her approach to politics, born out of the Franklin Street Methodist Church and her father's grocer's shop. It was a response to the political climate of the mid-to-late 1970s.[12] As the crisis seemed to worsen, so Thatcher's public statements increasingly referenced her 'conviction(s)'. During 1975 and 1976 Thatcher used the term 'conviction(s)' six times. Between January 1978 and May 1979, she used the term sixteen times. During the remaining eight months of 1979 she used the word nine times. This was intended to garner electoral support by presenting the Conservative Party as being led by 'genuine conviction, in touch and in tune with the people'.[13]

To this end, it was successful. In 1979 May's Gallup Political Index found that 54 per cent of the sample questioned 'agreed a lot' with the statement that Mrs Thatcher was a 'strong personality'.[14] The poll found that 58 per cent agreed that Mrs Thatcher 'has good or new ideas'.[15] The following month Thatcher won the general election, seen by many as 'a victory for conviction and commitment'.[16] Given the policy-platform adopted by the Conservative Party, Thatcher's victory was brought about, in part, by her rhetorical style which resonated within the context of 1979, rather than by policy substance. *The Times* was correct to note that many commentators felt Thatcher's use of the 'language of conviction', had 'won her the election [in 1979]'.[17]

Given the resonance of Thatcher's 'language of conviction' during the 1979 election campaign, it is of little surprise that she and her speechwriters felt it politic to continue with it once in office. The word 'conviction' was used nine times in 1980 and nineteen times in 1981. Thatcher herself pushed such an approach, evident in her *penchant* for including the pronoun 'I'. In a speech delivered during the 1983 general election, Thatcher amended the original line: 'The British people want to see their country properly defended' to: '*I believe* [author's italics] our people want to see ... '.[18] Similarly, the line 'And we shall win' was edited by Thatcher to read: '*I believe* [author's italics] we shall win'.[19]

Thatcher's use of a 'language of conviction' was evident throughout her first government. In the summer of 1981 Hoskyns sent Thatcher a memo entitled *Political Survival*, warning her to 'say "we" and not "I"'.[20] Others, by contrast, encouraged her to continue to use 'I'. In 1981, advising on the prime minister's forthcoming PPB, Hart stressed that 'during the last election the electorate voted for you because they detected a courageous and determined personality utterly different from the past three Prime Ministers'.[21] 'Britain', he suggested, 'would like nothing more than to be led in a good cause by you'.[22] Thatcher responded positively to Hart's sycophancy. His suggestion was marked with two vertical lines to indicate her approval.[23] Fawning 'wordsmiths', combined with Thatcher's genuine belief that she was a 'conviction politician', ensured that she continued to deploy the 'language of conviction' beyond the specific political context in which it evolved.[24]

Yet whilst the language remained unchanged, the political environment into which it was deployed did not. Already, by January 1980, faced with a rise in the mortgage rate and the Cabinet's decision to tax domestic gas, the 'language of conviction' became less convincing. Such decisions, *The Times* noted, 'looked and sounded inconsistent with Mrs Thatcher's known philosophy and practice'.[25] There existed a 'fear that in less than a year, Mrs Thatcher, the great opponent of U-turns [was beginning] to retreat into pragmatism, as Mr Heath did'.[26] Just days before Thatcher addressed the Young Conservatives in 1980, a speech relying heavily on the 'language of conviction', Alan Clarke noted a distinct lack of conviction leadership.[27] The party, he recorded, was driven by *ad hoc* considerations, and was gripped by a 'panic of instant crises'.[28]

The government's decision, taken the following year, to find an additional £300–£400 million to avoid an early clash with the miners in 1981 and to keep open the pits earmarked for closure only added to a political climate which made Thatcher's continued use of a 'language of conviction' seem ever more incongruous. Terence Lancaster of the *Daily Mirror* noted:

> With a great crashing of gears and grinding of brakes Mrs Thatcher has avoided a head-on collision with the miners by swinging her government into one of the most spectacular U-turns in political history.[29]

The Observer taunted the government, suggesting that they 'had not even waited to see the whites of their [the NUM's] eyes before climbing down'.[30] Foot mocked Thatcher in the House of Commons.[31] Even the most 'devout Conservatives', *The Times* noted, were struggling 'to square' the new government's policies 'with the rhetoric and flavour of 1979'.[32] The *Occult Gazette*'s prediction, made in 1975, that Thatcher 'will merely become a second Ted Heath' was becoming a reality.[33]

The powers of the supernatural, which presumably informed the journalists of the *Occult Gazette*, were unable to help them foresee the actions of General Galtieri. The inhospitable landscape of 1979–82 was again shifted by the 'Falklands Factor', which, although not universally acknowledged, is cited by many as the moment when Thatcher was able to turn a potential crisis into political strength.[34] Yet the 'Falklands Factor' was not simply a form of warrior-worship. Unlike the NUM, Thatcher's response to the Argentine threat correlated with the 'language of conviction' which she used, in part, to describe her decisions.[35] 'Mrs Thatcher's views, prejudices and style', Peter Riddell told his readers in 1983:

> have determined the Government's actions more than any other single factor. As Sir John Nott, the Defence Secretary from 1981–3, remarked of her contribution to the Falklands victory, 'without [her] it would have been impossible.[36]

Simon Jenkins writing in *The Times* noted that Thatcher:

> was always the central driving force: it was 'she who must be persuaded' on any course of action. And her dominance was one of decisiveness not, as Eden's was over Suez, of hesitation.[37]

War and then victory in the South Atlantic altered the political context in which Thatcher's 'language of conviction' existed.[38] Two years after the conflict, David Watt noted that Thatcher 'was unashamedly a "conviction politician"', and that this had 'been said so often that it has achieved folklore status'.[39] In the context of the Falklands Crisis, Thatcher had bound herself to the positive attributes associated with the political label 'conviction politician'. In so doing, one later commentator noted that this 'set her on a pedestal of electoral invincibility from which she was not toppled for another eight years'.[40]

Nonetheless, the positive connotations associated with Thatcher's leadership, articulated by those such as Jenkins and Riddell, were not universally accepted. In 1984 Raymond Briggs published his satirical depiction of the Falklands Crisis, *The Tin-Pot Foreign General and the Old Iron Woman*. Briggs presents Thatcher's conviction not as decisive, but demonic. The book spent eleven weeks in the *Sunday Times* bestseller lists, and four at number one. This alternative understanding of 'conviction' gained ground when, in the mid-1980s, a disagreement between Michael Heseltine and Thatcher over the future of the British helicopter manufacturer Westland altered the political landscape once more. Heseltine wanted Westland to join a European consortium and Thatcher wanted it to be bought by the American firm Sikorsky. Heseltine resigned from government on 9 January 1985 following a Cabinet discussion of the issue. He claimed:

> [T]he concept of first amongst equals, which is the position constitutionally of the Prime Minister, was actually set on one side and the will of the Prime Minister was imposed ... [upon] the majority of colleagues who had heard the case.[41]

This relatively trivial disagreement over the future of a British helicopter manufacturer had been transformed into an indictment of Thatcher's leadership. 'We have a form of presidential government', an anonymous Cabinet member reported, 'in which she [Thatcher] operates like a sovereign in her court'.[42] 'She did warn us', Peter Hennessy told his readers:

> three months before becoming Prime Minister she told Kenneth Harris: 'It must be a conviction government. As Prime Minister I could not waste time having internal arguments.'[43]

Here, in these two sentences, the evolution of the meanings associated with the notion of political 'conviction' is made clear. Electorally advantageous for Thatcher in the late 1970s, by the mid-1980s Thatcher's 'language of conviction' took on a quite different meaning, especially when reprinted during the Westland Affair. 'Conviction' was now becoming understood in terms of stubbornness: 'It was no use asking her [Thatcher] to change her mind about something or other.'[44]

So widespread did this negative understanding of 'conviction' become that, in the summer of 1985, David Frost put it to Thatcher that: 'there have been lots of things you will have read in the papers about [...] people [...] talking about the "TBW [That Bloody Woman] factor".'[45] Thatcher responded, telling Frost that she had 'never heard it', demonstrating the point by misquoting the abbreviation, 'TVW?'[46] Her claim of ignorance seems to have been genuine. Thatcher was not briefed on the public's perception of her leadership, based on the findings of Saatchi & Saatchi's *Life in Britain* research, until a meeting held at Chequers on 13 April 1986.[47] The findings confirmed the TBW label. Her leadership was still understood in terms of 'strength', 'confidence' and 'conviction', but was now also seen to have 'lost its way' and as having 'no clear aim'.[48] The prime minister 'was thought to have become more extreme'.[49] These messages 'went down like a ton of bricks', somewhat proving the point.[50]

It was not until the policy debates surrounding the Community Charge that the alternative understanding of Thatcher as a 'conviction politician' made itself felt. Ian Aitken, writing in *The Guardian* noted like many commentators before him, that Thatcher was 'a conviction politician'.[51] Unlike similar statements made in 1979, 1983 or even 1985, this was not meant as a compliment. Aitken, in using the term as a means of justifying his criticism of the Community Charge, did so on the assumption that it would elicit a negative response from the reader. Thatcher was, Aitken pointed out, 'far too entrenched to contemplate even a modest withdrawal'[52] on the policy. Ronald Butt, writing in *The Times*, echoed the point. 'Mrs Thatcher has become more "presidential" than any other peacetime Prime Minister.'[53] From 1988 onwards Thatcher's 'language of conviction' had become politically hazardous.

This mutation continued at pace. Even Brian Walden, Thatcher's favourite television interviewer and sometime contributor to her public statements, promulgated the view that Thatcher was growing increasingly presidential. 'You come over [to the electorate]', Walden told Thatcher during his interview with her on *The Walden Interview* (1989):

> as being someone who one of your backbenchers said is slightly 'off her trolley', authoritarian, domineering, refusing to listen to anybody else – why?[54]

Perhaps Walden's comments were inspired by the recent resignation of Nigel Lawson. Perhaps they were a reaction to an article carried in that morning's *Independent* which accused Walden as being soft on Thatcher.[55] Either way, the comments hurt Thatcher (she did not speak to Walden again) and added momentum to the now widely held view of Thatcher's leadership.

Following the Conservative Party's defeat in Mid-Bedfordshire in 1990 commentators began to repeat that 'Mrs Thatcher's dominance of her Cabinet has turned into a dangerous liability', the word 'turned' suggesting that, as shown above, such dominance, such conviction, *had* been a political advantage. By late November 1990 the mutation was complete. It was Thatcher's position as a conviction politician that *The Guardian* saw as causing the political crisis around the Community Charge. 'She was a conviction politician', the piece noted, 'but too often scorned the reasoned statements of different convictions, sometimes by her closest colleagues. Arguments she relished, as long as she won, but persuasion she neglected'.[56]

However, talk of *Thatcher's* 'language of conviction' when assessing the prime minister's public discussion of the Community Charge is inaccurate. There is little evidence that Thatcher made great use of such language to discuss the policy. Instead, she deployed a language reliant upon statistics, intricate policy-based arguments and attacks on the Labour Party. Speaking to the Conservative Central Council in 1990, for example, Thatcher began by announcing that 'many of the bills for the Community Charge which people are now receiving are far too high. I share the outrage they feel'. She then went on to substantiate this assertion by noting that 'of the 37 million people who had a vote for local councils, only 17 million paid rates', a statistic Thatcher would repeat during a set-piece speech in Finchley.[57] The Scottish Conservatives were told that 'People don't want high spending paid for by high taxes. But that's what Labour want'.[58] After an awkward joke involving seagulls, chickens and Neil Kinnock, Thatcher launched into her defence of the Community Charge at the Conservative Party Conference of 1990:

> Labour's third pledge is to replace the Community Charge with the unfairness of rates with all the additional horrors of a revaluation. What Labour wants is for local authorities to be accountable not to the citizen but to its own Left-wing.[59]

Thatcher then did not discuss the Community Charge in a 'language of conviction'. Nevertheless, political commentators continued to employ such language as a means of understanding both the policy and its implications. By 1990 Thatcher's 'language of conviction' had mutated not only in terms of its meaning, but also in terms of how the language was used, by whom and when.

120   *Making Speeches*

The *raison d'etre* of Thatcher's 'language of conviction' was to oppose alternative political convictions (or, worse still, those deemed to have no conviction at all) which were held to have contributed to British decline. It was an integral part of Thatcher's waging of the 'Battle of Ideas'.[60] Consequently, Thatcher's rhetoric required opponents with whom to do battle. However, contrary to existing assumptions (and Thatcher's own stated assumption), her opponents should not be understood as autonomous entities, waiting for her to react against them. They were in fact political labels, reified by Thatcher.[61]

This is perhaps most evident in Thatcher's rhetorical crafting of the term 'Labour Party'. Like Churchill's unsuccessful attempt in 1945, and the Conservative Party more generally after 1918, Thatcher's construction of the term 'Labour Party' rested upon the stressing of characteristics which, it was felt, would create a political label which could be opposed for maximum political gain. It was John Hoskyns and Norman Strauss who, during the years of opposition, led the process of associating the 'Labour Party' with politically advantageous meanings. Although Hoskyns did not initially hit it off with the leader of the opposition (she was irritated by the amount of lamb that he consumed during their first meal together) she warmed to his proposition to transform 'Labour's secret weapon [the party's relationship with the trade unions] into its major electoral liability'.[62] This required a 'communications programme' that aimed to 'link the Labour Party and the [negative aspects of] union leadership in the public mind'.[63] *Stepping Stones*, the title given to Hoskyns' and Strauss' secret strategy, was presented to Thatcher on 17 November 1977.[64]

Hoskyns' suggestions seemed to have had an effect on Thatcher's set-piece speeches. Throughout 1975 the word 'union(s)' did not appear alongside the word 'Labour' in Thatcher's set-piece speeches. During 1976 and 1977 the word 'union(s)' was used in relation to the Labour Party just six times. When addressing the Conservative Party Conference in 1978 Thatcher made a point of ironically stressing the 'special relationship' between the Labour Party and the trade union movement.[65] From January until May 1979 Thatcher used the word 'union(s)' ten times. This had the desired electoral outcome. In April 1979 polling commissioned by the Conservative Party reported: 'The Labour Party are less likely to be seen as the party best able to deal with the Trade Unions than they were in September 1977'.[66] Though the electorate doubted whether the Conservative Party would be able to handle the unions,[67] Thatcher had successfully associated the label 'Labour Party' with meanings from which

The Speechwriter's Political Influence 121

she could derive political advantage. The 'trade union issue', contemporary political scientists concluded, 'became a liability for Labour in the 1979 general election ... because [amongst other things] of the voters' ... perception of Labour's closeness to the unions'.[68]

This was not solely the result of Hoskyns' and Strauss' strategy. The electoral success that Thatcher was able to gain from meanings associated with the 'Labour Party' was also the product of the industrial unrest that blighted the British economy during the winter of 1978–9. Despite *Stepping Stones* being adopted by the party in late 1977, almost one-third of instances of Thatcher associating the 'Labour Party' with the word 'union(s)' came in the first five months of 1979. Clearly, Hoskyns' and Strauss' desire to imprint the 'Labour Party' with certain meanings could only proceed when conditions allowed. Prior to this, as Hoskyns himself admitted, 'we had been cranking the *Stepping Stones* [engine] ... and had only managed to get it to fire fitfully on one or two cylinders'.[69] It was 'the nightly television pictures of [the strikes]' a consequence of the 'Winter of Discontent' that, as Bernard Donoughue recalled, 'damage[d] ... the government and the trade union movement'.[70] It was this that enabled Thatcher's association of the 'Labour Party' with the negative aspects of the trade unions to gain traction.

Thatcher's reification of the 'Labour Party' was not one dimensional. It did not rely solely upon associating the party with the trade union movement. Had this been the case it would have been difficult to profit from the label once the government had defeated the miners in 1984 and, in so doing, altered the political landscape. A quantitative analysis of Thatcher's prime ministerial rhetoric reveals that the two characteristics appearing most regularly in concordance with the label 'Labour Party' are the words 'tax' and 'defence'.[71] In isolation, both words appear politically neutral. Both took on negative political connotations when used by Thatcher in concordance with the label 'Labour Party'. Thatcher's statement to the Conservative Central Council in 1983 was typical:

> Labour put a tax on jobs twice. Firstly, they imposed the Selective Employment tax. We had to abolish it. Then they put on the National Insurance Surcharge. We have cut it by more than two-thirds.[72]

Thatcher was to repeat the same message when addressing a crowd in Harrogate:

> We had to reduce income tax to encourage managers and workers. And we have. The basic rate reached 35p in the pound under Labour. We cut it to 30p. We had to cut tax on business. And we did. We have slashed the National Insurance Surcharge.[73]

The frequency with which Thatcher linked the Labour Party with high taxation fell again in 1984, to just three speeches, before rising again to six speeches during the general election campaign of 1987. 'Labour', Thatcher told the Young Conservatives, 'is the party of high taxation'.[74] She went on to repeat this phrase twice more in her speech in Newport[75] before warning her audience in Solihull that the Labour Party 'are embarked on a moral crusade to increase income tax'.[76]

The same is true of Thatcher's rhetorical association of the Labour Party with a weak and ineffective defence policy. During 1983 Thatcher would associate the Labour Party with weak defence six times.[77] This was repeated during the 1987 election campaign, where Thatcher did so in eight speeches. The British electorate 'cannot trust a Labour Government', the prime minister told an audience in Newport, because it would 'leave Britain defenceless'.[78] Thatcher then, used her public set-piece speeches as a means not simply to attack her opponents, most often the Labour Party, but to construct a political label which, as discussed below, when attacked, offered the Conservative Party electoral advantages.

Thatcher herself was an important driving-force behind the authorship of this version of the 'Labour Party'. Whilst drafting the Conservative Central Council Speech in 1983, Number 10 circulated a document entitled *Information required by the Prime Minister*. Thatcher requested a 'List of the worst features of Healey's Budgets' and, so that a favourable comparison could be made, 'a jazzed up version of the most exciting features of Geoffrey Howe's five Budgets'.[79] The resultant breakdown of the Conservative record provided Thatcher with the statistics to underpin her association of the Labour Party with high taxation in both the Conservative Central Committee Speech and in her later speech in Harrogate.[80] Analysis of the handwritten notes from which Thatcher delivered her speech to an audience in Fleetwood in 1983 reveals that she herself also inspired the rhetorical association of the Labour Party with the charge that they would 'weaken our defences'.[81] Thatcher jotted the key points of the speech. Under the heading 'Choice at this election' and the subtitle, 'Issues' Thatcher noted, at the very top, 'Defence'.[82] Remembering the 1983 election, Thatcher recalled how 'I always realised that there were a few issues on which Labour was especially vulnerable'. Thatcher named these 'gut issues'[83] (including tax and defence) and associated them with the political label of the 'Labour Party'. That these associations were most pronounced during general election periods illustrates the political capital gained by this approach.[84]

Thatcher was not, however, the sole author of the political label the 'Labour Party' which existed during the late 1970s and 1980s, and which

The Speechwriter's Political Influence   123

the Conservative Party were able to benefit from electorally. Others in her speechwriting team played a part. Take Thatcher's Conservative Central Council Speech of 1983. It is likely that Ian Gow ensured that Thatcher and her 'wordsmiths' had access to the speeches of Cecil Parkinson and Winston Churchill Jnr., the former focusing attention on Labour's tax policy and the latter on Labour's policy of unilateral disarmament.[85] Sherman's submission, 'Fragments for Central Council Speech', covered as it is with blue felt-tip pen, seems also to have been positively received. Sherman's assertion that the speech should be used as a means of 'bringing home to the public what Labour really stands for, and why it won't work' met with particular approval.[86] To achieve this Sherman proposed that Thatcher should focus her attack on both tax and defence. In discussing the latter, Sherman suggested the following: 'Is it moderate to wish to give up our nuclear deterrent one-sidedly, to opt out of our defensive alliances against soviet aggression?' For the former, he urged Thatcher to reveal the threat posed by Labour of 'burden[ing] tax-payers'.[87] Although little of Sherman's suggested wording made it into the final draft, his suggestion of associating the Labour Party with high taxation certainly did.[88]

Thatcher's Prime Ministerial success aligned the political label of the 'Labour Party' with meanings that would provide her with electoral benefits. Although there was, of course, criticism of the Conservative Party's taxation policy, 'tax' was an area from which the Conservatives were able to profit electorally. Ipsos MORI's polling statistics reveal that the Conservative Party were regularly perceived to have the 'best policies' when it came to taxation.[89] During the 1983 general election, when Thatcher's set-piece speeches emphasized the threat of Labour's high taxation, the Conservatives were able to extend their lead over the Labour Party by eleven points on the specific issue of tax.[90] In 1983 Ipsos MORI polls showed that the Conservative Party had taken an eight point lead over the Labour Party in terms of approval ratings for defence policy. As Tim Bell recalls, 'the nuclear debate at the time was incredibly intense ... but there was no contest in the minds of the electorate as to who made them feel the safest on the world stage'.[91] This was repeated during the election month of 1987 when, on the issue of defence, the Conservative Party moved ahead of the Labour Party by nine points.[92]

But whilst Thatcher actively associated specific issues with the political label of the 'Labour Party', she did not herself create these issues, nor did her 'wordsmiths'. Thatcher took great pleasure in quoting the opposition, to an audience in Harrogate:

> Listen to what they [the Labour Party] say about defence: 'Labour will reduce the proportion of the nation's resources devoted to defence' ... To do that would mean cutting Britain's defence by ... [the] equivalent ... [of] the entire budget of the Royal Navy.[93]

Here, Thatcher's construction of a certain understanding of the 'Labour Party' reflected, rather than created, a contemporary understanding of the political label. Conservative Party polling identified that the policy of unilateral nuclear disarmament, articulated by Foot (a lifelong member of CND) and Kinnock (until he dropped the policy following Labour's defeat in the 1987 general election) was electorally beneficial for the Conservative Party.[94] Such campaigning 'tapped into the cold war paranoia that was at its height in British society in 1983'.[95] The way an unknown author, probably Ingham, recorded the Conservative Party's use of the issue of defence during the 1987 election is telling. The Conservative Party's focus upon defence was thought to be having a 'damaging' effect upon Kinnock's presentation 'as a credible defender of Britain'. The issue, the report noted, had been 'milked' to great success.[96]

Similarly, the Gallup Index Poll, for example, showed that in the spring of 1979, 57 per cent of those surveyed agreed that income tax should be cut, an increase of 5 percentage points since October 1978.[97] The Conservative Party's own polling had identified 'tax' as a potentially fruitful topic only eight months into office.[98] This was further confirmed as Parliament prepared to dissolve for the 1983 general election. The Labour Party, taking advantage of the negotiations being held to ensure that the Finance Bill was passed, forced the removal of tax-cutting proposals, underlining its commitment to the 'tax and spend' policies articulated in *The New Hope for Britain*, 1983. Such a policy-agenda 'kept the party's reputation for extremism [...] before the public, a fact which Kinnock's Policy Review (established in 1986) was unable to rectify in time for the following year's general election.[99] The Labour Party, Thatcher recalled after she had left office, 'were quite happy to brand Labour the party of higher taxation: and so were we'.[100]

Established understanding of political labels enabled Thatcher to successfully shape the 'Labour Party', but the political label of the 'SDP', and then the 'SDP-Liberal Alliance' was new, with few entrenched meanings already associated with them. As John Gummer noted, 'neither the party at large nor our back benchers quite know how to handle the SDP – it is all too unfamiliar'.[101] As a result, the rise of the SDP was seen by those such as Michael Jopling (chief whip, 1979–83) as a 'political threat to the Party'.[102] 'The break-up of the Labour Party and the emergence of the SDP/Liberal alliance', wrote Peter Walker (minister

The Speechwriter's Political Influence   125

for agriculture, fisheries and food, 1979–83), 'is the most serious threat to the Tory vote in this century'.[103] Such was the concern that John Gummer suggested that a small group be set up, 'perhaps under Francis Pym's chairmanship, with Ministerial/Central Office membership whose one purpose would be to monitor and counter the Social Democrats'.[104] This perceived threat was the product, in part, of Thatcher's own binary distinctions between Left and Right, a division with which the SDP (and later the SDP-Liberal Alliance) did not conform, and which thus afforded this new political grouping electoral potency. Walker noted how the 'Conservative move to the right and Labour's swing to the left has left a vacuum in the centre which the new alliance has rushed to fill', and to which, it should be added, Thatcherite rhetoric struggled to respond.[105]

It seems that Thatcher's speechwriters responded to this new political threat by attempting to identify the SDP not as a distinct political label – a potentially dangerous tactic since their distinction from the Labour Party and Conservative Party was a source of political strength – but to associate it with the Labour Party. Preparing thoughts for the 1981 Conference Speech, Hoskyns argued that the SDP should be presented as 'the old Labour Party which Heath, Macmillan etc all fought against'. The SDP, Hoskyns stressed, 'stands for everything that got us into the present mess'.[106] Such rhetorical tactics were used throughout the 1983 election campaign. Thatcher, for example, addressed an election rally in Edinburgh by noting how:

> The last Labour Government, in which Mr. Healey was Chancellor and the SDP were prominent members, and which latterly the Liberals kept in office – that was the government which had to be rescued by the international community from the folly of the very policies which Labour would now like to try again.[107]

The same message was repeated a few days later in Birmingham:

> Today the Liberals have new allies: the SDP – the very men (and women, I regret to say, Mr Chairman) who sat in that self-same Labour Government who voted yet more powers for the trade unions, who ran up inflation to twenty-seven per cent, who saddled Britain with debt, led us into the Winter of Discontent, destroyed our Grammar schools and voted for more nationalisation of industry.[108]

Although Thatcher's rhetorical handling of the SDP-Liberal Alliance altered by the time of the 1987 election, the period 1981–3 saw Thatcher and her speechwriters attempt to cast the SDP-Liberal Alliance as the Labour Party of pre-1979. This, it appears, gained only limited traction. The failure of the SDP-Liberal Alliance's 1983 election campaign was less the product of Thatcher's rhetorical tactics than a result, as David Owen recalls, of the electorate, 'quite rightly', associating the SDP-Liberal Alliance with a series of policy and leadership 'fudges'.[109]

Thatcher's post-1990 recollection of her willingness to shape, or at least attempt to shape, political labels such as the 'Labour Party' sits awkwardly alongside statements she had made in opposition. 'We must get rid of labels', Thatcher told the 1922 Committee in 1975. 'We must not attach labels to groups of people. Politics are bedevilled by such labels.'[110] Given that Thatcher had, in the past, been associated with the labels of 'Milk snatcher' and 'Hoarder', it is perhaps more realistic to say that Thatcher did not dislike political labels per se, but disliked those that could damage her own electoral chances.

That Thatcher made such a pronouncement in 1975 is no coincidence. The political label 'Thatcherism', used by Thatcher's opponents to cast her as some sort of right-wing ideologue, was gaining popularity. Nigel Lawson, in *The View from No. 11* suggests that, although it was he who had popularized the term in his speech *Thatcherism in Practice* (1981), he 'later discovered it had been used in [...] *Marxism Today*'. 'But', he continued, 'no one had taken any notice'.[111] Such an explanation seems questionable. Thatcher, when addressing the Conservative Central Council on 15 March 1975, felt that the party had to 'deal' with 'tired and silly slogans' such as 'Thatcherism'. That Thatcher had identified the label as a threat, and that it was the sentence containing the term which the BBC decided to air in their news bulletin, suggests that the term was not only in existence prior to 1979, but that it was popular currency. Clearly, as commentators have suggested, the term was theorized – but not coined – by *Marxism Today* and popularized by Lawson.[112]

Once Thatcher entered office, the term 'Thatcherism' began to shift in meaning. Although in 1980 Thatcher's opponents were attempting 'to make "Thatcherism" the dirtiest word in the country' only a year later Lawson was using the term in a positive manner.[113] By the time of the 1983 general election, the term was becoming a means by which the political landscape could be mapped and understood.[114] By 1984 Thatcher herself was using the term and, in so doing, she captured it from the opposition in the same way that she had annexed the intended insult 'Iron Lady'.[115] 'It's interesting', Thatcher told a Conservative Rally at Westminster, 'to see how catching these policies of sound finance have become – whether they're called honest money, or monetarism, just plain common sense, or Thatcherism'.[116] Thatcher again used the term in a positive manner in 1987 when she appeared on *Panorama*. Though she was hesitant to embrace the term, she nonetheless offered a definition:

> [Thatcherism] stands for sound finance and Government running the affairs of the nation in a sound financial way. It stands for honest money – not inflation. It stands for living within your means. It stands for incentives because we know full well that the growth, the economic strength of the nation comes from the efforts of its people [...] It stands for the wider [...] spread of ownership of property, of houses, of shares, of savings. It stands for being strong in defence.[117]

Similarly, Hart, writing to Stephen Sherbourne, suggested that Thatcher's 1985 Conference Speech 'should speak of Thatcherism. It should mention it by name. It should define it'.[118] Presumably, this would be in the terms that Hart had suggested four years previously: 'Thatcherite policies have two very simple ingredients: common sense and good old-fashioned morality.'[119]

Though sycophantic speechwriters approved of the label, and Thatcher did, at times, use the term in a positive manner, she treated it with caution. Hart's contribution to the 1985 Conference Speech was not taken seriously. The speech Thatcher delivered did not include a definition of Thatcherism, or any mention of it at all. Indeed, she regularly removed any mention of 'Thatcherism' from her set-piece speeches. Although a definition did make it into the final draft of a speech she delivered during the 1983 election campaign, it was Thatcher herself who removed the line: 'Some people call this Thatcherism. I say it is simply common sense. And there is not a patent on common sense.'[120] This reflected Thatcher's dislike of the term. Though the label was in common usage by the mind-1970s, she used the term just once during the period 1975–9. 'She was worried that people could have too much of her'[121] recalled Robin Harris, 'she thought that if people thought she said, "I have created a new ideology" – people would want to see the back of her'.[122] Those advising Thatcher were also cautious of the label. On the odd occasion when Thatcher did use the term (often during unscripted dialogue) Tim Bell 'rebuked' the prime minister 'for using "Thatcherism"'.[123] Thatcher then seemed to represent a continuation of Conservative prime ministers' traditional unease with ideology (though not 'conviction'), or at least with the possibility of being perceived as ideological.[124]

Thatcher was unsuccessful in achieving this goal. Despite rarely using the term 'Thatcherism', it nonetheless came to play an important role in discussing and assessing Thatcher's period in office. From the day Thatcher took office until the day she departed, *The Times* used the word 974 times. During the same period, Thatcher used the term in public addresses just nineteen times. Discussing the Labour Party's 1986 'jobs pledge', Hugo Young commented that: 'For the jobs pledge to cease to appear insane, we need to be able to fit it into a wider landscape: the landscape of socialism, an intelligible replacement for Thatcherism.'[125] Young clearly expected his readers to not only be familiar with the word 'Thatcherism', but to understand that it denoted a coherent ideological position.

Even those close to Thatcher came to understand the term as expressing a coherent ideological position against which their own place in the political landscape could be judged. Tebbit, speaking at the Conservative Party Conference in 1987, made clear his loyalty to Thatcher: 'They [the Labour Party] would be wise to brace themselves for a lot more of the Thatcher era before we come to post-Thatcherism.'[126] It is little wonder that Tebbit's position within the Conservative Party came to be understood in relation to 'Thatcherism'. In 1986 for example, Tebbit's rebuttal to those who criticized the party's policy-agenda was interpreted by James Naughtie as 'Tebbit demands Thatcherism at a faster pace.'[127] Recalling his reaction to Anthony Meyer's 1989 leadership challenge, Howe employed the political label of 'Thatcherism' to describe his and Lawson's complicated relationship with the prime minister:[128]

> The recklessness with which Margaret had been ready, within the last three months, to downgrade or discard two card-carrying foundation members of Thatcherism [Lawson and himself] had done nothing to endear her leadership to me.[129]

Hart was correct when he informed Stephen Sherbourne that the term 'Thatcherism' was being used by 'friend and foe alike'.[130] Despite Thatcher's efforts, 'Thatcherism' came to provide not only a term that journalists could employ to describe the political landscape and manoeuvrings of politicians, but also a term that politicians could use to describe their own positions. Unlike the political label of the 'Labour Party', Thatcher was unable to achieve her intended outcomes with the political label of 'Thatcherism', namely to avoid being associated with the term and its politically dangerous suggestion of ideological coherence.

On 19 January 1979, at the height of the 'Winter of Discontent', Chris Patten wrote to Keith Joseph. He noted how the Labour Party was starting to struggle in the polls: 'things are moving quite nicely in our direction'. This, he continued, was 'because we have moved skilfully in the wake of events, rather than because events have moved in the wake of our rhetoric'.[131] Patten was, of course, bound to say this. He, along with Lord Thorneycroft, tried to kill Hoskyns' and Strauss' *Stepping Stones* project which, by early 1979, seemed to be working.[132]

Nevertheless, Patten's judgement was not unsound. In many ways the success of Thatcher's rhetoric was reliant upon events. As Robin Harris recalled, Thatcher's 'language of conviction', especially that which referenced her childhood, was chronologically specific: 'It was good in 1979.'[133] The political landscape of the 1970s meant that an appeal to conviction evoked a sense of 'resolution' in contrast to 'cynical weakness'.[134] From the mid-1980s onwards, in a political landscape shaped by the Westland Affair and later the 'Poll Tax', Thatcher's 'language of conviction' came increasingly to conjure up notions of presidential leadership and stubbornness. Similarly, Thatcher's successful construction of a politically advantageous 'Labour Party', both in opposition and in government, relied not so much on her shaping of rhetoric, as on alignment with pre-existing electorally useful connotations.

But it was challenging to alter the pre-existing (though not static) meanings associated with certain political labels. Thatcher and her 'wordsmiths' struggled to shape, or disengage from, the ideological coherence associated with the term 'Thatcherism'. Her rhetorical strategy of erasing the word in her set-piece speeches or attempting to align it with 'common sense' in unscripted discussions had little impact. The word became part of the common lexicon employed by commentators to report the internal manoeuvrings within the Conservative Party, as well as to analyse the government's various policies.

Despite Thatcher's and her speechwriters' attempt to carefully construct political labels, based either on 'gut issues', polling research, political pragmatism or, as is more likely, a combination of all three, the authorship of labels came not from the pen of a speechwriter, but from the existing contemporary environment. The success of Thatcher's oracy in achieving its goals, to present the Labour Party as high spending and weak on defence, to portray Thatcher as a 'conviction politician', and to avoid any suggestion that Thatcher represented some sort of ideologue, was not the product of speechwriters' originality but of speechwriters' ability to identify and exploit existing popular perceptions. The success of Thatcher's language was conditioned by her context.

Conclusion

At 6.05am on 2 April 1982 Moody Brook, the Royal Marines' barracks on the Falkland Islands came under attack from *Commandos Anfibios* (special amphibious operations force of the Argentine Marines). 7,920 miles away in London it was 9.05am. Thatcher sat in the flat above Number 10, interviewing Ferdinand Mount and discussing a serious 'problem' – she had nobody who was able to write her set-piece speeches.[1] Mount, she hoped, once appointed to head her Policy Unit, would provide the solution. That Thatcher's mind was preoccupied with the mechanics of speechwriting was, in some ways, the result of poor communications between London and Stanley. She would not be made aware of the Argentine invasion of the Falkland Islands until lunchtime. But it was also a consequence of the importance Thatcher attached to speechwriting. After all, the prime minister was aware that the invasion was imminent. Despite this, Thatcher still devoted time, thought and energy to improving the mechanics of her speechwriting process. Clearly, speechmaking ranked highly in Thatcher's list of priorities.

This was typical of Thatcher. Her engagement diary is full of meetings devoted to speechwriting. On Tuesday 8 May 1979 she spent an hour and a half writing her Scottish Conservative Party speech. She would devote only approximately forty-five additional minutes to meeting her newly assembled Shadow Cabinet. A typical week in 1985 included approximately seven and a half hours of speechwriting, and five hours of preparation for PMQs. On two occasions (25 and 27 November 1985) Thatcher scheduled speechwriting sessions in the evening but did not indicate an end point.[2] So it is likely that Thatcher devoted more than the total twelve and a half hours recorded to the preparation of her set-piece rhetoric.

The importance of speechwriting

Given that Thatcher spent so much of her week writing speeches (not to mention delivering them) it seems strange that her speechwriting, and speechmaking in general, has, until now, been overlooked as a principal topic of study. This is not to say that Thatcher's speeches have been ignored. Contemporaneous political journalists and political scientists referred to Thatcher's public words in their studies of Thatcher and 'Thatcherism'. Historians' early accounts of the topic, written before the archives were fully opened, were forced to rely, amongst other things, on Thatcher's public statements. Later works use Thatcher's words, along with archival sources, to explore specific historical topics. Studies of Thatcher's rhetoric analyse her most famous speeches. Such diversity is unified by one commonality: all use Thatcher's speeches, and sources pertaining to their creation, as a means to an end, rather than an end in itself. This book has shown that Thatcher's speechmaking process is worthy of study in its own right. To suggest otherwise is to ignore an activity that Thatcher valued and prioritized and which, consequently, came to absorb so much of her time.

But the time that Thatcher, and others, devoted to speechmaking was not, as is often assumed, confined to the period preceding the delivery of a speech. David Owen and Neil Kinnock used pre-prepared scripts as a 'first draft' which could change significantly during delivery.[3] Kinnock, for example, could double the length of his initial drafts. A speech delivered by Owen, but more particularly Kinnock, was thus a 'creation of its occasion'.[4] Although Thatcher did deliver un-scripted 'minor' speeches she, like Reagan, rarely departed significantly from pre-prepared speaking notes which, from the mid-1980s, would be read from an autocue. But the reaction of the audience did, at times, cause Thatcher to make changes to her speaking text mid-delivery. Even when Thatcher stepped down from the platform the speech continued to evolve. Press releases were used to tweak and, in some cases, re-write sections of the speech that had been delivered. Yet this, and the growing passivity of the news media, did not afford the party or the government the opportunity to produce a 'final' speech. The Birtist tendency to explain rather than to report Thatcher's words, combined with news media's desire to set the news-agenda continued the speechwriting process beyond the point of delivery. The speech that reached the national audience could, at times, bear little resemblance to the speech that Thatcher had delivered from the platform, or indeed the same speech being reported by other news media. Thatcher's speeches, when they reached the wider, national audience, were thus a negotiated product, formed by 'wordsmiths', the speaker,

Conclusion

the audience, government or party apparatus and the news media. An analysis of Thatcher's multifaceted speechmaking not only reveals a hitherto overlooked area of Thatcher's career, but also furthers our understanding of areas familiar to students of the topic, each of which is addressed below.

'Chaos': Thatcher's speechwriting process

At 9.00am on Wednesday 8 October 1975 Ronnie Millar was in his London flat, in bed and suffering a hangover. The fact that Thatcher was due to address the Conservative Party Conference in two days' time did not enter his thoughts. To his 'great relief' he had been assured that he would not be included in the writing of the speech.[5] Thatcher would write the first draft herself and Patten and Ridley would edit. At 9.01am he was woken by Thatcher's first diary secretary, Caroline Stephens, buzzing on his intercom. His heart sank as he opened the door and noticed that Stephens was clutching a typewriter. Fuelled by coffee, fried liver and Disprin, Millar was put to work. All day Stephens tapped away at her typewriter as he spoke. By the evening Millar was reduced to nursing his hangover with Chardonnay. Word came through that Thatcher had requested that Millar join the writing party in Blackpool. At 7.28am the following day Millar pulled out of Euston, heading north. He continued to write on the train. Adam Ridley greeted Millar: 'You're very welcome', he told Millar, 'mad – but welcome'.[6] Millar continued to work on the speech throughout the rest of the day, that night and into the early hours of the following morning. He completed his final edits minutes before Thatcher delivered the speech at 11.30am. The 'Blackpool experience' of 1975 left an indelible mark upon Thatcher's speechwriting process.[7]

As leader of the opposition, and later as prime minister, Thatcher found scripting major set-piece speeches 'awkward and rather difficult'.[8] The writing of the 1975 Conference Speech taught her that although she could write the notes, or the text, of a 'minor' speech, she 'must have a text in front of [her]' before she involved herself in the writing process of 'middling' and 'major' speeches.[9]

The 'Blackpool experience' also generated the process by which these first drafts would be produced. One author would produce the first draft of 'middling' speeches, whereas an array of contributors would be commissioned to write the composite parts of 'major' speeches which would then be combined to form the first draft. Once in Number 10, civil servants, mostly drawn from her Private Office, were deployed to provide first drafts of Thatcher's speeches dealing with government policy. That Thatcher recalled the creation of her set-piece speeches in terms of 'general rules', and that these were formalized by Ken Stowe within days of entering Number 10, suggests that her speeches were created through a process that emerged organically, but which came to be codified and formalized.[10] It should not be assumed however that Stowe's document, which aimed to formalize the new prime minister's speechwriting process, achieved its intended purpose.

In fact, viewed from the perspective of the speechwriter, Thatcher's speechwriting was characterized by 'chaos', and this chaos was the product of her insecurity in her own ability to write.[11] Thatcher reached out for help in drafting her words. This was not unusual. Churchill's private secretary John Colville recalls 'while the Prime Minister always wrote his own speeches' and was 'beyond plagiarism', after 1951, 'I [...] acquired a certain ability to imitate his style'. As a result, Colville wrote 'quite a number' of Churchill's speeches.[12] Prime ministers from Baldwin to Blair have employed the services of their 'wordsmiths'. What was unusual was the number of speechwriters that Thatcher used. Philip Collins, Blair's speechwriter, notes that unlike presidential 'wordsmiths', 'British speechwriters tend to be cats who prowl alone'.[13] Broadly, this observation is correct. Tom Jones wrote for Baldwin, Joe Haines for Harold Wilson and Collins himself for Blair. Ted Heath relied upon a core team of speechwriters, but they numbered only four. Thatcher, on the other hand, reached out to a multitude of speechwriters. This willingness to gather around her an array of speechwriters reflected the fact that, unlike other prime ministers, Thatcher felt no embarrassment in calling on the skills of others. Tony Benn's observation of Harold Wilson, that he was 'sensitive about any suggestion that he [Wilson] did not write his own speeches',[14] was not applicable to Thatcher.

In opposition, when Thatcher struggled to attract speechwriters and was denied access to the machinery of Whitehall, she regularly worked with approximately twenty-eight individuals.[15] Once in Number 10, dozens of 'wordsmiths' would be recruited, often in an *ad hoc* fashion, to contribute to just one prime ministerial speech. Often Thatcher would demand, on a whim, individuals such as George Urban, men from outside the immediate writing team, to contribute to her speech drafts. This slowed and disrupted the writing process, as well as allowing individuals who operated close to the centre of power but separate from the 'Home Team' (men such as Jeffrey Archer or David Hart, for example) the opportunity to make uninvited contributions. This in turn encouraged individuals to attempt 'to take control of events [in the speechmaking process]', destabilizing the process still further.[16] At times,

Conclusion

this reduced Thatcher's speechwriting to 'madness'.[17] The distinction between political speechwriters and governmental speechwriters broke down. Sections of major speeches would be written by one author and then, without warning, re-written by another. On at least one occasion two teams of speechwriters, working independently of each other, wrote two separate drafts for the same Conference Speech. Thatcher's well-publicized disregard for consensus seemed not to apply when it came to writing speeches.

Although Thatcher accepted that she needed the help of 'wordsmiths' she, unlike Reagan or Heath (both of whom used speechwriters), was heavily involved in the speechwriting process. Her decision to become involved in speechwriting was not unusual for a prime minister. Baldwin had also occasionally composed his own words. Collins remembers that 'Blair often took his fountain pen and scribbled his own words in a spider hand'.[18] Churchill and Wilson regularly wrote their own set-piece speeches. The former tended to dictate his speeches 'in short bursts', and then rework the speech several times.[19] Yet the regularity with which Thatcher involved herself in speechwriting, and the time she devoted to the process, despite her use of speechwriters, is unusual for one in her position. Thatcher regularly took up her felt-tip pen, spending hours editing her speech drafts, often in the company of her 'wordsmiths'. She challenged every sentence and every word. Although this ensured that Thatcher's words, though perhaps scripted by others, were always genuine, it did slow the speechwriting process.

During the early 1980s, Hoskyns remembers, Ronnie Millar and David Howell were working with Thatcher on an upcoming speech. The three played around with ideas. David Howell absent-mindedly suggested the phrase 'a deeper democracy'.[20] Thatcher who, no doubt, had spent the previous hours dismissing her speechwriters' suggestions, latched onto the phrase. She started crooning the words to herself in a low voice: 'Deeper democracy! Deeper democracy!' Howell's relief at having hit upon a phrase that met with Thatcher's approval turned slowly to concern. Minutes ticked by as Thatcher metronomically repeated the words. Howell became increasingly uneasy. He tried to explain that the phrase 'wasn't some "big idea," just a couple of words'. It was no use. 'The more he [Howell] objected, the more enthusiastic she became.' Panicking, Howell changed tactics. He declared that the more he re-read the words the less he was happy with them and suggested an alternative phrase. Thatcher accepted the new suggestion and Howell breathed a sigh of relief. The threesome were able to 'get back to work'.[21] The pain of Thatcher's speechwriting became well known. When Cecil Parkinson, in opposition, was called upon to contribute to

Thatcher's speechwriting he would claim 'quite sensibly, that he had a dentist appointment to attend'.[22]

Any 'rules' supposedly governing Thatcher's speechwriting process tended to break down when applied to the reality of the writing of her speeches. Thatcher's speechmaking process displayed features shared with other prime ministers and leading political figures. Nevertheless, Thatcher's peculiar contribution to this process, and her use of many speechwriters, meant that her approach to speechmaking, if not unique, was unusual.

'Dental technicians': The political significance of Thatcher's 'wordsmiths'

Thatcher's Mansion House Speech in 1990, written in part by Andrew Turnbull (principal private secretary to the prime minister, 1988–92), included the line: 'There will be no ducking bouncers, no stonewalling, no playing for time. The bowling's going to get hit all around the ground'.[23] This defiant line was a gift for the broadcast media. It expressed Thatcher's determination to face-down the mounting criticism of her leadership. Yet this phrase clearly did not originate from Thatcher, who had little interest in sport. 'We, [Thatcher's "Home Team"]' Robin Harris recalls, 'would never have allowed that' to make it into her final speech draft. It was clearly a 'civil service joke' which, as a result, appeared 'old' and out of touch.[24] Words had been put in Thatcher's mouth. In this case, the effect was stylistically jarring, similar to her likening the Labour Party to a pint of bitter, a singularly un-Thatcher-like comment.[25] At other times, Thatcher's use of lines written by others became politically sensitive. Mount claimed that Thatcher delivered a line drafted by John Gummer, that 'the National Health Service is safe with us' in the same way a hostage might deliver a script drafted by her captors.[26] To gain access to the speechwriting circle, Tebbit suggests, was to gain a 'privileged position' as it allowed him to 'make policy contributions' from time to time.[27]

The political agency afforded to Thatcher's speechwriters is perhaps more impressive in their autobiographical recollections than in a more objective assessment. Thatcher welcomed the opportunity to debate and discuss policy with her speechwriters, but she did so precisely because they did not sit in the Cabinet. Though the likes of Hoskyns, Sherman and Gummer may have understood the act of speechwriting as being a politicized process, Thatcher did not. Her speechwriters were 'wordsmiths'. They served a technical rather than

Conclusion 137

a political function. She compared them to 'dental technicians'.[28] Peter McKay of the *Daily Express* likened them to 'worker bees' who 'work themselves to death in a mere eight weeks. Mrs Thatcher's worker bees', McKay continued, 'last slightly longer than that'.[29] Whether viewed as a bee or as a technician, Thatcher saw her speechwriters as providing an answer to a prosaic problem – the need to write speeches. Therefore, though Thatcher did articulate positions that ran counter to her own political beliefs, she did so knowingly, and not as a result of any sort of cajoling from her 'wordsmiths'. The archive is littered with marginalia testifying to this fact. She chose to publicly pledge her support for the NHS and offered to work with the Labour government during the winter of 1978–9. These were not the acts of a prime minister being captured by her speechwriters, but of one who knew what to say in public and when, in order to achieve tactical objectives. Whilst Thatcher may not have been able to write speeches with ease, she did recognize her words' relationship with the policy-agendas of her party and, later, her governments. Thatcher used her public language to say the unsayable and, in so doing, forced the agenda. When she told Gordon Burns that 'people are really rather afraid that this country might be [...] swamped by people with a different culture' she bounced her party into immediately modifying its position on the issue of immigration. Thatcher's abandonment, in early 1979, of 'moderation and quietness' over the issue of union power broke the 'paralysis' in policy formation that had hitherto gripped the party.[30] This began the gradual process of union reform that was to become a characteristic of Thatcher's premiership and draws attention to the limitations of assessing Thatcher's government policy-agenda in isolation from the policy discussions taking place in opposition. In government, her declaration that she was 'not for turning', that she was opposed to a 'United States of Europe' and that she welcomed 'independent state schools' all made public the policy wranglings that had hitherto been taking place in private and, in so doing, enabled her to get 'her way'.[31]

The speechmaking process offers a fresh vantage point from which to assess the articulation, and thus the shaping, of Thatcher's policy-agenda. Thatcher's speeches, and the policy-agenda with which they were so closely related, were shaped not solely by Thatcher's convictions, or by a coherent 'Thatcherite' ideology. Whether 'attack[ing]' the idea of a 'United States of Europe'[32] (Bruges Speech, 1988), or sanctioning the chancellor's policy of shadowing the Deutschmark (PMQs, May 1988), all statements, and their associated political implications, were coloured by the organizational 'chaos' of the speechwriting process. The former, for example, resulted from a form of speech draft 'ping-pong' between the FCO and Number 10, whilst the latter was the product of a hastily convened speechwriting session between the prime minister and the chancellor, in which policy commitments were exchanged for public words of support. Thus, the analysis of Thatcher's speechmaking process suggests that the effect of the prosaic, day-to-day organizational chaos of running the government or, for that matter, the opposition, of which speechmaking is part, has perhaps been overlooked in studies of Thatcher's Conservative Party, and the policy-agendas it pursued.

'Outsiders': who were Thatcher's 'wordsmiths'?

The Old Rose pub, which closed its doors in early 2011, is situated in Wapping. Its nondescript exterior of London red-brick and red-painted columns looks much like any other pub in the East End of London. From the mid-1980s onward it served a mixed clientele. Local residents propping up the bar of their 'local' drank alongside 'media types' who had stopped for a drink on their way home from work. Situated no more than five miles from Downing Street (as the crow flies), its beer-stained wooden chairs, glasses of Fanta and fluorescent lighting seemed a world away from Number 10.[33] Yet, from 1987 onward, The Old Rose regularly played host to Ronnie Millar, Woodrow Wyatt and David Hart – who, at various moments in time, contributed to Thatcher's speechmaking and as a consequence could claim to have held positions of significance within Thatcher's 'court'. That they met in The Old Rose seemed to epitomize the assumption that Thatcher's courtiers were somehow 'outsiders'.[34] Reflecting upon Thatcher's election to the party's leadership in 1975, Simon Jenkins of *The Times* recalled how she was 'an outsider, the candidate of the "peasants' revolt", of the dispossessed right wing'.[35] Thatcher herself encouraged this characterization.[36]

In the case of Alfred Sherman, a former Communist who experienced poverty in the East End, such an interpretation seems plausible. However, a study of Thatcher's speechmaking shows that many of those upon whom she relied were not maverick outsiders. Thatcher's private secretaries, men who epitomized the establishment, played a significant role in the scripting of the words that would articulate her governments' policy-agenda. Ferdinand Mount, an old-Etonian, shaped many of Thatcher's political speeches from his position as head of the Number 10 Policy Unit. In reality, Thatcher's 'wordsmiths' defied categorization. This is best illustrated by Mount's predecessor. Hoskyns, unlike many of those working on Thatcher's speeches, did not spend his formative years at Oxbridge. Yet, perhaps because of this, he was proud of his regimental tie (Rifle Brigade)

Conclusion

which he wore at regimental dinners. Here he socialized with, amongst others, fellow Wykamists. Despite his suggestions to the contrary, Hoskyns was hardly an establishment 'outsider'. Instead, he personifies the nebulous nature of the term 'establishment', and so its consequent limited value as a means of categorization.

A study of Thatcher's 'wordsmiths' also reveals the limitation of using the political spectrum as a means of categorization. Hoskyns remembers being part of a small 'band of revolutionaries'[37] who transformed the political orientation of the Conservative Party. Alongside others such as Sherman, he fought to ensure that Thatcher's major set-piece speeches bore the hallmark of the Right. Yet Thatcher did not necessarily agree with his approach. In the factious context of Conservative Party politics of 1981 the emollient language provided by the 'wet' John Gummer was preferred over that scripted by wordsmiths associated with the CPS. Chris Patten, like Gummer, was well-known for his 'wet' tendencies and, again like Gummer, shaped much of Thatcher's articulation of her policy-agenda both in opposition and in government. When addressing the House of Commons from the opposition's benches at critical moments, a skill that Thatcher was never able to master, Sherman's scripts were jettisoned in favour of those penned by party grandees. Chris Patten remained a key contributor to Thatcher's speeches from opposition until the later years of her premiership. In speechmaking at least, Thatcher did not simply rely upon 'the dispossessed right wing' or allow ideological dogmatism to shape the team of individuals on whom she relied.

'Thatcher's people', viewed from the perspective of speechmaking, cannot be defined by a set of shared characteristics. Her speechwriters, many of whom have been overlooked in studies of Thatcher's leadership of both party and government, included those of great wealth, and those who relied upon speechwriting as a source of income. They included those who had attended Oxbridge, and those who had not received a university education at all. They included men who were 'wet' and men who were 'dry', men who drank in Whites, and those who drank in The Old Rose.

'Verbal combat': Thatcher and the platform

According to Thatcher's reminiscences, her platform speeches could be lively affairs where she engaged in 'verbal combat' with her immediate audience.[38] But this was not always the case. During a visit to Tiptree in Essex during the 1987 election campaign, Thatcher 'set up a soapbox, summoning the local shoppers to hear her message.[39] What the locals of Tiptree heard has not been recorded in any detail. When one audience member was asked to recall Thatcher's words, she responded simply that it was 'a lot of rubbish'.[40] The audience member's disenchantment with Thatcher's words may have been the result of her political leanings. Equally, it may have been a symptom of Thatcher's inability to connect with an immediate audience. Often during election campaigns, Thatcher made use of 'template' speeches, worked up the night before, and designed to communicate national messages with only a token reference to the locality.[41] Logistical convenience seemed to be the overwhelming consideration in deciding where she should speak. Thatcher's speechmaking therefore reflected the wider historical trend of a 'decline of the platform'. The interaction between 'high' and 'low' politics migrated to the television studio, or sometimes, to the radio studio. This, it would seem, reduced the political significance of the location of the platform and the immediate audience surrounding it.

But a quantitative analysis of Thatcher's campaigning suggests a different scenario. In the month leading up to the general election of 1987 for example, Thatcher gave a total of five speeches, three of which were in London, one in the West Midlands and one in the South East. During the election campaign itself, Thatcher's speechmaking increased, with her delivering twenty-seven speeches. London was the most used location, with nine speeches, two of which were in her constituency of Finchley. North Yorkshire, Wales and the South East hosted just one speech each. The month following the election saw Thatcher's monthly speechmaking fall to just seven speeches, six in London (two in her constituency) and one speech abroad. London proved to be the most frequent location for Thatcher's platform (as it was in the months before and after an election campaign) but, during election campaigns, this was complemented by a wider variety of alternative geographical locations. This was driven, in part, by Thatcher's determination to *show* local party workers and Conservative Party candidates that they had not 'been written off'.[42] Despite delivering regionally unspecific language, the location of Thatcher's platform remained significant.

The geographical importance of the platform was not restricted to periods of electioneering. The location of the platform was used to emphasize the key messages contained within her speeches. The speech Thatcher delivered to an American audience whilst receiving the Winston Churchill Foundation Award (1983) 'provided an ideal setting for a major speech on her new thinking about cold war strategy', namely that it should be understood as a battle of ideas which could be won.[43] In 1984 Thatcher delivered a speech reaffirming Britain's relationship with the United States. She travelled for more than two days to deliver this message from Camp David, a location selected to amplify Thatcher's message of transatlantic unity. The opposite was also true. She avoided locations that had the potential to undermine her rhetorical goals. Thatcher spoke only to receptive audiences when she toured the United States in opposition. During the early 1980s, when Thatcher was declaring that 'there is no alternative' to her government's economic policies, or variations on this theme, she avoided locations experiencing high levels of unemployment.[44] Thatcher recognized the interplay between her words and her platform and sought to use this to her advantage.

She recognized also that the immediate and the national audiences were not mutually exclusive; the former taking on barometric significance for the latter. A favourable audience reaction to Thatcher's words would be reported to the wider, national audience, casting Thatcher's messages in a positive light. The inevitable standing ovation that greeted Thatcher's conclusion of her annual Party Conference Speech became a staple of reports, and cast the broadcast of her speeches, and the messages that had been articulated, in a positive light. Thatcher, and those who advised her, was keen to avoid any shots that could be used to undermine the presentation of her words. When Thatcher delivered her speech, Britain Awake, to a half-empty Kensington Town Hall, Reece made the television crews promise to not capture any 'cut away' shots. To the viewing public it would look as though 'nobody cared what she [Thatcher] had to say'.[45]

It was for this reason that Thatcher's aides advised that she always pay attention to 'the audience that [… she was] giving the speech to'.[46] Though Thatcher and her speechwriters were no experts in classical rhetoric, they nonetheless ensured that her speeches elicited positive responses from the immediate audience. 'Clap lines', the consequence of a variety of rhetorical devices, were of vital importance to Thatcher, as was her ability to deliver them correctly. The platform itself was utilized as a means of encouraging positive audience reactions. Under Harvey Thomas' supervision, Thatcher's speeches evolved into celebrity-studded affairs complete with music, lasers and dry-ice. This was designed to 'let off a huge emotional [… release] in the audience' and so provide positive barometric shots for the evening's news.[47] This is not to say that Thatcher was able to marshal the reaction of the immediate audience at will. The audience could, and did, react to Thatcher's words in unpredictable ways. This in turn had the potential to alter the language she had intended to deliver. In the case of her 1981 Conference Speech, this could lead to the formation of some of her most iconic utterances. Contrary to current assumptions, the importance of the immediate audience

142   *Making Speeches*

surrounding the platform was not eclipsed by the media landscape of the late twentieth century, it was a feature of it, a fact that Thatcher and her aides were aware of and responded to.

Creating the news: The media landscape of the 1970s and 1980s

On 6 January 1980 Thatcher gave her first television interview since winning the previous year's general election. The interview, conducted by Brian Walden, bore all the hallmarks of a 'blockbuster' interview which was felt, by those advising Thatcher on her media appearances, to be 'very important' in setting the news-agenda and thus 'influenc[ing] national thinking'.[48] The questions, whilst not pre-planned, were the product of discussions between London Weekend Television and Number 10.[49] David Cox and Bernard Ingham had first met for a 'drink and a talk' some weeks before.[50] Careful thought had been given to where in Number 10's White Drawing Room Thatcher would sit, what would be in shot (it was decided that the fireplace was an appropriate backdrop), and how many cameras were to be used. It took five hours for the set to be completed. Thatcher arrived thirty minutes before filming was due to begin at 12.00. This gave her time to pull her lime green purse from her bag, remove unwanted lipstick from her teeth with a tissue and pop a mint into her mouth. Just under an hour later the interview came to an end. Denis Healey promptly took to the airwaves. Interviewed on Radio 4's *The World This Weekend* he questioned the 'ambiguity'[51] that Thatcher had shown in the interview. The following day Fred Emery covered Walden's interview, and Healey's reaction to it, on the front page of *The Times*.[52] No wonder those around Thatcher felt that set-piece television interviews were key in setting the news-agenda. The interview had become 'the news', setting the agenda of the press and radio. In October of the following year *The Times* carried an article dedicated to Walden's *Weekend World*, marvelling at the programme's success in 'getting itself reported'.[53] Unsurprisingly television was regarded by Thatcher's aides as the 'most persuasive medium', a view echoed by later scholars.[54]

Yet the fact that the same aides, at various times, contradict themselves suggests that such a conclusion is too simplistic.[55] Radio, especially BBC Radio 4's morning programmes, had the ability to set the news-agenda. To do so was the stated objective of the *Today* programme.[56] To overlook radio in the media landscape of the 1970s and 1980s, as many studies do, is to ignore an influential medium. Coverage of the 1983 Conservative Party Conference, specifically Kenny Everett's antics, stands as an example of the way that the press, unhindered by the impartiality of the broadcast media, were also able to set 'the news'. The news-agenda of the 1970s and 1980s was the product not simply of television, or even the broadcast media. It was the product of three competing media.

Only rarely, it seems, was the news-agenda set by the set-piece speech. Accepting the leadership of the Conservative Party in 1975, Thatcher told the party that '[i]t is no good having a first-class product unless people know about it. And they won't know about it unless we tell them about it.' Set-piece speeches were not, however, the answer: 'old politicians learnt to use oratory'. 'A different technique' must now be 'mastered'.[57] Such a position was understandable. A decline in verbatim reporting, a shift in the social and academic composition of journalists, and the corresponding tendency to explain rather than report 'the news', meant that the set-piece speech was ill-suited to the media landscape of the 1970s and 1980s; it appeared a hangover from an earlier age.

The irony of using part of her acceptance speech to proclaim the ineffectiveness of set-piece speeches was almost certainly lost on Thatcher. It does however raise questions about the supposed decline in significance of the set-piece speech as a means of political communication, capable of dictating the news-agenda. In the hands of skilled 'wordsmiths', Thatcher's set-piece speeches were written in such a way as to exploit the media landscape of the 1970s and 1980s. 'Tight and taut' phrases, encapsulating Thatcher's central messages, were deployed to exploit the brevity that characterized news media's style of reporting.[58] Repetition of phrases and themes allowed her to shape the interpretative 'tracks' along which journalists travelled when approaching, interpreting and reporting upon her speeches.[59] Thatcher, Reece, Thomas and Ingham used television's need for quality pictures and sound, and 'news' in general, to ensure that Thatcher's speeches were reported in the most advantageous way possible. Press releases were used to focus journalistic attention upon the central messages Thatcher wished to communicate to the national and, at times, international audience. When Millar died in 1998 *The Herald* published an obituary. The article quoted Thatcher: 'He [Millar] made a real difference to getting our political message across successfully.'[60] The ex-premier's remarks stood testament not only to her former 'wordsmith's' talents, but also to the effectiveness of the set-piece speech as a form of political communication.

Given this, it is useful to return to the interview Thatcher gave to Walden in early 1980. Though the interview was widely reported, the news-agenda was, at least in part, shaped by the set-piece speech she had delivered at the Guildhall some weeks before. It was 'difficult', the prime minister had told her audience, to:

> put across the message that the only cash the Government has comes from taxation and borrowing ... [the] same borrowing whose scale is pushing interest rates up, and which has to be repaid. Pennies don't fall from heaven, they have to be earned here on earth.[61]

Thatcher referenced the speech, and her point, in her later interview with Walden. 'There isn't a pot of gold to draw on', Thatcher told Walden:

> there is either your own extra effort, working machinery better, or you're taking something from your fellow citizens, and I am saying to you, as I said at that speech which I did in the Guildhall, pennies don't come from heaven, they have to be earned here on earth.[62]

She labelled this approach the 'Thatcher experiment'.[63] It was this that later media channels reported. Far from representing an outdated form of political communication, a leftover from the 'Golden Age' of rhetoric, Thatcher's set-piece speeches were part of the fabric of the 1970s' and 1980s' political communications environment. They were not simply 'the news'; they had the potential to shape 'the news'.

Thatcherism: Shifting the debate

In the summer of 1995 Margaret Thatcher appeared on the BBC's *Good Morning Summer* show. The set – a mock kitchen decorated in pale blues and yellows – was designed to not only tap into the Mayle-inspired middle-class Provencal *zeitgeist*, but also echo the show's 'relaxed' approach to reporting the news. Thatcher's uniform of pearls, bouffant hair and black-and-white checked jacket jarred with Sarah Greene's 'on-trend' pastel blouse and Will Hanrahan's casual shirt (no tie) and jacket. The ex-premier, who had become emblematic of Britain in the 1980s, seemed detached from the 1990s.

This sense of detachment was underlined by the subject of the interview, Thatcher's recently published *The Path to Power*. Thatcher regurgitated anecdotes from the book: family trips to the cinema, her mother's skills as a seamstress, her father's position as an alderman. Only when the subject of Major's government was raised did Thatcher come alive. Deflecting Greene's suggestion that she define 'Majorism', Thatcher asserted that, having left office, she was in a 'good position to define Thatcherism'.[64] Indeed, Thatcher used such interviews to do

Conclusion

145

just that. CBC News's Peter Mansbridge began his interview with Thatcher by informing her that he had 'watched many of the seemingly dozens of interviews you have given over the past few weeks in America and in Britain about [...] Thatcherism'.[65]

This sat at odds with her relationship with the term 'Thatcherism' during the period 1975–90. Perhaps, by the mid-1990s, Thatcher had allowed herself to have become persuaded that she had invented an 'ism'. During the preceding two decades she had avoided the term, preferring instead the 'language of conviction', rooted in her lower-middle-class Methodist upbringing. Such language supports an understanding of 'Thatcherism' put forward by those such as Peter Riddell, which underplays any suggestion of 'ideology' and instead focuses upon Thatcher's personal convictions. Thatcher herself avoided, in her set-piece speeches, any suggestion that she had 'created a new ideology'.[66] 'It is not a name', Thatcher told Robin Day, 'that I created, in the sense of calling it an "ism"'.[67] Thatcher appears to have continued the Conservative Party's traditional mistrust of doctrine, preferring instead to stress that the policy-agenda presented by her speeches was defined by 'common sense'.[68]

Yet, on occasion, Thatcher did use the political label 'Thatcherism' to describe the policy-agenda pursued by her government, articulated in, and influenced by, political language which was, in part, scripted by ideologically aware 'wordsmiths'. Those around Thatcher, such as Parkinson and Howe, also used the political label 'Thatcherism', and did so to describe an ideologically coherent position.

There exists no one definition of 'Thatcherism'. Questions must therefore be raised over the scholarly debate around 'Thatcherism' – a debate that is characterized by a determination, itself a product of the 1980s, to find 'the right' definition of the term.[69] Whilst, to varying degrees, some commentators stress that 'Thatcherism' should be defined in ideological terms, others present a non-ideological definition. Some stress Thatcher's centrality to the development of 'Thatcherism', and view 1975 and 1979 as moments of great importance, others have depersonalized the term by setting it in its historical context. Some have engaged with the term through an economic lens whilst others, echoing Keith Joseph's declaration that 'monetarism is not enough', stress the multifaceted concerns of 'Thatcherism'. Thus, attempts to define 'Thatcherism' are conducted through a series of inter-related debates ranging across time, disciplines and the political spectrum.

Political labels such as 'Thatcherism' have no single meaning. Even when Thatcher was able to associate a political label such as the 'Labour Party' with

146 *Making Speeches*

electorally advantageous meanings, alternative definitions of the term existed concurrently. To seek one, authentic definition of 'Thatcherism' is thus a futile endeavour. Consequently, this book adds to the body of work that suggests that a more fruitful debate should consider the 'varieties of Thatcherism' that exist and their relationship with the agendas pursued by political actors.[70]

A Thatcher era?

To implement a particular policy-agenda, Lord Tebbit notes, 'you start off by changing the climate [of public opinion]'.[71] Prime ministerial set-piece speeches were 'part of changing it', although, he admitted, 'there is a degree of art in that'.[72] John O'Sullivan too, recalled that prime ministerial phrases used in set-piece speeches 'were very important' because of the effect they could have on the political and public climate. It was for this reason that they were 'fought over [...] bitterly'[73] and why the archive is littered with documentary evidence of the pedantry with which Thatcher and her 'wordsmiths' approached the speechwriting process.[74]

Yet the influence of the speechwriter should not be overstated. The contemporary context in which they worked, and in which Thatcher delivered her speeches, had a profound effect upon the degree to which Thatcher was able to achieve her rhetorical ambitions. The contemporary context in which the political label 'Thatcherism' existed could, for example, limit the degree to which she was able to distance herself from the term, and its suggestion of an ideological approach to government. Despite her efforts, commentators and politicians from across the political spectrum insisted on using the term to describe a coherent ideological position unique to Thatcher. Similarly, the degree to which Thatcher's set-piece speeches could achieve their intended outcomes was governed not only by the work of those who scripted them, but also by the ebb and flow of their political context. Whilst Thatcher's 'language of conviction' gained traction in the political context of the late 1970s, it struggled to resonate with the electorate when describing Thatcher's pragmatic policy decisions of the period 1980–3, and later, the Community Charge of 1989–90. In contrast, Thatcher's shaping of the political label 'Labour Party' was successful precisely because it relied on a current understanding of the 'Labour Party'.

Thus, whilst the role played by 'wordsmiths' must be taken seriously, it should be acknowledged that their effectiveness was, at least in part, reliant upon the contemporary political context in which they operated. This being the case, the

Conclusion 147

view that Thatcher 'changed everything' and that her governments represented a 'distinct "Thatcher Era"' detached from, yet shaping their contemporary contexts, is open to question.[75] This study of Thatcher's speechmaking process demonstrates that her political language, and its ability to achieve its predetermined goals, can only be understood when set in its contemporary political context.

'Transcend the divisions'.[76] Thatcher, speechwriting and British political history

As scholars have long recognized, language and action are intimately intertwined; one affects the other. However, this book has intended to shift attention beyond a study of discourse and meaning. It has looked beyond 'analytical narratives' and has introduced the prosaic into the study of public, political language.[77] The speechwriting process should not be seen as a self-contained act of drafting of words and phrases, but as a continual process from the initial putting of pen to paper, through Thatcher's delivery of a speech to an immediate audience, its dissemination through the news media and finally to its interaction with the wider political landscape. The intention of this work has thus been to 'transcend the divisions' within the study of public, political language in British political history, in terms of both content and methodology.[78] It has revealed Thatcher's unique speechmaking process, as well as engaging with broader questions associated with her three governments, and the contemporary media and political landscape in which they existed. Thus, Thatcher's set-piece speeches, far from representing hangovers from a bygone age,[79] an 'archaic, subsidiary method' of political communication,[80] already in 'decline' by 1979,[81] remained politically significant. As a result, Thatcher's speeches, and the documents related to their construction, should not be viewed as a source-base of secondary importance. Instead, Thatcher's speechmaking, and the documents related to this process, offers the opportunity to undertake original archival research, allowing one to assess Thatcher's leadership of the opposition, and then government, from a fresh vantage point.

Notes

Where a document is located on the Margaret Thatcher Foundation's website (MTF), and also in hardcopy at the Churchill Archive Centre (CAC) the reader is provided with information pertaining to both locations. A unique number – used to identify each document on the Margaret Thatcher Foundation's website is provided first, followed by the alpha-numerical catalogue reference for documents held at the Churchill Archive Centre.

Introduction

1 Unnamed, 'In Her Own Words', *Daily Telegraph*, 1 April 2013, 16. Unnamed, 'In Her Own Words', *The Guardian*, 9 April 2013, 4.

2 Tom Newton Dunn, 'Good Way to Go – The End of a World Political Legend', *Sun*, 9 April 2013, 3. Thatcher is one of several prime ministers whose words act as points around which memories of their legacy coalesced. For other examples, see John Ramsden, *The Man of the Century: Winston Churchill and His Legend since 1945* (London: HarperCollins, 2003), 51 and David McLoughlin, 'The Origins and Reception of Harold Wilson's 1963 "White Heat" Speech' (MSc diss., London Centre for the History of Science, Medicine and Technology, London, 2010).

3 See, for example, Philip Williamson, *Stanley Baldwin: Conservative Leadership and National Values* (Cambridge: Cambridge University Press, 1999).

4 See, for example, Gareth Stedman Jones, *Languages of Class: Studies in English Working Class History, 1832–1982* (Cambridge: Cambridge University Press, [1983] 1993), discussed below.

5 See Robert Saunders, '"Crisis? What Crisis?" Making Thatcherism and the Seventies', in *Making Thatcher's Britain*, ed. Ben Jackson and Robert Saunders (Cambridge: Cambridge University Press, 2012).

6 Christopher Collins, 'Editorial Policy of Site: Preface to Complete Public Statements of Margaret Thatcher, 1945–90 on CD-ROM', in *Complete Public Statements of Margaret Thatcher, 1945–90*, ed. Christopher Collins (Oxford: Oxford University Press, 1998).

7 Ibid.

8 Joseph Meisel, 'Words by the Numbers: A Quantitative Analysis and Comparison of the Oratorical Careers of William Ewart Gladstone and Winston Spencer Churchill', *Historical Research*, 73, no. 182 (2000): 262–96, 268.

9 Ed. Collins, *Margaret Thatcher: Complete Public Statements 1945–1990 on CD-ROM*, Speech at Fornham All Saints, 29 May 1987, UDN: 87_225.

10 Paul Readman, 'The State of Twentieth-Century British Political History', *The Journal of Policy History*, 21, no. 3 (2009): 323.

11 Quentin Skinner, 'The Principles and Practices of Opposition: The Case of Bolingbroke versus Walpole', in *Historical Perspective. Studies in English Thought and Society in Honour of J. H. Plumb*, ed. Neil McKendrick (London: Europa Publications, 1974), 94.

12 Maurice Cowling, *The Impact of Labour, 1920–1924. The Beginnings of Modern British Politics* (Cambridge: Cambridge University Press, 1971), 4. The introduction to Cowling's work demonstrates that he was acutely aware of the importance of language.

13 James Vernon, *Politics and the People: A Study in English Political Culture, 1815–67* (Cambridge: Cambridge University Press, 1993), 1.

14 Stedman Jones, *Languages of Class*, 243.

15 Stedman Jones, when recalling the period, underplays such a direct correlation between contemporary politics and historical methodological development. See Gareth Stedman Jones, 'History and Theory: An English Story', *Historein*, 3 (2001): 119. www.historeinonline.org (accessed 15 June 2015).

16 Robert Blake, *The Conservative Party from Peel to Thatcher* (London: Fontana Press, 1985), 367.

17 Maurice Cowling, *1867, Disraeli, Gladstone and Revolution. The Passing of the Second Reform Bill* (Cambridge: Cambridge University Press, 1967).

18 Jonathan Parry, 'Maurice Cowling: A Brief Life', in *The Philosophy, Politics and Religion of British Democracy. Maurice Cowling and Conservatism*, ed. Robert Crowcroft, S. J. D. Green and Richard Whiting (London: I. B. Tauris, 2010), 21.

19 Dror Wahrman, 'The New Political History: A Review Essay', *Social History*, 21, no. 3 (1996): 343.

20 Williamson, *Stanley Baldwin*, 14.

21 Karen Musolf, *From Plymouth to Parliament. A Rhetorical History of Nancy Astor's 1919 Campaign* (London: Palgrave Macmillan, 1999), x. See also Matthew Roberts, 'Constructing a Tory World-View: Popular Politics and the Conservative Press in Late Victorian Leeds', *Historical Research*, 79, no. 203 (2006): 115–43.

22 Musolf, *From Plymouth to Parliament*, ix.

23 Luke Blaxill, 'Quantifying the Language of British Politics, 1880–1910', *Historical Research*, 86, no. 232 (2013): 315.

150   *Notes*

24 Jon Lawrence and Alexandre Campsie, 'Political History', in *Writing History Theory and Practice*, ed. Stefan Berger, Heiko Feldner and Kevin Passmore (London: Bloomsbury Academic, 2010), 209.

25 See Hugo Young, *One of Us: A Biography of Margaret Thatcher* (London: Macmillan, 1990); Andrew Gamble, 'Thatcherism and Conservative Politics', in *The Politics of Thatcherism*, ed. Stuart Hall and Martin Jacques (London: Lawrence & Wishart Ltd., 1983), 109–31; Andrew Gamble, *The Free Economy and the Strong State: The Politics of Thatcherism* (Basingstoke: Palgrave, 1994).

26 John Campbell, for example, notes that '[t]he turning point in Mrs Thatcher's public attitude to the community was her speech to the College of Europe in Bruges in September 1988'. John Campbell, *Margaret Thatcher. Volume Two: The Iron Lady* (London: Vintage, 2012), 602.

27 Jim Prior, *A Balance of Power* (London: Hamish Hamilton, 1986); Norman Tebbit, *Upwardly Mobile* (London: Weidenfeld & Nicolson, 1988); William Whitelaw, *The Whitelaw Memoirs* (London: Aurum Press, 1989); John Nott, *Here Today, Gone Tomorrow, Recollections of an Errant Politician* (London: Methuen Publishing Ltd., 2002); Peter Carrington, *Reflect on Things Past: The Memoirs of Lord Carrington* (London: Fontana Press, 1988); Geoffrey Howe, *Conflict of Loyalty* (London: Macmillan, [1994] 2008); Nigel Lawson, *The View from No. 11: Memoirs of a Tory Radical* (London: Bantam Press, 1992); Nicholas Ridley, *My Style of Government: The Thatcher Years* (London: Hutchinson, 1991); Margaret Thatcher, *The Downing Street Years* (London: HarperCollins, 1993); John Major, *John Major: The Autobiography* (London: HarperCollins, 1999); Douglas Hurd, *Memoirs* (London: Abacus, 2004); William Waldegrave, *A Different Kind of Weather: A Memoir* (London: Constable, 2015).

28 Interview with Chris Collins, email exchanges, 18 December 2017.

29 Peter Clark, 'The Rise and Fall of Thatcherism', *London Review of Books*, 20, no. 24 (1998). www.lrb.co.uk/v20/n24/peter-clarke/the-rise-and-fall-of-thatcherism (accessed 27 July 2015).

30 Ferdinand Mount, *Cold Cream: My Early Life and Other Mistakes* (London: Bloomsbury Publishing, 2008), 337.

31 Interview with Robin Harris, Somerset House, London, 11 June 2014.

32 Eds. Ben Jackson and Robert Saunders, *Making Thatcher's Britain* (Cambridge: Cambridge University Press, 2012), 17.

33 See Jon Lawrence and Florence Sutcliffe-Braithwaite, 'Margaret Thatcher and the Decline of Class Politics', in *Making Thatcher's Britain*, ed. Ben Jackson and Robert Saunders (Cambridge: Cambridge University Press, 2012), 132–47.

34 There are, of course, exceptions. Eliza Filby, for example, has paid some attention to the speech-drafting process. See Eliza Filby, *God & Mrs Thatcher: The Battle for Britain's Soul* (London: Biteback Publishing, 2015), 113–15 and 124–6. Yet such

analysis is undertaken as a means to an end – the analysis of Thatcher's use of religious rhetoric, rather than as an end in itself.

35 Charles Moore, *Margaret Thatcher: The Authorised Biography, Volume Three: Herself Alone* (London: Allen Lane, 2019). David Cannadine notes that the publication of Moore's final volume will 'signal the end of another phase of interpretation and historiography', namely that based on traditional archival work. David Cannadine, *Margaret Thatcher. A Life and Legacy* (Oxford: Oxford University Press, 2017), 136.

36 MTF, 112545, (THCR 2-6-2-2). Ken Stowe minute to Margaret Thatcher, 8 May 1979, page 1.

37 See Quentin Skinner, *Visions of Politics. Volume I: Regarding Method* (Cambridge: Cambridge University Press, 2002), 87. For a similar approach, see Ben Jackson, *Equality and the British Left. A Study in Progressive Political Thought, 1900–64* (Manchester: Manchester University Press, 2007).

38 The word 'prosaic' brings to mind an activity which is boring and mundane. For scholars, this is often how Thatcher's speechmaking has been understood. However, this work will show how apparently mundane, prosaic activities such as speechwriting should not be assumed to lack political significance.

39 Skinner, 'The Principles and Practices of Opposition'.

40 Joseph Meisel, 'Review of *Margaret Thatcher: Complete Public Statements 1945–1990*', review no. 133. Available online: https://reviews.history.ac.uk/review/133 (accessed 30 October 2023).

41 Ibid. It should be kept in mind that there are around 400 speeches where the speaking text cannot be located, and several speeches that have not been included due to copyright issues.

42 Ibid.

43 Luke Blaxill, *The War of Words. The Language of British Elections, 1880–1914* (Woodbridge: The Royal Historical Association, 2000), 25.

44 For more details about Antconc, see www.laurenceanthony.net/software/antconc/.

45 See below, Chapter 7.

46 Paul Readman, 'Speeches', in *Reading Primary Sources, Routledge Guide to Using Primary Sources*, ed. M. Dobson and B. Ziemann (London: Routledge, 2008), 211. See also Wahrman, 'The New Political History'.

47 Blaxill, *The War of Words*, 26.

48 For similar examples, see Robert Schlesinger, *White House Ghosts, Presidents and Their Speechwriters* (New York: Simon & Schuster, 2008) and Richard Aldous, *Schlesinger: The Imperial Historian* (New York: W. W. Norton & Company, 2017). The latter book is about the former author's father who, although most famed for his role as a historian and biographer, also contributed to the speeches of President Kennedy.

49 See, for example, Alan Clark's claims to have shaped Thatcher's Bruges Speech (1988). Ed. Ion Trewin, *Alan Clark Diaries: Into Power 1983–1992* (London: Phoenix,

2001), 226. Harvey Thomas too was keen to stress the role he played in writing Thatcher's speeches. 'I did a lot of work on changing [Thatcher's] words'. Interview with Harvey Thomas, Potters Bar, 30 July 2015.

50 Lawrence and Campsie, 'Political History', 221.

51 Robert Saunders, 'The Many Lives of Margaret Thatcher', *English Historical Review*, 132, no. 556 (2017): 638.

52 See eds. Jackson and Saunders, *Making Thatcher's Britain* and Richard Vinen, *Thatcher's Britain. The Politics and Social Upheaval of the 1980s* (London: Simon and Schuster, 2009).

53 Current debate revolves around two opposing positions. On the one hand, there are those who suggest that 'Thatcherism' is best understood as an ideologically coherent whole. These include: Young, *One of Us*; Gamble, 'Thatcherism and Conservative Politics' and Gamble, *The Free Economy and the Strong State*. On the other hand, there are those who see 'Thatcherism' as being defined more by instinct than ideology. See Peter Riddell, *The Thatcher Government* (Oxford: Martin Robertson, 1983) and Shirley Robin Letwin, *The Anatomy of Thatcherism* (London: Routledge, 1992).

54 Of course, there are always exceptions. See, for example, E. H. H. Green, *Thatcher* (London: Bloomsbury Academic, 2006); and Vinen, *Thatcher's Britain*.

55 MTF, 103807, Thatcher interview on London Weekend Television's *Weekend World*, 7 January 1979.

56 See, for example, eds. R. A. W. Rhodes and Patrick Dunleavy, *Prime Ministers, Cabinet and Core Executive* (London: Palgrave, 1995).

57 Austin coined the term 'speech acts' to describe the illocutionary and perlocutionary power of words. See J. L. Austin, *How to Do Things with Words* (Oxford: Oxford University Press, 1962). See also ed. J. R. Searle, *The Philosophy of Language* (Oxford: Oxford University Press, 1971).

58 Tebbit, *Upwardly Mobile*, 142.

59 Interestingly, more attention has been paid to speechwriters in works concerned with the presidents of the United States. See, for example, Schlesinger, *White House Ghosts, Presidents and Their Speechwriters* and Aldous, *Schlesinger*.

60 Richard Vinen, 'A War of Position? The Thatcher Government's Preparation for the 1984 Miners' Strike', *English Historical Review*, 134, no. 566 (2019).

61 Saunders, 'The Many Lives of Margaret Thatcher', 655.

62 See Vinen, *Thatcher's Britain*.

63 Interview with Bernard Ingham, Purley, 27 February 2015.

64 CAC, minute from John Whittingdale to Ronald Millar, 9 June 1989, Ronald Millar's Papers, unpublished.

65 See Henry Jephson, *The Platform: Its Rise and Progress* (London: Frank Cass and Company Ltd. [1892]. Vol. I, 1968).

Notes 153

66 See Luke Blaxill, *The War of Words: The Language of British Elections, 1880–1914* (Woodbridge: Royal Historical Society, 2020) and Jon Lawrence, *Electing Our Masters: The Hustings in British Politics from Hogarth to Blair* (Oxford: Oxford University Press, 2008).

67 Ronald Millar, *A View from the Wings* (London: Weidenfeld and Nicolson, 1993), 282.

68 Ibid.

Chapter 1

* Millar, *A View from the Wings*, 275.

1 Millar, *A View from the Wings*, 275.

2 Thatcher, *The Downing Street Years*, 301.

3 Ibid., 301. See also, MTF, 205253, Chris Patten Speech Draft, 1 October 1987.

4 Thatcher, *The Downing Street Years*, 567.

5 Ibid., 5.

6 Millar, *A View from the Wings*, 275.

7 Dennis Kavanagh and Anthony Seldon, *The Powers behind the Prime Minister: The Hidden Influence of Number 10* (London: HarperCollins, 2000), 172.

8 Anonymous information obtained by the author.

9 Ibid.

10 Ranelagh's account of 'Thatcher's People' does not include O'Sullivan or Harris. John Ranelagh, *Thatcher's People: An Insider's Account of the Politics, the Power and the Personalities* (London: HarperCollins, 1991).

11 Margaret Thatcher, *The Path to Power* (London: HarperCollins, 1995), 280.

12 Charles Moore, *Margaret Thatcher: The Authorised Biography, Volume One: Not for Turning* (London: Allen Lane, 2013), 299.

13 Anonymous interview.

14 MTF, 131056 (THCR 1-11-18 f4). Minute from Tim Flesher to Margaret Thatcher, 26 April 1983.

15 Interview with Michael Scholar, Oxford, 24 August 2016.

16 Ibid. This does not sound like a phrase that Thatcher would have uttered. Perhaps such a phrase reflects the manner in which private secretaries viewed Thatcher's political advisers.

17 Ibid.

18 Interview with Robin Harris, Somerset House, London, 11 June 2014.

19 Ibid.

20 Telephone interview with Adam Ridley, 2 February 2021.

21 MTF, 104604, Margaret Thatcher, Speech to Conservative Central Council, 28 March 1981.

22 Thatcher, *The Downing Street Years*, 139.

23 John Hoskyns, *Just in Time: Inside the Thatcher Revolution* (London: Aurum Press, 2000), 52. Churchill Archives Centre, Hosk1/75, Peter Thorneycroft to John Hoskyns, undated. MTF, 104604, Margaret Thatcher, Speech to Conservative Central Council, 28 March 1981.

24 See Ranelagh, *Thatcher's People.*

25 George Younger, Ian Gow, William Whitelaw, Geoffrey Howe and Jock Bruce-Gardyne all attended Winchester College.

26 Jonathan Aitken, for example, graduated from Christ Church, Oxford, pursuing careers in both journalism and politics, via the Conservative Research Department. Like Mount, Aitken was well-connected and wealthy, but adopted an 'anti-establishment' stance.

27 Simon Jenkins, 'I Have Not Finished Yet', *The Times*, 19 November 1990, 14.

28 Thatcher, *The Path to Power*, 305.

29 CAC, THCR5-1-2-38, Thatcher's handwritten Conservative Party speech draft, undated. The draft includes what was page 18 of Sherman's draft. For Sherman's draft, see THCR5-1-2-39, *A Strategy for Restoring Britain / for Recovery, for Renewal,* undated.

30 Thatcher, *The Path to Power*, 280.

31 Ibid., 306.

32 Millar, *A View from the Wings*, 234.

33 Ibid., 234.

34 Ibid., 241.

35 Mount, *Cold Cream*, 328.

36 Thatcher, *The Downing Street Years*, 567.

37 Interview with John O'Sullivan, Reform Club, London, 10 April 2015.

38 Thatcher, *The Downing Street Years*, 567.

39 Ibid., 567.

40 Millar graduated from King's College, Cambridge, Harris from Exeter College, Oxford and O'Sullivan graduated from the University of London.

41 Thatcher, *The Downing Street Years*, 567.

42 Interview with John O'Sullivan, Reform Club, London, 10 April 2015.

43 Thatcher, *The Downing Street Years*, 567.

44 Interview with John O'Sullivan, Reform Club, London, 10 April 2015.

45 Interview with Charles Powell, Millbank, London, 10 November 2016.

46 CAC, THCR2-6-2-118, Stowe minute, 1 June 1979, 1.

47 Interview with Michael Scholar, Oxford, 24 August 2016.

48 Ibid.

Notes

49 Ibid.

50 Ibid.

51 Ibid.

52 Ibid.

53 Ibid.

54 Ibid.

55 CAC, THCR 5/1/5/172. Part 2 of 2. Handwritten first draft of Thatcher's Berlin 'Golden Book Ceremony' Speech, 29 October 1982.

56 Ibid.

57 Telephone interview with Adam Ridley, 2 February 2021.

58 Ibid.

59 Ibid.

60 MTF, 109842 (MSS 2/6/1/233) Steering Committee: Minutes of 61st Meeting, 15 January 1979, 1. The draft does not have a title but is marked 'Intro', 1–16.

61 CAC, THCR2-6-235, Conquest to Ryder, 28 June 1978.

62 George Gardiner, *A Bastard's Tale. The Political Memoirs of George Gardiner* (London: Aurum Press, 1990), 116.

63 Ibid., 116.

64 Tebbit, *Upwardly Mobile*, 144.

65 Telephone interview with Adam Ridley, 2 February 2021.

66 Tebbit, *Upwardly Mobile*, 144.

67 MTF, 149564 (THCR 5-1-5-370 f144). MT speech draft ('Mark 2'), 14 January 1986, 39.

68 Interview with William Rickett, Saxmundham, Suffolk, 17 August 2016. See CAC, THCR 2/6/2/69, Ian Gow minute to Margaret Thatcher, 9 November 1979.

69 Interview with William Rickett, Saxmundham, Suffolk, 17 August 2016.

70 Ibid.

71 MTF, 105294 (Hansard HC [41/158-62]). Prime Minister's Questions, 19 April 1983.

72 MTF, 104996 (Hansard HC [27/850-54]). Prime Minister's Questions, 13 July 1983.

73 Interview with William Rickett, Saxmundham, Suffolk, 17 August 2016. Thatcher used the phrase again, for example, during PMQs in 1984. MTF, 105675, PMQs, House of Commons, Westminster, 3 May 1984.

74 See, for example, CAC, THCR 5-1-4-105, Robert Armstrong to Tim Flesher, 19 November 1985.

75 Quoted in Philip Ziegler, *Wilson: The Authorised Life* (London: Weidenfeld & Nicolson, 1993), 155.

76 Interview with William Rickett, Saxmundham, Suffolk, 17 August 2016.

77 Ibid.

78 Interview with Charles Powell, Millbank, London, 10 November 2016.

79 Interview with John Whittingdale, Portcullis House, London, 19 January 2010.

80 Interview with Charles Powell, Millbank, London, 10 November 2016.

81 MTF, 142256 (THCR 1-1-25 f199). Charles Powell speech draft to Margaret Thatcher, 7 October 1985.

82 Ibid. For the final script see MTF, 106145, Margaret Thatcher's speech to the Conservative Party Conference, 11 October 1985.

83 Interview with William Rickett, Saxmundham, Suffolk, 17 August 2016.

84 Ibid.

85 Ibid.

86 Mount, *Cold Cream*, 285.

87 Thatcher, *The Downing Street Years*, 579.

88 Interview with William Rickett, Saxmundham, Suffolk, 17 August 2016.

89 MTF, 112003 (Sherman MSS [Royal Holloway Library] Box 7). Letter from Utley to Wolfson, 6 December 1978.

90 MTF, 111755 (Ronnie Millar MSS [Charterhouse School] 10480/42). Letter from Thatcher to Millar, 16 October 1990.

91 Kavanagh and Seldon, *The Powers behind the Prime Minister*, 172.

92 Mount, *Cold Cream*, 328.

93 Hoskyns, *Just in Time,* 230.

94 CAC, THCR 5-1-5-172. Part 2 of 2. Handwritten first draft of Thatcher's Berlin 'Golden Book Ceremony' Speech, delivered on 29 October 1982. MTF, 105043, Margaret Thatcher's speech at the Golden Book Ceremony, 29 October 1982.

95 CAC, THCR 5-1-5-172. Part 2 of 2. Handwritten first draft of Thatcher's Berlin 'Golden Book Ceremony' Speech, delivered on 29 October 1982.

96 MTF, 105043, Margaret Thatcher's speech at the Golden Book Ceremony, 29 October 1982. Such alterations by the prime minister proved significant as it was these lines which were reported by BBC Radio News.

97 Thatcher, *The Downing Street Years*, 301.

98 George R. Urban, *Diplomacy and Disillusion at the Court of Margaret Thatcher: An Insider's View* (London: I. B. Tauris, 1996), 40.

99 Hoskyns, *Just in Time*, 131.

100 Carol Thatcher, *Diary of an Election with Margaret Thatcher on the Campaign Trail: A Personal Account by Carol Thatcher* (Letchworth: Sidgwick & Jackson Ltd., 1983), 104.

101 Ibid., 104.

102 Hoskyns, *Just in Time,* 134.

103 Ibid., 134.

104 Ibid., 131.

105 Meisel, 'Words by the Numbers', 262–96, 269.

106 Interview with Michael Scholar, Oxford, 24 August 2016.

Notes

107 Ibid.

108 Ibid.

109 Nick Thomas-Symonds, *Harold Wilson: The Winner* (London: W&N, 2022), 92.

110 CAC, THCR 1-20-1, Thatcher's speaking text for her speech to the Conservative Party Conference, 10 October 1980.

111 Ibid.

112 Anonymous interview.

113 Ibid.

114 Hoskyns, *Just in Time*, 131.

115 Urban, *Diplomacy and Disillusion at the Court of Margaret Thatcher*, 41.

116 Ibid., 41.

117 Ibid., 41.

118 Mount, *Cold Cream*, 330.

119 Millar, *A View from the Wings*, 278.

120 Telephone interview with Adam Ridley, 2 February 2021.

121 Ibid.

122 Ibid.

123 Mount, *Cold Cream,* 328.

124 Ibid., 329.

125 Ibid., 330.

126 Peter Stothard, *The Senecans. Four Men and Margaret Thatcher* (London: Gerald Duckworth & Co. Ltd, 2016), 156.

127 Ibid., 51.

128 David Young, *Inside Thatcher's Last Election. Diaries of the Campaign that Saved Enterprise* (London: Biteback Publishing, 2021), 33.

129 Mount, *Cold Cream,* 329.

130 Millar, *A View from the Wings*, 278.

131 Urban, *Diplomacy and Disillusion at the Court of Margaret Thatcher*, 58.

132 Ibid., 36.

133 Ibid., 90.

134 Telephone interview with Adam Ridley, 2 February 2021.

135 CAC, THCR 5-1-2-248, Ridley to Thatcher, 19 January 1979.

136 Mount, *Cold Cream*, 329.

137 Urban, *Diplomacy and Disillusion at the Court of Margaret Thatcher*, 91.

138 Ibid., 91.

139 Ibid., 93.

140 CAC, THCR 5-1-5-43, Preparation regarding Thatcher's speech to Franco-British Council, 19 September 1980.

141 Ibid.

142 CAC, Hosk 2-411, Letter from Hoskyns to Millar, 30 November 1981.

158   *Notes*

143   Ibid.

144   Anonymous interview.

145   See, for example, Peter Hennessy, *The Prime Minister: The Office and Its Holders since 1945* (London: Penguin, 2001), 400–1 and Young, *One of Us,* 324.

146   Millar, *A View from the Wings*, 235.

147   Ranelagh, *Thatcher's People*, 52.

148   Millar, *A View from the Wings*, 282.

149   Ibid., 282.

Chapter 2

*   Tebbit, *Upwardly Mobile*, 142.

1   For a rare example of Thatcher writing her own speech drafts, see MTF, 205250, Thatcher handwritten 1987 Conference Speech draft, 26 September 1987.

2   Williamson, *Stanley Baldwin*, 157.

3   Ibid., 161. This is not surprising given that at times, Jones held political opinions which were at odds with Baldwin.

4   Thatcher, *The Downing Street Years*, 579. References to Thatcher's use of speechmaking appear in Prior, *A Balance of Power*; Whitelaw, *The Whitelaw Memoirs*; Howe, *Conflict of Loyalty*.

5   Anthony King, 'Margaret Thatcher as a Political Leader', in *Thatcherism,* ed. Robert Skidelsky (London: Chatto and Windus, 1988), 62.

6   Riddell, *The Thatcher Government*, 6.

7   Lawson, *The View from No. 11*, 837.

8   Thatcher, *The Downing Street Years*, 579.

9   Campbell, *Margaret Thatcher. Volume Two*, 543.

10   MTF, 106941, Margaret Thatcher's Conservative Party Conference Speech, Winter Gardens, Blackpool, 9 October 1987.

11   Interview with John O'Sullivan, Reform Club, London, 10 April 2015.

12   Ibid.

13   Kenneth Baker, *The Turbulent Years* (London: Faber & Faber, 1993), 220.

14   Ed. Ion Trewin, *The Hugo Young Papers: Thirty Years of British Politics – Off the Record* (London: Allen Lane, 2008), 300.

15   Howe, *Conflict of Loyalty*, 103.

16   MTF,103485, TV Interview for Granada *World in Action,* 27 January 1978.

17   Ibid.

18   CAC, THCR5-1-2-164, Copy of Mr Whitelaw's Speech, 26 January 1978.

19   Thatcher, *The Path to Power*, 407.

20   Green, *Thatcher*, 135.

21 Ibid., 135.

22 Prior, *A Balance of Power*, 107.

23 Howe, *Conflict of Loyalty*, 104.

24 Prior, *A Balance of Power*, 107.

25 MTF, 103763, TV interview for ITN, 10 October 1978.

26 Fred Emery, 'Tory Leaders Angered as Mr Heath Backs Pay Guidelines', *The Times*, 12 October 1978, 1.

27 Alan Wood et al., 'Thatcher Plea for Responsibility by Unions', *The Times*, 14 October 1978, 3.

28 MTF, 110797, *Conservative Campaign Guide Supplement*, 1 March 1978, 27.

29 Telephone interview with Adam Ridley, 2 February 2021.

30 Thatcher, *The Path to Power*, 122.

31 Ibid., 425.

32 Ibid.

33 Ibid.

34 MTF, 103807, TV interview for London Weekend Television *Weekend World*, 7 January 1979.

35 Ibid.

36 John Campbell, *Margaret Thatcher. Volume One: The Grocer's Daughter* (London: Vintage, 2000), 420.

37 MTF, 103807, TV interview for London Weekend Television *Weekend World*, 7 January 1979.

38 Eric Caines, *Heath and Thatcher in Opposition* (London: Palgrave Macmillan, 2017), 255.

39 Hugh Stephenson, *Mrs Thatcher's First Year* (London: Jill Norman Ltd, 1980), rear cover.

40 MTF, 103807, TV interview for London Weekend Television *Weekend World*, 7 January 1979.

41 Ibid.

42 Ibid.

43 Peter Thorneycroft memo to Thatcher, 13 December 1978 quoted in Stanley Crooks, *Peter Thorneycroft* (Winchester: George Mann Publications, 2007), 273.

44 Hoskyns, *Just in Time,* 40.

45 CAC, Hosk 1–27, *Record of meeting with John Biffen*, 4 August 1977, 4.

46 MTF, 103807, TV interview for London Weekend Television *Weekend World*, 7 January 1979.

47 Hoskyns, *Just in Time,* 252.

48 Tebbit, *Upwardly Mobile*, 186.

49 MTF, 134178 (PREM19/1281 f240). *Department of Employment letter to Number 10*, 20 April 1983, 3.

50 MTF, 110859, *Conservative Party General Election Manifesto*, 18 May 1983.

51 John O'Sullivan (2016), 'John O'Sullivan Discusses Robert Conquest's Influence on Margaret Thatcher', Hoover Institution, 25 January. Available online: https://www.hoover.org/research/john-osullivan-discusses-robert-conquests-influence-margaret-thatcher (accessed 29 May 2023).

52 Interview with John O'Sullivan, Reform Club, London, 10 April 2015.

53 Moore, *Margaret Thatcher: The Authorised Biography, Volume One*, 650.

54 Ibid., 537.

55 MTF, 111772, Letter from David Hannay to John Kerr, 29 March 1988.

56 Ibid.

57 Ibid.

58 Howe, *Conflict of Loyalty*, 537.

59 Ibid., 537.

60 Ibid.

61 Lawson, *The View from No. 11*, 907.

62 Howe, *Conflict of Loyalty*, 537.

63 Ibid., 538.

64 MTF, 108234, House of Commons Statement: Rome European Council, 30 October 1990.

65 Howe, *Conflict of Loyalty*, 644.

66 Eds. Salmon, Hamilton and Twigge, *Documents on British Policy Overseas. Series III, Volume II*, Letter from Sir C. Mallaby (Bonn) to Mr Ratford. 23 October 1989, Letter from Sir P. Wright to Mr Wall. 30 October 1989, 79.

67 Ibid., 79.

68 Ibid., 80.

69 Hurd, *Memoirs*, 425.

70 MTF, 108050, Joint Press Conference with German Chancellor Kohl, 30 March 1990.

71 Lawson, *The View from No. 11*, 835.

72 Ibid., 834.

73 Ibid., 835.

74 Ibid.

75 Ibid.

76 Ibid., 836.

77 MTF, 107242, House of Commons PQs, 17 May 1988.

78 Lawson, *The View from No. 11*, 837.

79 O'Sullivan, 'John O'Sullivan Discusses Robert Conquest's Influence on Margaret Thatcher'.

80 Ibid.

81 Thatcher, *Path to Power*, 429.

82 MTF, 103926, *Conservative Party Political Broadcast*, 17 January 1979.

83 For further discussion of this point see Moore, *Margaret Thatcher: The Authorised Biography, Volume One*, 398.
84 Millar, *A View from the Wings*, 247.
85 Mount, *Cold Cream*, 331.
86 Ibid., 331.
87 Interview with William Rickett, Saxmundham, Suffolk, 17 August 2016.
88 Ibid.
89 Stothard, *The Senecans*, 31.
90 Peter Stothard, 'Mrs Thatcher's Three Wise Men', *The Times*, 4 October 1982, 6.
91 Stothard, *The Senecans*, 84.
92 Ibid.
93 MTF, 111983 (Sherman MSS [Royal Holloway Library] Box 3). Letter from Sherman to Thatcher, 17 June 1977.
94 Ibid.
95 Alfred Sherman, *Paradoxes of Power: Reflections on the Thatcher Interlude* (Exeter: Imprint Academic, 2005), 90.
96 Ibid., 90.
97 Ibid.
98 Mount, *Cold Cream*, 328.
99 Hoskyns, *Just in Time*, 133.
100 Ibid., 134.
101 George Clark et al., 'Heath Blasts at Thatcher's "Dreary Path"', *The Times*, 7 October 1981, 1.
102 Hoskyns, *Just in Time*, 338.
103 Ibid., 339.
104 Millar, *A View from the Wings*, 290.
105 Ibid., 290.
106 John Walden, 'Maggie Canes Her Critics', *Daily Express*, 17 October 1982, 1. Unfortunately, little record remains of what Thatcher said to the overflow crowd.
107 Ibid., 6.
108 MTF, 111746 (Ronnie Millar MSS [Charterhouse School] 10480-42). Letter from Thatcher to Millar, 12 June 1987.
109 Ibid.
110 MTF, 112637, Thatcher's speech to the Conservative Party Conference, 10 October 1980.
111 Ed. Trewin, *The Hugo Young Papers*, 157.
112 Ibid., 157.
113 Mount, *Cold Cream*, 331.
114 Ibid.
115 Ibid.
116 Ian Aitken, 'Fight Goes On, Says Thatcher', *The Guardian*, 17 September 1981, 1.

117 Telephone interview with Adam Ridley, 2 February 2021.

118 Millar, *A View from the Wings*, 235.

119 Ibid.

120 Ibid.

121 MTF, 112202 (THCR 2-6-2-133). Ronnie Millar draft Party Election Broadcast, 30 May 1979.

122 Filby, *God & Mrs Thatcher*, 124.

123 Thatcher, *The Path to Power*, 427.

124 Ibid., 428.

125 Mount, *Cold Cream,* 331.

126 Tebbit, *Upwardly Mobile*, 142.

127 O'Sullivan, 'John O'Sullivan Discusses Robert Conquest's Influence on Margaret Thatcher'.

128 Mount, *Cold Cream,* 331.

129 Thatcher, *The Path to Power*, 316.

130 Ibid., 316.

131 Frank Johnson, 'Off-TV triumph for real Ms Thatcher', *The Daily Telegraph*, 9 October 1976, 30.

132 Ibid.

133 Tebbit, *Upwardly Mobile*, 142.

134 CAC, THCR 5-1-5-5 part 2. Early drafts of Thatcher's Conservative Party Conference Speech, 1979. For the final text, see MTF, 104147, Thatcher's speech to the Conservative Party Conference, 12 October 1979.

135 Geoffrey Goodman, *Daily Mirror*, 16 October 1979, 11.

136 MTF, 108217, Speech to the Conservative Party Conference, 12 October 1990.

137 John Whittingdale, 'Margaret Thatcher', in *Eminent Parliamentarians*, ed. Philip Norton (London: Biteback Publishing, 2012), 246.

138 Ibid.

139 Interview with John O'Sullivan, Reform Club, London, 10 April 2015.

140 Ibid.

141 Caroline Slocock (2022), 'Breaking the Glass Chamber: Caroline Slocock in Conversation with Dr Emily Stacey', Mile End Institute, 15 September 2022. Available online: www.youtube.com/watch?reload=9&app=desktop&v=IRkMosjHUow&list=PLgHM2qlXTAXtHahHiX18XvSTwBCw_bIov&index=4 (accessed 14 April 2023).

142 See Gamble, *The Free Economy and the Strong State* and Young, *One of Us.*

143 Thatcher, *The Path to Power*, 395.

144 Interview with Robin Harris, Somerset House, London, 11 June 2014.

145 Ibid.

Notes

146 Julian Critchley, *A Bag of Boiled Sweets: An Autobiography* (London: Faber & Faber, 1994), 169. According to Critchley, it was Whitelaw who was responsible for this exact phrase. Critchley was later outed by *The Observer*. Ian Aiken, 'Critchley Admits Writing Attack on Thatcher', *The Observer*, 26 February 1980, 26.

147 Chris Patten, *First Confessions. A Sort of Memoir* (London: Penguin, 2017), 149.

148 For example, Patten wrote large parts of Thatcher's 1987 Conference Speech.

149 Mount, *Cold Cream*, 287.

150 Hoskyns remembers similar conversations with Thatcher. Hoskyns, *Just in Time*, 345.

151 Mount, *Cold Cream*, 287.

152 George Walden, *Lucky George, Memoirs of an Anti-Politician* (London: Allen Lane, 1999), 301.

153 Thatcher, *The Path to Power*, 429.

154 Millar, *A View from the Wings*, 280.

155 Hurd, *Memoirs*, 213.

Chapter 3

* MTF, 131383 (THCR 2/7/3/2 f3). Shrimsley minute, 7 April 1983, 5.

1 Jephson, *The Platform*, 572. For examples of how Jephson's work has influenced later studies see, Joseph Meisel, *Public Speech and the Culture of Public Life in the Age of Gladstone* (New York: Columbia University Press, 2001).

2 Jephson, *The Platform*, 573.

3 Blaxill, *The War of Words*, 1.

4 See Blaxill, *The War of Words*; Meisel, 'Words by the Numbers' and Lawrence, *Electing Our Masters*.

5 MTF, 105147, TV Interview for BBC1 *Nationwide*, 24 May 1983.

6 Ibid.

7 Ibid.

8 Thatcher even turned down Lawley's request for an interview on *Desert Island Discs*.

9 Martin Westlake, *Kinnock. The Biography* (London: Little, Brown and Company, 2001), 207.

10 CAC, THCR 2-7-3-38, Letter from Sue Lawley to Margaret Thatcher, 6 June 1983.

11 Though it should be noted that newspaper coverage allowed for the widespread broadcasting of some political speeches.

12 See Meisel, 'Words by the Numbers'.

13 MTF, 104047, General Election Press Conference, 27 April 1979.

14 Ibid.

15 For further discussion of this article, see Roderick P. Hart, *The Sound of Leadership: Presidential Communication in the Modern Age* (Chicago: University of Chicago Press, 1987), 155.

16 Hart, *The Sound of Leadership*, 157.

17 Patrick Cosgrave, *Margaret Thatcher. A Tory and Her Party* (London: Hutchinson, 1978), 17.

18 Caroline Slocock, *People Like Us: Margaret Thatcher and Me* (London: Biteback Publishing, 2018), 71.

19 CAC, THCR 2-7-1-57, Reece letter to A. Garner, 5 September 1978.

20 Thatcher, *Path to Power*, 457.

21 Hart has shown that presidents of the United States increased their rhetorical output consistently during election periods. Hart, *The Sound of Leadership*, 183.

22 See Moore, *Margaret Thatcher: The Authorised Biography, Volume One* and Campbell, *Margaret Thatcher, Volume Two*.

23 See Moore, *Margaret Thatcher: The Authorised Biography, Volume One*, 444.

24 For the purpose of this discussion, the speeches Thatcher made in the House of Commons have not been included.

25 Northern Ireland is a unique example. Thatcher spoke in Northern Ireland six times, yet none of these speeches took place in an election year. This is hardly surprising given the unique political climate of the six counties, detached as they were from the domestic rivalries of the mainland.

26 Hart, *The Sound of Leadership*, 183.

27 Thatcher, *Path to Power*, 448.

28 CAC, THCR 2-7-1-57, 'Election Strategy', undated, 1.

29 Thatcher, *The Downing Street Years*, 292.

30 Cecil Parkinson, *Right at the Centre* (London: Weidenfeld and Nicolson, 1992), 226.

31 MTF, 132466 (THCR -7-3-2 f66). Garner minute, 22 December 1982, 6.

32 Hart, *The Sound of Leadership*, 189.

33 Thatcher, *The Downing Street Years*, 293.

34 MTF, 132466 (THCR 2-7-3-2 f66). Garner minute, 22 December 1982, 6.

35 Ibid., 6.

36 Thatcher, *The Downing Street Years*, 293.

37 Ibid.

38 MTF,132466 (THCR 2-7-3-2 f66). Garner minute, 22 December 1982, 6.

39 Thatcher, *The Downing Street Years*, 293.

40 MTF, 131383 (THCR 2-7-3-2 f3). Shrimsley minute, 7 April 1983, 5.

41 Thatcher, *The Downing Street Years*, 293.

42 MTF, 106345, Thatcher's speech to the Anglo-Italian Summit, 12 March 1986.

43 MTF, 106348, Thatcher's speech to the Conservative Central Council, 15 March 1986.

Notes

44 CAC, THCR 2-7-1-5-7, Minutes of a meeting held in the Deputy Chairman's Office on Monday, 26 March 1979, 1.

45 CAC, THCR, 2-7-1-5-7, Election meeting agenda, undated but likely to be June 1978.

46 MTF, 105332, Cardiff Speech, 23 May 1983.

47 MTF,106855, IRN report on Thatcher's speech in Tiptree, Essex, 29 May 1983.

48 Thatcher, *The Downing Street Years*, 292.

49 MTF,105139, Speech to Conservative Candidates, 18 May 1983.

50 Thatcher, *The Downing Street Years*, 292.

51 Ibid.

52 MTF, 105332, Cardiff Speech, 23 May 1983.

53 MTF, 105349, Harrogate Speech, 26 May 1983.

54 Thatcher, *The Downing Street Years*, 577.

55 Ibid.

56 MTF, 106861, Speech to a Conservative Rally in Scotland, 2 June 1987.

57 MTF, 106874, Speech to Conservative Family Rally, 7 June 1987.

58 MTF, 106843, Newport Speech, 26 May 1987.

59 Thatcher, *The Downing Street Years*, 295.

60 Thatcher, *Path to Power*, 455.

61 Ibid., 459.

62 Interview with Robin Harris, Somerset House, London, 11 June 2014.

63 CAC, THCR 2-7-1-5-7, Leader's General Election Meeting, 26 June 1978, 1.

64 MTF, 131370, (THCR 2-7-3-36 f46). Mount minute to Thatcher, 24 January 1983. Wilson did indeed use a similar approach, see Ziegler, *Wilson*, 155.

65 Ibid.

66 Ibid. In the speech Thatcher told her audience 'I would like, if I may, to offer you some encouragement tonight by telling you how we as a nation are going to recover from the recession'. She then went on to discuss, in detail, four 'signposts of recovery'. MTF, 105244, Speech to Glasgow Chamber of Commerce, Glasgow, 28 January 1983.

67 MTF, 131370 (THCR 2-7-3-36 f46). Mount minute to Thatcher, 24 January 1983.

68 Interview with Robin Harris, Somerset House, London, 11 June 2014. Harris notes 'How much she [Thatcher] actually used them [the modules] I do not know'.

69 Thatcher, *The Downing Street Years*, 292. No trace of these remains in the archives.

70 For a full list see MTF, 131370, (THCR 2-7-3-36 f46). Mount minute to Thatcher, 24 January 1983.

71 MTF, 132466 (THCR 2/7/3/2 f66). Garner minute, 22 December 1982, 11.

72 Ibid., 11.

73 Thatcher, *The Downing Street Years*, 295.

74 Ibid.

75 Ibid.

Chapter 4

*   MTF, 109408 (Reagan Library: European &amp); Soviet Directorate NSC (Thatcher Visit – Dec 84 [4] Box 90902). US ambassador (London) to secretary of state, 15 September 1983.

1   MTF, 102629, Speech Accepting Conservative Party Leadership, 20 February 1975.

2   This statistic is adjusted to take into account the speech that Thatcher delivered to a Conservative Party rally in Bolton. Here she used the word 'jobs' eighteen times but did so without making any substantial references to the region in which she spoke. This speech thus acts to distort the geographical, statistical analysis of Thatcher's use of the word 'jobs' in opposition.

3   Ian Aitken, 'Thatcher Plays on Threat of Left', *The Guardian*, 11 October 1980, 1.

4   Ibid.

5   MTF, 104043, Speech to Conservative Rally in Edinburgh, 25 April 1979.

6   MTF, 104002, Adoption speech in Finchley, 11 April 1979.

7   MTF, 103420, Speech to Conservative Rally at Blenheim Palace, 16 July 1977; MTF, 103708, Speech to Welsh Party Conference, 10 June 1978.

8   MTF, 104375, Speech at ICI Plant. Runcorn, 6 June 1980.

9   MTF, 105617, Speech to Small Business Bureau Conference, 8 February 1984.

10   Arthur Marwick, *British Society Since 1945* (London: Penguin, 2003), 248–52.

11   Interview with Michael Scholar, Oxford, 24 August 2016. For variations on this template see MTF, 105260, Speech to the Institute of Directors, 23 February 1983 or MTF, 105295, Speech to Confederation of British Industry Annual Dinner, 19 April 1983.

12   CAC, THCR 4-1-4-44, Ian Gow note to Ferdinand Mount, 23 February 1983.

13   Ibid.

14   CAC, THCR 4-1-4-44, Ferdinand Mount letter to Margaret Thatcher, 18 March 1983.

15   MTF,123663 (THCR 5-1-5-169 Part 2 f94). No.10 letter to FCO concerning Foreign Affairs draft section of Conference Speech, 10 September 1982.

16   CAC, TCHR 2-1-1-32, Geoffrey Howe letter to Margaret Thatcher, 6 March 1978. Thatcher, it turned out, did not use the speech.

17   Slocock, *People Like Us*, 74.

18   Interview with Harvey Thomas, Potters Bar, 30 July 2015.

19   MTF, 114199 (THCR 5-1-5-105 f5). John Hoskyns minute to Margaret Thatcher, 7 July 1981.

20   Northern Ireland provided a unique context in which Thatcher's speeches could make an 'impact'. Attacks on the Labour Party or Social Democratic Party bore little relevance to her audience. Thatcher's Party Conference Speeches made

mention of the 'Labour Party' 160 times. The 'Labour Party' however, was not mentioned at all in any of the speeches delivered in Northern Ireland.

21 MTF, 102853, Speech to Faversham Conservatives, 13 February 1976.

22 MTF, 109393, Reagan Library: European & Soviet Directorate, NSC: Records (Thatcher Visit – Dec 84 [1] Box 90902). Burt briefing to Shultz, 19 December 1984.

23 MTF, 109392, Margaret Thatcher, 'Camp David Declaration', 22 December 1984.

24 Christopher Thomas, 'US Looks to Thatcher for Support', *The Times*, 22 December 1984, 1.

25 MTF, 109392, 'Camp David Declaration', 22 December 1984. The location of the platform was also an initial factor in Thatcher's speaking at the College of Europe in 1988. 'My own view', David Hannay wrote to John Kerr 'is that, if the Prime Minister is minded to make a speech with a European theme this [the College of Europe] is as good a platform as any for doing so'. MTF, 111772, David Hannay (Britain's Permanent Representative) to John Kerr (responsible for the European Community within the FCO), 29 March 1988.

26 MTF, 109408, Reagan Library: European & Soviet Directorate NSC (Thatcher Visit – Dec 84 [4] Box 90902). US ambassador (London) to secretary of state, 15 September 1983. The importance of location was also understood by Charles Powell in 1987. When organizing Thatcher's trip to the United States in 1987 Powell was keen to remind Thatcher of the 'symbolic importance' of the location from which she would deliver her planned set-piece speeches. It would, he suggested, 'underline the central importance of the transatlantic relationship in our foreign policy'. MTF, 205268 (THCR 1-9-18A8 f67). Charles Powell note to Thatcher, 11 July 1987, 2.

27 Remote interview with Adam Ridley, 26 March 2021.

28 Ibid.

29 MTF, 112664 (THCR 6-2-4-7 f108). Sally Dixon note to Margaret Thatcher, 29 January 1980.

30 MTF, 112670 (THCR 6-2-4-9 f73). Mike Pattison minute to Margaret Thatcher, 29 February 1980.

31 See MTF, 113388 (THCR 6-1-2-2). Margaret Thatcher's engagement diary, 14 March 1980.

32 MTF, 104587, Speech at St Lawrence Jewry, 4 March 1981.

33 Alun Rees, 'A Gospel of Hate', *Daily Express*, 5 March 1981, 1.

34 Ibid.

35 Interview with John O'Sullivan, Reform Club, London, 10 April 2015.

36 Max Atkinson, *Our Masters' Voices: The Language and Body Language of Politics* (London: Routledge, 1989), 13. Atkinson has shown that applause usually lasts for between seven and nine seconds. Anything outside these timings is considered

abnormal. Indeed, enthusiastic applause which gained attention in the news media has been shown to last for ten or more seconds. Ibid., 28.

37 ITNVA, 1133633105, Speech to Young Conservatives, 10 February 1979. Available online: https://www.gettyimages.co.uk/detail/video/margaret-thatcher-speech-at-young-conservatives-news-footage/1133633105?adppopup=true (accessed 29 May 2023).

38 BFIA, TX5.6.83, *BBC News at Nine O'Clock*, 5 June 1983.

39 BFIA, TX13.12.84, *BBC News at Nine O'Clock*, 13 December 1984.

40 Interview with John O'Sullivan, Reform Club, London, 10 April 2015.

41 Interview with Harvey Thomas, Potters Bar, 30 July 2015.

42 Thatcher, *The Downing Street Years*, 580.

43 Celebrities such as Ken Dodd, Bob Monkhouse and Jimmy Tarbuck were deployed to entertain the audience. These celebrities 'were not the message' but were used as a means of preparing the audience for Thatcher's appearance.

44 Interview with Harvey Thomas, Potters Bar, 30 July 2015.

45 ITNVA, 131089004, Conservative Party Conference Speech, 13 October 1989. Available online: www.itnsource.com/en/shotlist/ITN/1989/10/13/BSP131089004/?s=Thatcher (accessed 10 November 2015).

46 CAC, THCR5-1-3-11.

47 Robin Harris, *Not for Turning: The Life of Margaret Thatcher* (London: Bantam Press, 2013), 19.

48 MTF, 104074, Remarks on the counting of chickens, 3 May 1979.

49 MTF, 108256, Confidence in Her Majesty's Government, 22 November 1990.

50 CAC, THCR5-1-2-39, Lord Mancroft, The British Genius, undated, 3.

51 CAC, THCR5-1-38, Thatcher's handwritten speech draft, undated, 6.

52 MTF, 102777, Conservative Party Conference Speech, 10 October 1979.

53 Thatcher noted: 'I regarded the *quid pro quo* for my strong public support of the President as being the right to be direct with him and members of his Administration in private' (Thatcher, *The Downing Street Years*, 469).

54 ITNVA, 210285010, Speech at the British Residence in Washington, 2 February 1985. Available online: www.itnsource.com/en/shotlist/ITN/1985/02/21/AS210285010/?s=Thatcher (accessed 10 November 2015).

55 The impact which this rhetorical device had on the President himself is questionable. He makes no mention of the speech in his diary. See ed. Douglas Brinkley, *The Reagan Diaries* (New York: HarperCollins, 2007).

56 ITNVA, 141088022, Conservative Party Conference Speech, 14 October 1988. Available online: www.itnsource.com/en/shotlist/ITN/1988/10/14/AS141088022/?s=Thatcher (accessed 10 November 2015).

57 Ibid.

58 Ibid.

Notes

59 Often the *tricolon* was used to signal applause. See, for example, the 1980 Conference Speech. 'This week has demonstrated that we are a party united in purpose, strategy and resolve.' MTF, 112637, Conservative Conference Speech text complete with annotations, 10 October 1980.

60 ITNVA, 141088022, Conservative Party Conference Speech, 14 October 1988. Available online: www.itnsource.com/en/shotlist/ITN/1988/10/14/AS141088022/?s=Thatcher (accessed 10 November 2015).

61 Ibid.

62 Remote interview with Adam Ridley, 26 March 2021.

63 Interview with Michael Scholar, Oxford, 24 August 2016.

64 Interview with Robin Harris, Somerset House, London, 11 June 2014.

65 Ibid.

66 Interview with Robin Harris, Somerset House, London, 11 June 2014.

67 John Ramsden, *Man of the Century: Winston Churchill and His Legacy Since 1945* (London: HarperCollins, 2003), 576–8.

68 Powell was a gifted Classicist. Not only was he a Fellow of Trinity College, Cambridge by the age of twenty-two, but he was Professor of Greek at the University of Sydney by the age of twenty-five. However, he did not specialize in the works of classical rhetoricians. Churchill was denied a classical education. 'I have never', recalled Churchill, 'had the practise which comes to young men at the university of speaking in small debating societies'. Meisel, 'Words by the Numbers', 268.

69 Interview with Michael Scholar, Oxford, 24 August 2016.

70 Sherman, *Paradoxes of Power*, 90.

71 ITNVA, 1133633105, Speech to Young Conservatives, 10 February 1979. Available online: https://www.gettyimages.co.uk/detail/video/margaret-thatcher-speech-at-young-conservatives-news-footage/1133633105?adppopup=true (accessed 29 May 2023).

72 MTF, 121230, Speech to the Gala Lunch, Bonn, 18 November 1981.

73 MTF, 114248 (THCR 1-3-6 f18). Letter from Sir Michael Palliser to Margaret Thatcher, 20 November 1981.

74 Thatcher, *The Downing Street Years*, 568.

75 CAC, THCR, 5-1-2-37, Conference Speech speaking text, undated, 1.

76 Interview with Harvey Thomas, Potters Bar, 30 July 2015.

77 Ibid.

78 Ibid.

79 MTF, 107789, Speech to the Conservative Party Conference, 13 October 1989.

80 Millar, *A View from the Wings*, 287.

81 Ibid.

170   *Notes*

82 MTF, 112637, 1980 Conference Speech text complete with annotations, 10 October 1980.

83 For Thatcher's recollections see Thatcher, *The Downing Street Years*, 122.

84 MTF, 112637 (THCR 5-1-4-16 f97). 1980 Conference Speech text complete with annotations, 10 October 1980.

85 Ibid.

86 See visual record of Thatcher delivering the line, MTF, 11266, Speech to the Conservative Party Conference, 10 October 1980.

87 Lawrence, *Electing Our Masters*, 152. See also eds. David Butler and Dennis Kavanagh, *The British General Election of 1983* (London: Palgrave Macmillan, London, 1984), 166.

88 Ed. Collins, *Margaret Thatcher: Complete Public Statements 1945–1990 on CD-ROM*, Thatcher's interview on BBC 4's *Woman's Hour*, 28 November 1986, UDN86_361.

89 Thatcher, *Diary of an Election*, 54.

90 Ibid.

91 Ibid.

92 MTF,112637 (THCR 5-1-4-16 f97). 1980 Conference Speech text complete with annotations, 10 October 1980.

93 Thatcher, *The Downing Street Years*, 293.

94 MTF, 106888, Re-election Speech, Finchley, 12 June 1987.

95 Interview with Bernard Ingham, Purley, 27 February 2015.

96 See Lawrence, *Electing Our Masters*, 146–70.

97 Sherman, *Paradoxes of Power*, 90.

Chapter 5

* CAC, THCR 2-6-2-135 part 1 f173, Ingham minute to Thatcher, 20 May 1981.

1 MTF, 110260 (Thatcher MSS 2-6-1-162). Circulated Paper (Shadow Cabinet), 28 April 1978.

2 Meisel, *Public Speech and the Culture of Public Life in the Age of Gladstone*, 288.

3 Stephen Koss, *The Rise and Fall of the Political Press in Britain, 1955–1974*, Vol. V (Oxford: Oxford University Press, 1995), 1096. See also Kevin Williams, *Read All about It! A History of the British Newspaper* (London: Routledge, 2010), 221–43; Graham Stewart, *The History of The Times. Volume VII, 1981–2002. The Murdoch Years* (London: HarperCollins, 2005), 316.

4 Peter Riddell remembers that, whilst Political Editor of the *Financial Times* between 1981 and 1988, he decided to end 'the traditional distinction between gallery coverage and lobby stories' which led to 'reports on speeches or exchanges in the Chamber form[ing] just a few paragraphs or sentences within a broader political story'. Peter Riddell, 'Members and Millbank: The Media and Parliament', in *Politics*

and the Media: Harlots and Prerogatives at the Turn of the Millennium, ed. Jean Seaton (Oxford: Wiley-Blackwell, 1998), 12.

5 Fred Emery, 'Mrs Thatcher's Pledge to Restore Free Wage Bargaining', *The Times*, 14 October 1978, 1.

6 Robin Oakley, 'Thatcher Ends Conference on a Note of Victory', *The Times*, 11 October 1988, 1.

7 Nicholas Wood, 'Europe Fears Battle ahead with Thatcher', *The Times*, 22 September 1988, 1.

8 George Lockhead, 'The Power and the Glory', *Daily Express*, 13 October 1979, 5.

9 Interview with Bernard Ingham, Purley, 27 February 2015.

10 Riddell, 'Members and Millbank', 17. Riddell attended Dulwich College, then Sidney Sussex College, Cambridge.

11 David McKie (2016), 'Simon Hoggart Obituary', *The Guardian*, 6 January 2014. Available online: www.theguardian.com/media/2014/jan/06/simon-hoggart-obituary (accessed 2 December 2015).

12 Alan Watkins, *A Short Walk Down Fleet Street: From Beaverbrook to Boycott* (London: Gerald Duckworth and Co. Ltd., 2000), 29.

13 Ibid., 29.

14 Tony Gray, *Fleet Street Remembered* (London: William Heinemann Ltd., 1990), 137.

15 Ibid., 227.

16 Bernard Ingham, *Kill the Messenger* (London: HarperCollins, 1991), 23.

17 Deedes first entered the Cabinet under Harold Macmillan in 1962, as minister without portfolio. He was later appointed minister of information.

18 Geoffrey Goodman (2007), 'Terence Lancaster', *The Guardian*, 9 October 2007. Available online: www.theguardian.com/news/2007/oct/09/guardianobituaries. pressandpublishing (accessed 2 December 2015).

19 Ibid.

20 Ingham, *Kill the Messenger*, 356.

21 MTF, 131493 (THCR 2-10-27 f44). Derek Howe minute to Margaret Thatcher, 9 February 1983.

22 MTF, 105252, Speech to the Young Conservatives Conference, 12 February 1983.

23 Ibid.

24 Simon Hoggart, 'Thatcher to Fight on CND', *The Guardian*, 13 February 1983, 2.

25 MTF, 131493 (THCR 2-10-27 f44). Derek Howe minute to Margaret Thatcher, 9 February 1983.

26 Terence Lancaster, 'Maggie's Cue for an Election', *Daily Mirror*, 9 October 1982, 2.

27 Ibid.

28 John Warden, 'Maggie Triumphant', *Daily Express*, 9 October 1982, 5.

29 Julian Haviland, 'Thatcher Says There Will Be No NHS Break-up', *The Times*, 9 October 1982, 1; Terence Lancaster, 'Maggie's Cue for an Election', *Daily Mirror*, 9 October 1982, 2.

30 MTF, 104119, Speech at the Birmingham Press Club lunch, 20 July 1979.

172   *Notes*

31 Koss, *The Rise and Fall of the Political Press in Britain*, 1105.

32 Woodrow Wyatt, *The Journals of Woodrow Wyatt*, Vol. 1 (London: Pan Books, 1999), 61–3.

33 Jeremy Tunstall, *Newspaper Power: The New National Press in Britain* (Oxford: Clarendon Press, 1996), 88.

34 Harold Evans, *Good Times, Bad Times* (London: Weidenfeld and Nicolson, 1984), 236.

35 Ibid., 234.

36 MTF, 122759, Ian Gow minute to Margaret Thatcher, 23 March 1982.

37 Ibid.

38 Robin Oakley, 'Thatcher Ends Conference on a Note of Victory', *The Times*, 11 October 1988, 1.

39 Ibid.

40 Thatcher, *The Downing Street Years*, 568.

41 Unnamed, 'Thatcher Crusade for Popular Capitalism', *The Times*, 11 October 1986, 4.

42 Ibid.

43 Sheree Dodd, 'Thatcher Fires a Nuclear Missile', *Daily Mirror,* 11 October 1986, 2.

44 Ibid.

45 Ibid.

46 Ibid.

47 Evans, *Good Times, Bad Times*, 234.

48 MTF, 122759, Alan Waters minute to Ian Gow, 22 March 1982.

49 MTF, 131561 (THCR 3-1-33 Part 1 f45). Margaret Thatcher message to Ronald Reagan, 15 September 1983.

50 David Watt, 'The Dangers of a Churchill Posture', *The Times*, 7 October 1983, 11.

51 Ibid., 11. The *Daily Telegraph* adopted a similar position.

52 BFIA, TX5.6.83, *BBC News at Nine O'Clock*, 5 June 1983.

53 Ibid. *BBC Radio Four News* took a similar line. Although it did mention Kenny Everett, it focused more on Thatcher's speech, especially her discussion of the Labour Party.

54 Chris Potter, 'Superstar Maggie Is a Wow at Wembley!', *The Sun*, 6 June 1983, 1.

55 Philip Webster, 'Prime Minister Draws the Stars to Wembley', *The Times*, 6 June 1983, 1.

56 Tunstall, *Newspaper Power,* 1.

57 MTF, 122990 (THCR 1-12-16 Part 1f3.) Bernard Ingham minute to Margaret Thatcher, 'Media Relations: Stocktaking and Looking Ahead', 3 August 1982. Andrew Marr also recognizes this point. 'Journalists', Marr confessed, 'are not taught what news is. We learn by copying. We look at what news was in yesterday's papers, and the week before.' Andrew Marr, *My Trade: A Short History of British Journalism* (London: Picador, 2009), 57.

Notes

58 Thatcher, *The Path to Power*, 362.

59 MTF, 102947, Speech to Finchley Conservatives, 31 January 1976.

60 Ibid.

61 Readers were told that during her Conference Speech 'Mrs Thatcher also Played Iron Lady in Foreign Affairs'. Fred Emery, 'Mrs Thatcher Insists That She Will Not Give Way on Economic Policy', *The Times*, 11 October 1980, 1.

62 Nicholas Ashford, 'Thatcher Delivers Blistering Attack on Soviet Tyranny', *The Times*, 30 September 1983, 1.

63 Trevor Fishlock, 'Thatcher and Trudeau Discuss Arms Stance', *The Times*, 26 September 1983, 6.

64 Thatcher, *The Downing Street Years*, 325.

65 Quoted in Charles Moore, *Margaret Thatcher. The Authorised Biography. Volume Two: Everything She Wants* (London: Allen Lane, 2015), 114.

66 MTF, 122990 (THCR 1-12-16 Part 1 f3). Bernard Ingham minute to Margaret Thatcher, 'Media Relations: Stocktaking and Looking Ahead', 3 August 1982.

67 John Warden, 'I Won't Throw in the Towel', *Daily Mirror*, 17 October 1981, 5.

68 Marr, *My Trade*, 57.

69 John Warden, 'I Won't Throw in the Towel', *Daily Mirror*, 17 October 1981, 5.

70 Unnamed, 'The Lady's Not for Learning', *Daily Mirror*, 11 October 1980, 5.

71 John Warden, 'I Won't Throw in the Towel', *Daily Mirror*, 17 October 1981, 4.

72 MTF, 119211 (THCR 1-3-5 [50]). Michael Cole letter to Thatcher, 1 December 1980, 2.

73 This is particularly true of Harold Wilson and his dealings with prime ministerial communication surrounding the decision to devalue the pound. See Jeremy Tunstall, *The Westminster Lobby Correspondence: Sociological Study of National Political Journalism* (London: Routledge and Kegan Paul, 1970), 35–6 and 69–70.

74 Both the *Independent* and *The Guardian*, later followed by the *Scotsman*, refused to attend Lobby meetings and on 29 October 1986 the Lobby only narrowly voted to keep the briefings on non-attributable terms (by a margin of 67–55), showing just how concerned the press were that the Lobby was acting as a tool of Number 10.

75 Robert Harris, *Good and Faithful Servant: The Unauthorised Biography of Bernard Ingham* (London: Faber & Faber, 1991), 90.

76 Ibid.

77 Ibid.

78 Quoted in Ibid., 91.

79 Ibid.

80 The Lobby also turned on John Biffen following his appearance on Brian Walden's *Weekend World* (Sunday, 11 May 1986) where he had suggested that 'nobody seriously supposed that the Prime Minister would be Prime Minister throughout the entire period of the next parliament'. John Biffen, *Semi-detached* (London: Biteback Publishing, 2013). On the Tuesday Biffen recorded in his diary: 'There

174 *Notes*

has been powerful No. 10 briefing describing me as "maverick," "eccentric" and "semi-detached" etc'. Ibid., 401.

81 CAC, THCR 5-1-2-3, Patten to Thatcher, 11 March 1975.
82 Telephone interview with Adam Ridley, 2 February 2021.
83 Ibid.
84 Interview with John Whittingdale, Portcullis House, London, 19 January 2010.
85 MTF, 121351 (THCR 2-6-2-135 part 1 f173). Letter from Sir Harry Boyne to Bernard Ingham, 21 May 1981.
86 Ibid.
87 Ibid.
88 Ibid.
89 Interview with John Whittingdale, Portcullis House, London, 19 January 2010.
90 Thatcher, *The Path to Power*, 358.
91 Ibid.
92 Ibid., 359.
93 Ibid.
94 MTF, 121877 (THCR 5-1-5-125 f59). Bernard Ingham minute to Margaret Thatcher, 20 November 1981.
95 Ibid.
96 MTF, 105332, Speech at Cardiff City Hall, 23 May 1983.
97 Collins, 'Editorial Policy of Site'.
98 CAC, THCR 2/6/2/135 part 1 f173, Ingham minute to Thatcher, 20 May 1981.
99 Ibid.
100 Robin Oakley, 'Now It's Up to the People', *The Times*, 26 October 1988, 16.
101 William Rees-Mogg, *Memoirs* (London: Harper Press, 2011), 95.

Chapter 6

*   Millar, *A View from the Wings*, 276.
1   Interview with Bernard Ingham, Purley, 27 February 2015.
2   John Nott, *Here Today, Gone Tomorrow. Recollections of an Errant Politician* (London: Politico Publishing Ltd., 2002), ix.
3   There were, of course, exceptions. During the 1979 election BBC2 broadcast *On the Hustings* which played clips of set-piece speeches lasting up to 12 minutes. *Westminster* (Monday to Friday, 8.15–9.00pm, reaching an audience of 0.1 million), *Westminster Live* (Tuesday and Thursdays, 15.00–15.50pm, reaching an audience of 0.6 million) and *Westminster Week* (Sunday 12.00–12.35pm, reaching an audience of 0.2 million) broadcast substantial clips of parliamentary speeches.
4   MTF, 122990 (THCR 1-12-16 Part 1 f3). Ingham minute to Margaret Thatcher, 3 August 1982, 6.

Notes   175

5 Interview with Bernard Ingham, Purley, 27 February 2015.

6 MTF, 118897 (THCR 2-6-2-187). Reece note to Thatcher, 24 May 1978, 5.

7 Ibid., 1.

8 Ibid., 3.

9 Interview with Bernard Ingham, Purley, 27 February 2015. Such structured interviews were safer than the unscripted variety. Thatcher's disastrous encounter with Diana Gould regarding the sinking of the *Belgrano* (*Nationwide*, BBC, 24 May 1983) was the result of a 'phone-in' style of interview which was more difficult to manage than set-piece interviews. See MTF, 105147, Margaret Thatcher interview on the BBC's *Nationwide* programme, 24 May 1983.

10 It was agreed that the interview would be conducted with 'the fireplace as background, using three cameras, and with you [Thatcher] to the right of the fireplace looking at it'. MTF, 119980 (THCR 5-2-4 [78]). Bernard Ingham minute to Margaret Thatcher, 28 December 1979.

11 This was not restricted to Walden. David Frost rang Tim Bell before interviewing Thatcher to ask for the 'gut question'. Tim Bell, *Right or Wrong: The Memoirs of Lord Bell* (London: Bloomsbury Continuum, 2014), 77.

12 MTF, 119980 (THCR 5-2-4 [78]). Bernard Ingham minute to Margaret Thatcher, 28 December 1979.

13 For Ingham's advice see MTF, 119982 (THCR 5-2-4 [65]). Bernard Ingham minute to Margaret Thatcher, 5 January 1980, 3. MTF, 104210, Margaret Thatcher's interview on *Weekend World*, 6 January 1980.

14 MTF, 101632, Margaret Thatcher's Conservative Political Centre Lecture, 'What's Wrong with Politics', 11 October 1968.

15 MTF, 101632, Speech at Church of St Lawrence Jewry, 30 March 1978.

16 MTF, 122990, *Media Relations*, Ingham to Thatcher, 3 August 1983, 1.

17 Ibid., 12.

18 MTF, 112264 (THCR 2-6-2-134). Gordon Reece letter to Richard Ryder, 26 November 1979, 3.

19 Ibid., 3.

20 MTF, 118897 (THCR 2-6-2-187). Some guidelines on the media in a general election, 24 March 1978, 3.

21 Andrew Crisell, *An Introductory History of British Broadcasting* (London: Routledge, 2002), 223.

22 David Hendy, *Life on Air: A History of Radio Four* (Oxford: Oxford University Press, 2008), 268.

23 Ibid., 321.

24 Whitelaw, *The Whitelaw Memoirs*, 264.

25 Campbell, *Margaret Thatcher. Volume Two*, 401.

26 Paul Donovan, *All Our Todays: Forty Years of Radio 4's 'Today' Programme* (London: Jonathan Cape, 1997), 197.

Notes

27 Ibid., 194.

28 Ibid.

29 Ibid.

30 CAC, THCR 5-2-39 Neville Gaffin to Thatcher, 6 October 1980. The interview was finally given on 26 November 1980.

31 MTF, 123676 (THCR 5-2-78 f152). Ingham minute to Thatcher, 2 January 1982, 2.

32 Ibid., 1. Little written record survives of these supplementary briefing sessions.

33 Ibid., 1.

34 MTF, 123689, (THCR 5-2-85 f19). Ingham minute to Margaret Thatcher, 16 May 1982, 1.

35 Ibid.

36 MTF, 104938, Margaret Thatcher's radio interview for IRN, 17 May 1982.

37 See, for example, James Wightman, *The Telegraph*, 'Thatcher warns junta', 18 May 1982, 1.

38 CAC, THCR 5-2-39, Caroline Thomas to Thatcher, 27 November 1980.

39 Paul Corcoran, *Political Language and Rhetoric* (Austin: University of Texas Press, 1979), 199.

40 See Alistair Hetherington and Kay Weaver, 'Business as Usual: The Impact of Television Coverage on Press Reporting of the Commons', in *Televising Democracies*, ed. Bob Franklin (London: Routledge, 1992), 175.

41 Eds. Butler and Kavanagh, *The British General Election of 1983*, 166.

42 ITNVA, 808045098, Margaret Thatcher Visit to USA, 9 September 1977. Available online: https://www.gettyimages.co.uk/detail/video/margaret-thatcher-visit-to-usa-usa-new-york-cms-margaret-news-footage/808045098?adppopup=true (accessed 29 May 2023).

43 BFIA, TX6.6.83, *BBC News at Nine O'Clock*, 6 June 1983.

44 This was not unique. Thatcher's speech in Kuala Lumpur in 1985 was covered in a similar fashion. BFIA, TX5.4.85, *BBC News at Nine O'Clock*, 5 April 1985.

45 See, for example, John Birt and Peter Jay, 'Television Journalism: The Child Is an Unhappy Marriage between Newspapers and Film', *The Times*, 30 September 1975, 12.

46 Robin Aitken, *Can We Trust the BBC?* (London: Continuum, 2007), 31, 32.

47 Ibid., 32.

48 BFI, 'The Kinnock Report' in the BBC's *Tonight*, 10 October 1975.

49 Thatcher, *The Path to Power*, 308.

50 Interview with Harvey Thomas, Potters Bar, 30 July 2015.

51 Campbell, *Margaret Thatcher. Volume Two*, 608.

52 Ibid.

53 BFIA, TX20.9.88, *BBC News at Nine O'Clock*, 20 September 1988.

54 Ibid.

55 Ibid.

56 Ibid.

Notes

57 BBC Written Archives (BWA), 1263–4, *BBC Radio 4 News*, 6pm, 15 October 1983.

58 BWA, 1177–8, *BBC Radio 4 News*, 10.00pm, 10 October 1980.

59 BWA, 1177–8, *BBC Radio 4 News*, 9.00pm, 10 October 1980.

60 BWA, 1177–8, *BBC Radio 4 News*, 10.00pm, 10 October 1980.

61 BFIA, TX20.9.88, *BBC News at Nine O'Clock*, 20 September 1988.

62 Ibid.

63 BWA, 1409–10, *BBC Radio 4 News*, 6.00pm, 20 September 1988.

64 BWA, 1263–4, *BBC Radio 4 News*, 6.00pm, 15 October 1983.

65 Thatcher, *The Downing Street Years*, 311.

66 BWA, 1263–4, *BBC Radio 4 News*, 6.00pm, 15 October 1983.

67 Hendy, *Life on Air*, 319.

68 Ibid.

69 See MTF, 106318, (Hansard HC [90/651-58]). Margaret Thatcher's House of Commons Statement regarding Westland plc, 27 January 1986. See also MTF, 106314 (Hansard HC [90/449-60]). Margaret Thatcher's House of Commons Statement regarding Westland plc, 23 January 1986.

70 MTF, 106318, (Hansard HC [90/651-58]). Margaret Thatcher's House of Commons Statement regarding Westland plc, 27 January 1986.

71 Moore, *Margaret Thatcher: The Authorised Biography, Volume Two*, 502.

72 Ibid.

73 Bruce Anderson, 'Where Thatcher Went Wrong', *The Times*, 29 January 1986, 10.

74 MTF, 107188, Margaret Thatcher's 'Action for Cities' Speech, 7 March 1988.

75 MTF, 107191, Margaret Thatcher radio interview, IRN, 7 Match 1988.

76 Ibid.

77 MTF, 108108, Speech at a dinner hosted by Mikhail Gorbachev, 8 June 1990.

78 Ibid.

79 MTF, 108109, ITN interview, Moscow, 8 June 1990.

80 MTF, 108110, Channel 4 interview, Moscow, 8 June 1990. See also MTF, 108111, Margaret Thatcher TV-AM interview, 8 June 1990.

81 Baker, *The Turbulent Years*, 270.

82 MTF, 119213, (THCR 1-5-10). Hurd minute to Thatcher, 23 September 1980. Unemployment would actually reach the 3 million mark in 1983.

83 MTF, 112663, (THCR 2-6-2-39 f60). Ingham minute to Thatcher, 29 September 1980, 1.

84 MTF, 104439, Speech to the Conservative Trade Unionists Conference, 1 November 1980.

85 Ibid.

86 BWA, 1505–6, *Analysis*, 26 November 1980.

87 MTF, 120028, (THCR 5-2-39 [35]). Ingham minute to Thatcher, 25 November 1980, 1.

88 BWA, 1505–6, *Analysis*, 26 November 1980.

89 CAC, THCR 5-2-39 Ingham to Thatcher, 27 November 1980.

90 Michael Brunson, *A Ringside Seat: An Autobiography* (London: Hodder and Stoughton Ltd., 2000), 97.

91 Ibid., 98.

92 Ralph Negrine, *Politics and the Mass Media in Britain* (London: Routledge, 1994), 104.

93 Ibid.

94 Ibid., 124.

95 BFIA, TX20.9.88, *BBC News at One O'Clock*, 20 September 1988.

96 Burke does go on to say: 'In a speech she is due to deliver about now in Luxembourg'. BFIA, TX20.9.88, *BBC News at One O'Clock*, 20 September 1988.

97 Ibid.

98 No record of this press release survives in the Conservative Party Archive, Bodleian Libraries, Oxford.

99 BFIA, TX20.9.88, *BBC News at One O'Clock*, 20 September 1988.

100 Ibid.

101 Interview with Bernard Ingham, Purley, 27 February 2015.

102 Andrew Rawnsley, 'Lights But Not Much Action on MP-TV', *The Guardian*, 21 November 1989, 2. Presumably Thatcher, as prime minister, would be afforded more time.

103 Interview with Bernard Ingham, Purley, 27 February 2015.

104 *The Times*, 'Kinnock Continues the Windbag Tradition', 7 October 1983, 28.

105 At times Kinnock's pre-scripted points could double in length during delivery. See ed. Peter Kellner, *Thorns and Roses, Speeches of Neil Kinnock, 1983–1991* (London: Radius, 1992), 2.

106 Interview with Bernard Ingham, Purley, 27 February 2015.

107 MTF, 102629, Speech accepting the Conservative Party leadership, 20 February 1975.

108 Interview with John Whittingdale, Portcullis House, London, 19 January 2010.

109 Hoskyns, *Just in Time*, 131.

110 Interview with John Whittingdale, Portcullis House, London, 19 January 2010.

111 Millar, *A View from the Wings*, 276.

112 MTF, 112637, Speech to the Conservative Party Conference, 10 October 1980.

113 Millar, *A View from the Wings*, 289.

114 Ibid., 287.

115 Ibid.

116 Ibid., 288.

117 BFIA, TX10.10.80, *BBC News at Nine O'Clock*, 10 October 1980.

118 Millar, *A View from the Wings*, 288.

119 Hoskyns, *Just in Time*, 231.

120 Ibid.

121 Thatcher, *The Downing Street Years*, 122.

122 Interview with Bernard Ingham, Purley, 27 February 2015.

Notes

123 Ibid. This can be seen in Thatcher's 1981 Conference Speech. The use of repetition was picked up by the BBC. The BBC reported Thatcher's 1981 Conference Speech by noting that 'Mrs Thatcher has said it *again*... [author's italics]'. BFIA, TX16.10.81, *BBC News at Nine O'Clock*, 16 October 1981.

124 MTF, 103980, Speech to Conservative Central Council, 24 March 1979.

125 See, for example, MTF, 104026, Speech at Conservative Rally in Birmingham, 19 April 1979.

126 BFIA, TX21.9.88, *BBC News at One O'Clock*, 21 September 1988.

127 MTF,107332, Speech to the College of Europe, 20 September 1988.

128 MTF, 107333, Speech at a luncheon given by Jacques Santer, 21 September 1988.

129 BFIA, TX20.9.88, *BBC News at Nine O'Clock*, 20 September 1988.

130 BFIA, TX21.9.88, *BBC News at Nine O'Clock*, 21 September 1988.

131 Ibid.

132 Ibid.

133 Craig Brown, 'Love-Bombed to Submission', *The Times*, 11 June 1987, 24.

134 Atkinson, *Our Masters' Voices*, 165.

135 Eds. David Butler and Dennis Kavanagh, *The British General Election of 1987* (London: Palgrave Macmillan, London, 1988), 139.

136 Millar, *A View from the Wings*, 276.

137 Corcoran, *Political Language and Rhetoric*, 199.

Chapter 7

* Interview with Norman Tebbit, Bury-St-Edmunds, 24 October 2014.

1 CAC, THCR5-1-5-7 (Part 2), Letter from Hugh Thomas to Margaret Thatcher, 25 June 1979. Airey Neave Memorial lecture – transcript and notes. The assumption that words express fixed, lasting meanings was not confined to Thomas. Nigel Lawson confidently defined 'the right' definition of the word 'Thatcherism'. Lawson, *The View from No. 11*, 64.

2 Interview with Norman Tebbit, Bury-St-Edmunds, 24 October 2014.

3 Williamson, *Stanley Baldwin*, 15.

4 See Saunders, 'The Many Lives of Margaret Thatcher'.

5 Campbell, *Margaret Thatcher. Volume Two*, 352. Cannadine takes a similar approach. See Cannadine, *Margaret Thatcher*, 59.

6 The characterization of Thatcher as a 'conviction politician' has been widely used in the analysis of her premiership. Kwasi Kwarteng, for example, in his assessment of Thatcher's leadership from March to September 1981, does so with the understanding that Thatcher was a 'conviction politician'. Kwasi Kwarteng, *Thatcher's Trial. Six Months That Defined a Leader* (London: Bloomsbury, 2015), ix–xii. See also Green, *Thatcher*, 2.

180 *Notes*

7 Peter Riddell, *The Thatcher Decade: How Britain Has Changed during the* 1980s (London: Blackwell, 1989), 3.

8 Moore, *Margaret Thatcher: The Authorised Biography, Volume One*, 397.

9 Riddell, *The Thatcher Government*, 7.

10 For further discussion, see Antonio Weiss, *The Religious Mind of Mrs Thatcher*. Available online: www.margaretthatcher.org/document/11274 (accessed 17 April 2017), 26.

11 See Adam Sisman, *A.J.P. Taylor. A Biography* (London: Sinclair-Stevenson Ltd., 1994), 369.

12 Green, *Thatcher*, 17. See also Weiss, *The Religious Mind of Mrs Thatcher*, 20.

13 MTF, 103443, Conservative Party Conference Speech, 14 October 1977.

14 *Gallup Political Index*, Report number, 225, May 1979, 5.

15 Ibid.

16 MTF, 104147, Conservative Party Conference Speech, 12 October 1979.

17 Brian Connell, 'A Times Profile', *The Times*, 5 May 1980, 6.

18 MTF, 105349, Harrogate Speech, 26 May 1983.

19 Ibid.

20 Thatcher did not take the advice well. When she next saw Hoskyns she whispered to him 'I got your letter. Nobody has ever written to a Prime Minister like that before'. See Moore, *Margaret Thatcher, The Authorised Biography, Volume One*, 642.

21 CAC, THCR 1-13-6, Peter Hart draft of the PPB, 8 July 1981.

22 Ibid.

23 Ibid.

24 See MTF, 104569, Young Conservatives Conference Speech, 14 February 1981.

25 David Wood, 'The Importance of Being Mrs Thatcher', *The Times*, 21 January 1980, 13.

26 Ibid.

27 MTF, 104569, Young Conservatives Conference Speech, 14 February 1981.

28 Ed. Trewin, *Alan Clark Diaries*, 203.

29 Terence Lancaster, 'Mrs Thatcher's Pit Disaster', *Daily Mirror*, 20 February 1981, 10.

30 Campbell, *Margaret Thatcher. Volume Two, The Iron Lady*, 103.

31 David Wood, 'The Importance of Being Mrs Thatcher', *The Times*, 21 January 1980, 13.

32 Ibid.

33 MTF, 102456, Speech to Conservative Trade Unionists Conference, 1 March 1975.

34 Campbell, *Margaret Thatcher. Volume Two*, 126.

35 See, MTF, 104929, Speech to Mid-Bedfordshire Conservatives, 30 April 1982.

36 Riddell, *The Thatcher Government*, 6.

37 Simon Jenkins, 'The Birth of the Thatcher Factor', *The Times*, 31 March 1983, 14.

38 In 1982, 'conviction(s)' was used ten times, and eight times in 1983.

39 David Watt, 'Convicted of Failure to Debate', *The Times*, 11 January 1985, 12.

40 Campbell, *Margaret Thatcher. Volume Two,* 126.

41 Anthony Bevins, 'Heseltine Resigns over Westland', *The Times,* 10 January 1986, 1.

42 Peter Hennessey, 'Why Heseltine Finally Snapped', *The Times,* 10 January 1986, 10.

43 Ibid.

44 Ibid.

45 MTF, 105826, Interview with TV-AM, 7 June 1985.

46 Ibid.

47 The research showed that the prime minister 'was thought to have become more extreme' and that the Conservative government were now seen as similar to their predecessors, 'stumbling along from crisis to crisis with no clear aim'. Rodney Tyler, *Campaign! The Selling of the Prime Minister* (London: Grafton, 1987), 36.

48 Ibid., 38, 36.

49 Ibid., 36.

50 Ibid., 38.

51 Ian Aiken, 'The Illusion of Ideology which Obscures the Progress of Poll Tax Pragmatism: Commentary', *The Guardian,* 25 April 1988, 19.

52 Ibid.

53 Ronald Butt, 'Carving a Presidential Role', *The Times,* 27 July 1989, 16.

54 MTF, 107808, TV interview for *The Walden Interview,* 28 October 1989. For a fuller discussion of the interview, see Rob Burley, *Why Is This Lying Bastard Lying to Me? Searching for the Truth on Political TV* (London: Mudlark, 2023).

55 *Independent,* 28 October 1989.

56 Hugo Young, 'She Accumulated More Personal Power Than Any Peacetime Prime Minister in History', *The Guardian,* 23 November 1990, 22.

57 MTF, 108051, Speech to Conservative Central Council, 31 March 1990. See also MTF, 108030, Speech to Finchley Conservatives (Association AGM), 5 March 1990.

58 MTF, 108087, Speech to Scottish Conservative Party Conference, 21 May 1990.

59 MTF, 108217, Speech to Conservative Party Conference, 12 October 1990.

60 MTF, 102655, Speech to Conservative Central Council, 15 March 1975.

61 This is, of course, true of all the political labels employed by Thatcher and her peers. After all, language is not reflective. For the purposes of this book, such a discussion will be confined to Thatcher's construction of the 'Labour Party'.

62 MTF, 111771 (THCR 2-6-1-248). *Stepping Stones Report,* 14 November 1977, 1.

63 Ibid., 2.

64 CAC, Hosk 1–81, Memo from Keith Joseph to members of Stepping Stones Steering Group, 28 February. 1978.

65 MTF, 103764, Speech to Conservative Party Conference, 13 October 1978.

66 CAC, RDLY 2-9-1-20, *Attitudes of the Electorate to Trade Unions,* April 1979, 1.

67 Ed. Bo Särlvik and Ivor Crewe, *Decade of Dealignment. The Conservative Victory 1979 and the Electoral Trends in the 1970s* (Cambridge: Cambridge University Press, 1983), 148.

68 Ibid.

69 Hoskyns, *Just in Time*, 81.

70 Bernard Donoghue, *Prime Minister: The Conduct of Policy under Harold Wilson and James Callaghan* (London: Jonathan Cape, 1987), 174.

71 'Defence' is used thirty-five times in conjunction with the Labour Party, within a range of seven words either to the left and right. During the course of Thatcher's premiership, the word 'tax' is associated with the term 'Labour' thirty-nine times.

72 MTF, 105285, Speech to Conservative Central Council, 26 March 1983. For other examples, see also MTF, 105314, Speech to the Scottish Conservative Party Conference, 13 May 1983 and MTF, 105322, Speech at Adoption Meeting, 19 May 1983.

73 MTF, 105349, Harrogate Speech, 26 May 1983.

74 MTF, 106743, Speech to the Young Conservatives Conference, 7 February 1987.

75 Thatcher noted that 'Labour is the high tax party' and then later that 'Labour are the high tax party'. MTF, 106843, Speech to a Conservative Party Rally in Newport, 26 May 1987.

76 MTF, 106852, Speech to a Conservative Party Rally in Solihull, 28 May 1987.

77 MTF, 105385, Speech at Fleetwood, 7 June 1983.

78 MTF, 106843, Speech to a Conservative Party Rally in Newport, 26 May 1987.

79 CAC, THCR 5-1-4-44, 'Central Council Speech. Information Required by the Prime Minister' date unknown but likely to be March 1983. This identification of policies that the Conservatives could benefit from electorally was not restricted to the Conservative Party's interaction with the Labour Party. On 22 April 1987, Thatcher met with a group of MPs to discuss the Conservative Party's approach to the Alliance in the forthcoming general election. It was decided that John Major and Stephen Sherbourne would 'Identify Lib/SDP policy points which demage [*sic*] the self-interest of potential Tory defectors'. MTF, 205192, Sherbourne conversation record, 22 April 1987.

80 This was a central component of the speech as the speaking text carries extensive annotations on the sections which tackle the Labour Party and tax. 'We have slashed the National Insurance Surcharge – Labour Tax on jobs – giving £2,000 million back to industry'. Not only has Thatcher underlined her point on the National Insurance Surcharge, a reminder for her to stress the point when delivering the speech, but she has also highlighted the entire paragraph dealing with tax. MTF, 105349, Harrogate Speech, 26 May 1983.

81 MTF, 105385, Speech at Fleetwood, 7 June 1983.

82 Ibid.

83 Thatcher, *The Downing Street Years*, 297.

84	For example, Thatcher discussed the Labour Party and their fiscal policy in two speeches during 1979 and in only one in 1980, but this increased to five times in 1983, with an average reference of two per speech.
85	Four days earlier Parkinson had warned the Conference that: 'the trouble with Socialists, they think that every penny the nation earns belongs to them. You earn it and they spend it.' CAC, THCR 5-1-4-44, Press release of Cecil Parkinson's speech to the Council Central Council, 22 March 1983.
86	CAC, THCR 5-1-4-44, Alfred Sherman's 'Fragments for Central Council Speech', 25 March 1983.
87	Ibid.
88	It is clear that during late 1982 and 1983, Sherman was not alone in urging such an approach, especially in relation to Labour and Defence. Lord Beloff too demanded oppositional rhetoric: 'I shall not be content until it becomes as hazardous to wear a CND badge on the streets of London as it would be to sport a swastika in Tel Aviv.' MTF, 122590 (THCR 1-4-2 part 2 f9). Lord Beloff memo to Margaret Thatcher, 14 December 1982.
89	Ipsos Political Monitor Archive, 'Best Party on Key Issues: Taxation'. Available online: www.ipsos-mori.com/researchpublications/researcharchive/poll.aspx?oItemID=32&view=wide (accessed 19 December 2016). Interestingly, the Conservative Party's lead did drop to a two-point lead in late 1985. Unfortunately, there is no equivalent Ipsos Mori data for the 1987 general election.
90	Ibid.
91	Tim Bell, *Right or Wrong*, 79.
92	Ipsos Political Monitor Archive, 'Best Party on Key Issues: Defence / Disarmament / Nuclear Weapons'. Available online: www.ipsos-mori.com/researchpublications/researcharchive/poll.aspx?oItemID=21&view=wide (accessed 19 December 2016).
93	MTF, 105349, Harrogate Speech, 26 May 1983.
94	MTF, 123643 (THCR 2-11-9-35 f38). Public Opinion Background Note 132, 26 September 1982.
95	Sam Delaney, *Mad Men & Bad Men: What Happened When British Politics Met Advertising* (London: Faber & Faber, 2015), 87.
96	MTF, 205205, Unsigned Memo for Thatcher, *Election Analysis II*, 29 May 1987, 1.
97	*Gallup Political Index*, Report number 225, May 1979, 7.
98	MTF, 112198 (THCR 2-6-2-38). Keith Britto memo, 21 November 1979.
99	Martin Pugh, *Speak for Britain. A New History of the Labour Party* (London: Vintage, 2011), 370.
100	Thatcher, *The Downing Street Years*, 290.
101	MTF, 205205, (THCR 2-7-5-65 f108). Unsigned Memo for Thatcher, *Election Analysis II*, 29 May 1987, 3.

102 MTF, 151115 (THCR2-1-4-67 f72). Michael Jopling minute to Ian Gow, 21 August 1981.

103 MTF, 122920 (THCR 1-15-6 f3). Peter Walker minute to Margaret Thatcher, 16 February 1982, 2.

104 MTF,151115 (THCR2-1-4-67 f72). John Gummer, *The Tories and the Social Democrats*, 21 August 1981, 3.

105 MTF,122920 (THCR 1-15-6 f3). Peter Walker minute to Margaret Thatcher, 16 February 1982, 2.

106 MTF, 114220 (THCR 5-1-4-25 f145). John Hoskyns note to Margaret Thatcher, 1 September 1981, 2.

107 MTF, 105358, Thatcher's speech in Edinburgh, 31 May 1983.

108 MTF,105376, Thatcher's speech in Birmingham, 3 June 1983.

109 David Owen, *Time to Declare* (London: Michael Joseph, 1992), 585. Thatcher and her speechwriters would exploit this during the 1987 election campaign. Thatcher, for example, requested a '[l]ist of personal disagreements on policy between Steel and Owen which are on the record' for use in her, and the party's, political speeches. MTF, 205192 (THCR 2-7-5-41 f25). Sherbourne conversation record, 22 April 1987.

110 MTF, 102493, Speech to the 1922 Committee, 31 February 1975.

111 Lawson, *The View from No. 11*, 64.

112 See eds. Jackson and Saunders, *Making Thatcher's Britain*.

113 Collins, *Margaret Thatcher: Complete Public Statements 1945–1990 on CD-ROM*, Thatcher interview, *Daily Mail*, 1 May 1980, UD80_103.

114 'Would you agree', asked an unknown journalist, 'that it is essentially Thatcher and Thatcherism and whether the people believe which will win or lose you the election?' MTF,105320, General Election Press Conference launching the 1983 Conservative Party Manifesto, 18 March 1983.

115 MTF, 102939, Speech at Kensington Town Hall, 19 January 1976.

116 MTF, 105703, Speech at Conservative Election Rally, 11 June 1984.

117 MTF, 106647, Margaret Thatcher interviewed by Robin Day on BBC One's *Panorama*, 8 June 1987.

118 CAC, THCR, 5-1-4-101, The Conference Speech, David Hart to Stephen Sherbourne, 25 September 1985.

119 CAC, THCR 1-13-6, David Hart draft of the PPB, 8 July 1981.

120 MTF, 105349, Harrogate Speech, 26 May 1983.

121 Interview with Robin Harris, Somerset House, London, 11 June 2014.

122 Ibid.

123 Ibid.

124 See John Ramsden, *An Appetite for Power. A History of the Conservative Party since 1830* (London: HarperCollins, 1998).

Notes 185

125 Hugo Young, 'Has Labour an Intelligible Answer to Thatcherism?', *The Guardian,* 2 September 1986, 23.

126 Unnamed author, 'Tebbit Spurs Tories on Radical Path', *The Guardian,* 7 October 1987, 5.

127 James Naughtie, 'Tebbit Demands Thatcherism at a Faster Pace', *The Guardian,* 14 May 1986, 32.

128 See Vinen, *Thatcher's Britain*, 180.

129 Howe, *Conflict of Loyalty*, 609.

130 CAC, THCR 5-1-4-101, The Conference Speech, David Hart to Stephen Sherbourne, 25 September 1985.

131 Hoskyns, *Just in Time*, 85.

132 CAC, RDLY 2-9-1-20, *Attitudes of the Electorate to Trade Unions*, April 1979, 1.

133 Interview with Robin Harris, Somerset House, London, 11 June 2014. It should also be noted that much of the language on Christian morals originated from Alfred Sherman who, by the early 1980s, was losing influence in Thatcher's speechwriting sessions.

134 David Watt, 'Convicted of Failure to Debate', *The Times*, 11 January 1985, 12.

Conclusion

1 Mount, *Cold Cream*, 287.

2 For an example, see MTF, 214082, Engagement diary, 25 November 1985; MTF, 214084, Engagement diary, 27 November 1985; MTF, 214087, Engagement diary, 30 November 1985.

3 Ed. Kellner *Thorns and Roses*, 2 and Owen, *Time to Declare*, 602.

4 Ed. Kellner, *Thorns and Roses*, 4.

5 Millar, *A View from the Wings*, 231.

6 Ibid., 234.

7 Ibid.

8 Urban, *Diplomacy and Disillusion at The Court of Margaret Thatcher*, 41.

9 Millar, *A View from the Wings*, 41.

10 CAC, THCR2-6-2-118 Stowe minute, 1 June 1979, 1.

11 Eds. Kavanagh and Seldon, *The Powers behind the Prime Minister*, 172.

12 John Colville, *The Fringes of Power. Downing Street Diaries, 1939–1955* (London: Hodder and Stoughton, 1985), 367.

13 Philip Collins, *When They Go Low, We Go High. Speeches That Shape the World – and Why We Need Them* (London: Fourth Estate, 2018), 7.

14 Quoted in Ziegler, *Wilson*, 155.

15 Anonymous interview.

16 Hoskyns, *Just in Time*, 339.

17 MTF, 112003, (Sherman MSS [Royal Holloway Library] Box 7). Letter from Utley to Wolfson, 6 December 1978.

18 Collins, *When They Go Low, We Go High*, 6.

19 Elizabeth Nel, *Winston Churchill by His Personal Secretary* (New York: iUniverse, Inc. 2021), 11.

20 Hoskyns, *Just in Time*, 131.

21 Ibid.

22 Anonymous interview.

23 MTF, 108241, Speech at Lord Mayor's Banquet, 12 November 1990.

24 Interview with Robin Harris, Somerset House, London, 11 June 2014.

25 'I sometimes think the Labour Party is like a pub where the mild is running out. If someone doesn't do something soon, all that's Left will be bitter. And all that's bitter will be Left.' MTF, 102777, Speech to the Conservative Party Conference, 10 October 1975.

26 Mount, *Cold Cream*, 331.

27 Tebbit, *Upwardly Mobile*, 146.

28 Hoskyns, *Just in Time*, 278.

29 Peter McKay, 'The Court of the Queen Bee', *Daily Express*, 4 October 1982, 6.

30 CAC, Hosk 1–27, *Record of meeting with John Biffen*, 4 August 1977, 4.

31 Prior, *A Balance of Power*, 107.

32 BFIA, TX21.9.88, *BBC News at Nine O'Clock*, 21 September 1988.

33 For a full description see Stothard, *The Senecans*.

34 See, for example, Ranelagh, *Thatcher's People*.

35 Simon Jenkins, 'I Have Not Finished Yet', *The Times*, 19 November 1990, 14.

36 See for example, MTF, 104849, TV interview for De Wolfe Productions, 30 December 1982.

37 Hoskyns, *Just in Time*, 100.

38 Thatcher. *The Downing Street Years*, 293.

39 MTF, 106855, Speech in Tiptree, 29 May 1987.

40 Ibid., 2.

41 Parkinson, *Right at the Centre*, 226.

42 Thatcher, *The Downing Street Years*, 295.

43 Richard Aldous, *Reagan and Thatcher. The Difficult Relationship* (London: W. W. Norton & Company, 2012), 145.

44 MTF, 112664, (THCR 6-2-4-7 f108). Sally Dixon note to Margaret Thatcher, 29 January 1980.

45 Anonymous interview.

46 Interview with Bernard Ingham, Purley, 27 February 2015.

47 Interview with Harvey Thomas, Potters Bar, 30 July 2015.

Notes

48 Interview with Bernard Ingham, Purley, 27 February 2015.

49 MTF, 119982 (THCR 5/2/4 [65]). Ingham minute to Thatcher, 5 January 1980.

50 MTF, 119978 (THCR 5/2/4 [108]). Ingham letter to David Cox, 27 November 1979.

51 Fred Emery, 'More Public Spending Cuts Essential for Growth, Mrs Thatcher Says', *The Times*, 7 January 1980, 1.

52 Ibid.

53 Geoffrey Wansell, 'Why Walden's Words Grab Headlines', *The Times*, 11 September 1981, 40.

54 Interview with Bernard Ingham, Purley, 27 February 2015.

55 MTF, 122990 (THCR 1-12-16 Part 1 f3). Ingham minute to Margaret Thatcher, 3 August 1982, 6.

56 Hendy, *Life on Air*, 319.

57 MTF, 102629, Speech Accepting Conservative Party Leadership, 20 February 1975.

58 Millar, *A View from the Wings*, 276.

59 MTF, 122990, (THCR 1-12-16 Part 1 f3). Bernard Ingham minute to Margaret Thatcher, 'Media Relations: Stocktaking and Looking Ahead', 3 August 1982.

60 'Sir Ronald Millar' (1998) in *The Herald*, 18 April 1998. Available online: www.heraldscotland.com/news/12300229.sir-ronald-millar/ (accessed 30 May 2023).

61 MTF, 104167, Speech at Lord Mayor's Banquet, 12 November 1979.

62 MTF, 104210, TV interview for London Weekend Television *Weekend World*, 6 January 1980.

63 Ibid.

64 *Good Morning Summer* (1995), Interview with Thatcher, BBC, exact date unknown. Available online: www.youtube.com/watch?v=zBEREJpOvNo (accessed 15 July 2023).

65 Peter Mansbridge (1993), '*Mansbridge One on One*, interview with Thatcher', CBC News, 8 November 1993. Available online: www.youtube.com/watch?v=3w0U1aYyGc8 (accessed 15 July 2023).

66 Interview with Robin Harris, Somerset House, London, 11 June 2014.

67 MTF, 106647, TV interview for BBC1 *Panorama*, 8 June 1987.

68 MTF,105703, Speech at Conservative Election Rally, Central Hall, Westminster, 11 June 1984.

69 Lawson, *The View from Number 11*, 64.

70 See the introduction to Eds. Jackson and Saunders, *Making Thatcher's Britain*.

71 Interview with Norman Tebbit, Bury St Edmunds, 24 October 2014.

72 Ibid.

73 Interview with John O'Sullivan, Reform Club, London, 10 April 2015.

74 See CAC, Hosk 2–180. 'Preparations for the Conference Speech', 3 October 1980.

75 Eric J. Evans, *Thatcher and Thatcherism* (London: Routledge, 2008), 1. Ed. Subroto Roy and John Clarke, *Margaret Thatcher's Revolution: How It Happened and What It Meant* (London: Continuum, 2005), 1.

76 Lawrence and Campsie, 'Political History', 221.

77 Musolf, *From Plymouth to Parliament*, ix.

78 Lawrence and Campsie, 'Political History', 221.

79 See Macmillan's comments to Kennedy, discussed in Chapter 6.

80 Corcoran, *Political Language and Rhetoric*, 199.

81 Lawrence, *Electing Our Masters*, Chapter 6, 146–70.

Bibliography

Richard Aldous, *Reagan and Thatcher. The Difficult Relationship* (London: W. W. Norton & Company, 2012).

Richard Aldous, *Schlesinger: The Imperial Historian* (New York: Norton, 2017).

Max Atkinson, Our *Masters' Voices: The Language and Body Language of Politics* (London: Routledge, 1989).

J. L. Austin, *How to Do Things with Words* (Oxford: Oxford University Press, 1962).

Kenneth Baker, *The Turbulent Years* (London: Faber and Faber, 1993).

Tim Bell, *Right or Wrong: The Memoirs of Lord Bell* (London: Bloomsbury Continuum, 2014).

Robert Blake, *The Conservative Party from Peel to Thatcher* (London: Fontana Press, 1985).

Luke Blaxill, 'Quantifying the Language of British Politics, 1880–1910', *Historical Research*, 86, no. 232 (2013): 313–41.

Luke Blaxill, *The War of Words. The Language of British Elections, 1880–1914* (Woodbridge: The Royal Historical Association, 2000).

Ed. Douglas Brinkley, *The Reagan Diaries* (New York: HarperCollins, 2007).

Michael Brunson, *A Ringside Seat: An Autobiography* (London: Hodder and Stoughton Ltd., 2000).

Rob Burley, *Why Is This Lying Bastard Lying to Me? Searching for the Truth on Political TV* (London: Mudlark, 2023).

Eds. David Butler and Dennis Kavanagh, *The British General Election of 1983* (London: Palgrave Macmillan, 1984).

Eds. David Butler and Dennis Kavanagh, *The British General Election of 1987* (London: Palgrave Macmillan, 1988).

Eric Caines, *Heath and Thatcher in Opposition* (London: Palgrave Macmillan, 2017).

John Campbell, *Margaret Thatcher. Volume One: The Grocer's Daughter* (London: Vintage, 2000).

John Campbell, *Margaret Thatcher. Volume Two: The Iron Lady* (London: Vintage, 2012).

David Cannadine, *Margaret Thatcher. A Life and Legacy* (Oxford: Oxford University Press, 2017).

Peter Carrington, *Reflect on Things Past: The Memoirs of Lord Carrington* (London: Fontana Press, 1988).

Peter Clarke (1998), 'The Rise and Fall of Thatcherism', *London Review of Books*, 10 December 1998 (www.lrb.co.uk/the-paper/v20/n24/peter-clarke/the-rise-and-fall-of-thatcherism, accessed 21 July 2024).

Christopher Collins, 'Editorial Policy of Site: Preface to Complete Public Statements of Margaret Thatcher, 1945–90 on CD-ROM', in *Complete Public Statements of Margaret Thatcher, 1945–90*, ed. Christopher Collins (Oxford: Oxford University Press, 1998).

Philip Collins, *When They Go Low, We Go High. Speeches That Shape the World – And Why We Need Them* (London: Fourth Estate, 2018).

John Colville, *The Fringes of Power. Downing Street Diaries, 1939–1955* (London: Hodder and Stoughton, 1985).

Paul Corcoran, *Political Language and Rhetoric* (Austin: University of Texas Press, 1979).

Patrick Cosgrave, *Margaret Thatcher. A Tory and Her Party* (London: Hutchinson, 1978).

Maurice Cowling, *1867, Disraeli, Gladstone and Revolution. The Passing of the Second Reform Bill* (Cambridge: Cambridge University Press, 1967).

Maurice Cowling, *The Impact of Labour, 1920–1924. The Beginnings of Modern British Politics* (Cambridge: Cambridge University Press, 1971).

Andrew Crisell, *An Introductory History of British Broadcasting* (London: Routledge, 2002).

Julian Critchley, *A Bag of Boiled Sweets: An Autobiography* (London: Faber and Faber, 1994).

Stanley Crooks, *Peter Thorneycroft* (Winchester: George Mann Publications, 2007).

Sam Delaney, *Mad Men & Bad Men: What Happened When British Politics Met Advertising* (London: Faber and Faber, 2015).

Bernard Donoghue, *Prime Minister: The Conduct of Policy under Harold Wilson and James Callaghan* (London: Jonathan Cape, 1987).

Paul Donovan, *All Our Todays: Forty Years of Radio 4's 'Today' Programme* (London: Jonathan Cape, 1997).

Eric J. Evans, *Thatcher and Thatcherism* (London: Routledge, 2008).

Harold Evans, *Good Times, Bad Times* (London: Weidenfeld and Nicolson, 1984).

Eliza Filby, *God & Mrs Thatcher: The Battle for Britain's Soul* (London: Biteback Publishing, 2015).

Ed. Bob Franklin, *Televising Democracies* (London: Routledge, 1992).

Andrew Gamble, *The Free Economy and the Strong State: The Politics of Thatcherism* (Basingstoke: Palgrave, 1994).

Tony Gray, *Fleet Street Remembered* (London: William Heinemann Ltd., 1990).

E. H. H. Green, *Thatcher* (London: Bloomsbury Academic, 2006).

Eds. Stuart Hall and Martin Jacques, *The Politics of Thatcherism* (London: Lawrence & Wishart Ltd., 1983).

Robert Harris, *Good and Faithful Servant: The Unauthorised Biography of Bernard Ingham* (London: Faber and Faber, 1991).

Robin Harris, *Not for Turning: The Life of Margaret Thatcher* (London: Bantam Press, 2013).

Roderick P. Hart, *The Sound of Leadership: Presidential Communication in the Modern Age* (Chicago: The University of Chicago Press, 1987).

David Hendy, *Life on Air: A History of Radio Four* (Oxford: Oxford University Press, 2008).

John Hoskyns, *Just in Time: Inside the Thatcher Revolution* (London: Aurum Press, 2000).

Geoffrey Howe, *Conflict of Loyalty* (London: Macmillan, [1994] 2008).

Douglas Hurd, *Memoirs* (London: Abacus, 2004).

Bernard Ingham, *Kill the Messenger* (London: HarperCollins, 1991).

Ben Jackson, *Equality and the British Left. A Study in Progressive Political Thought, 1900–64* (Manchester: Manchester University Press, 2007).

Eds. Ben Jackson and Robert Saunders, *Making Thatcher's Britain* (Cambridge: Cambridge University Press, 2012).

Henry Jephson, *The Platform: Its Rise and Progress*, Vol. I (London: Frank Cass and Company Ltd. [1892] 1968).

Dennis Kavanagh and Anthony Seldon, *The Powers behind the Prime Minister: The Hidden Influence of Number 10* (London: HarperCollins, 2000).

Ed. Peter Kellner, *Thorns and Roses, Speeches of Neil Kinnock, 1983–1991* (London: Radius, 1992).

Anthony King, 'Margaret Thatcher as a Political Leader', in *Thatcherism*, ed. Robert Skidelsky (London: Chatto and Windus, 1988).

Stephen Koss, *The Rise and Fall of the Political Press in Britain, 1955–1974*, Vol. V (Oxford: Oxford University Press, 1995).

Kwasi Kwarteng, *Thatcher's Trial. Six Months That Defined a Leader* (London: Bloomsbury, 2015).

Jon Lawrence, *Electing Our Masters: The Hustings in British Politics from Hogarth to Blair* (Oxford: Oxford University Press, 2008).

Jon Lawrence and Alexandre Campsie, 'Political History', in *Writing History Theory and Practice*, ed. Stefan Berger, Heiko Feldner and Kevin Passmore (London: Bloomsbury Academic, 2010).

Nigel Lawson, *The View from No. 11: Memoirs of a Tory Radical* (London: Bantam Press, 1992).

Shirley Robin Letwin, *The Anatomy of Thatcherism* (London: Routledge, 1992).

David McLoughlin, 'The Origins and Reception of Harold Wilson's 1963 "White Heat" Speech' (MSc diss., London Centre for the History of Science, Medicine and Technology, London, 2010).

John Major, *John Major: The Autobiography* (London: HarperCollins, 1999).

Andrew Marr, *My Trade: A Short History of British Journalism* (London: Picador, 2009).

Joseph Meisel, *Public Speech and the Culture of Public Life in the Age of Gladstone* (New York: Columbia University Press, 2001).

Joseph Meisel, 'Review of Margaret Thatcher: Complete Public Statements 1945–1990', review no. 133 (https://reviews.history.ac.uk/review/133, accessed 30 October 2023).

Joseph Meisel, 'Words by the Numbers: A Quantitative Analysis and Comparison of the Oratorical Careers of William Ewart Gladstone and Winston Spencer Churchill', *Historical Research*, 73, no. 182 (2000): 262–96.

Ronald Millar, *A View from the Wings* (London: Weidenfeld and Nicolson, 1993).

Charles Moore, *Margaret Thatcher: The Authorised Biography, Volume One: Not for Turning* (London: Allen Lane, 2013).

Charles Moore, *Margaret Thatcher. The Authorised Biography, Volume Two: Everything She Wants* (London: Allen Lane, 2015).

Charles Moore, *Margaret Thatcher: The Authorised Biography, Volume Three: Herself Alone* (London: Allen Lane, 2019).

Ferdinand Mount, *Cold Cream: My Early Life and Other Mistakes* (London: Bloomsbury Publishing, 2008).

Karen Musolf, *From Plymouth to Parliament. A Rhetorical History of Nancy Astor's 1919 Campaign* (London: Palgrave Macmillan, 1999).

Ralph Negrine, *Politics and the Mass Media in Britain* (London: Routledge, 1994).

Elizabeth Nel, *Winston Churchill by His Personal Secretary* (New York: iUniverse, Inc. 2021).

Ed. Philip Norton, *Eminent Parliamentarians* (London: Biteback Publishing, 2012).

John Nott, *Here Today, Gone Tomorrow, Recollections of an Errant Politician* (London: Methuen Publishing Ltd., 2002).

David Owen, *Time to Declare* (London: Michael Joseph, 1992).

Cecil Parkinson, *Right at the Centre* (London: Weidenfeld and Nicolson, 1992).

Jonathan Parry, 'Maurice Cowling: A Brief Life', in *The Philosophy, Politics and Religion of British Democracy. Maurice Cowling and Conservatism*, ed. Robert Crowcroft, S. J. D. Green and Richard Whiting (London: I. B. Tauris, 2010).

Chris Patten, *First Confessions. A Sort of Memoir* (London: Penguin, 2017).

Jim Prior, *A Balance of Power* (London: Hamish Hamilton, 1986).

John Ramsden, *An Appetite for Power. A History of the Conservative Party since 1830* (London: HarperCollins, 1998).

John Ramsden, *The Man of the Century: Winston Churchill and His Legend since 1945* (London: HarperCollins, 2003).

John Ranelagh, *Thatcher's People: An Insider's Account of the Politics, the Power and the Personalities* (London: HarperCollins, 1991).

Paul Readman, 'Speeches', in *Reading Primary Sources, Routledge Guide to Using Primary Sources,* ed. Miriam Dobson and Benjamin Ziemann (London: Routledge, 2008).

Paul Readman, 'The State of Twentieth-Century British Political History', *The Journal of Policy History*, 21, no. 3 (2009): 219–38.

William Rees-Mogg, *Memoirs* (London: Harper Press, 2011).

Ed. R. A. W. Rhodes and Patrick Dunleavy, *Prime Ministers, Cabinet and Core Executive* (London: Palgrave, 1995).

Peter Riddell, *The Thatcher Decade: How Britain Has Changed during the 1980s* (London: Blackwell, 1989).

Peter Riddell, *The Thatcher Government* (Oxford: Martin Robertson, 1983).

Nicholas Ridley, *My Style of Government: The Thatcher Years* (London: Hutchinson, 1991).

Matthew Roberts, 'Constructing a Tory World-View: Popular Politics and the Conservative Press in Late Victorian Leeds', *Historical Research*, 79, no. 203 (2006): 115–43.

Ed. Subroto Roy and John Clarke, *Margaret Thatcher's Revolution: How It Happened and What It Meant* (London: Continuum, 2005).

Ed. Bo Särlvik and Ivor Crewe, *Decade of Dealignment. The Conservative Victory 1979 and the Electoral Trends in the 1970s* (Cambridge: Cambridge University Press, 1983).

Robert Saunders, 'The Many Lives of Margaret Thatcher', *English Historical Review*, 132, no. 556 (2017): 638–58.

Robert Schlesinger, *White House Ghosts, Presidents and Their Speechwriters* (New York: Simon & Schuster, 2008).

Ed. Jean Seaton, *Politics and the Media: Harlots and Prerogatives at the Turn of the Millennium* (Oxford: Wiley-Blackwell, 1998).

Alfred Sherman, *Paradoxes of Power: Reflections on the Thatcher Interlude* (Exeter: Imprint Academic, 2005).

Adam Sisman, *A.J.P. Taylor. A Biography* (London: Sinclair-Stevenson Ltd., 1994).

Quentin Skinner, 'The Principles and Practices of Opposition: The Case of Bolingbroke versus Walpole', in *Historical Perspective. Studies in English Thought and Society in Honour of J. H. Plumb*, ed. Neil McKendrick (London: Europa Publications, 1974).

Quentin Skinner, *Visions of Politics. Volume I: Regarding Method* (Cambridge: Cambridge University Press, 2002).

Caroline Slocock, *People Like Us: Margaret Thatcher and Me* (London: Biteback Publishing, 2018).

Gareth Stedman Jones, 'History and Theory: An English Story', *Historein*, 3 (2001): 119 (www.historeinonline.org, accessed 15 June 2015).

Gareth Stedman Jones, *Languages of Class: Studies in English Working Class History, 1832–1982* (Cambridge: Cambridge University Press, [1983] 1993).

Hugh Stephenson, *Mrs Thatcher's First Year* (London: Jill Norman Ltd, 1980).

Graham Stewart, *The History of the Times. Volume VII, 1981–2002. The Murdoch Years* (London: HarperCollins, 2005).

Peter Stothard, *The Senecans. Four Men and Margaret Thatcher* (London: Gerald Duckworth & Co. Ltd, 2016).

Norman Tebbit, *Upwardly Mobile* (London: Weidenfeld & Nicolson, 1988).

Carol Thatcher, *Diary of an Election with Margaret Thatcher on the Campaign Trail: A Personal Account by Carol Thatcher* (Letchworth: Sidgwick & Jackson Ltd., 1983).

Margaret Thatcher, *The Downing Street Years* (London: HarperCollins, 1993).

Margaret Thatcher, *The Path to Power* (London: HarperCollins, 1995).

Nick Thomas-Symonds, *Harold Wilson: The Winner* (London: W&N, 2022).

Ed. Ion Trewin, *Alan Clark Diaries: Into Power 1983–1992* (London: Phoenix, 2001).

Ed. Ion Trewin, *The Hugo Young Papers*: Thirty Years of British Politics – Off the record (London: Allen Lane, 2008).

Jeremy Tunstall, *Newspaper Power: The New National Press in Britain* (Oxford: Clarendon Press, 1996).

Rodney Tyler, *Campaign! The Selling of the Prime Minister* (London: Grafton, 1987).

George R. Urban, *Diplomacy and Disillusion at The Court of Margaret Thatcher: An Insider's View* (London: I. B. Tauris, 1996).

James Vernon, *Politics and the People: A Study in English Political Culture, 1815–1867* (Cambridge: Cambridge University Press, 1993).

Richard Vinen, *Thatcher's Britain. The Politics and Social Upheaval of the 1980s* (London: Simon and Schuster, 2009).

Richard Vinen, 'A War of Position? The Thatcher Government's Preparation for the 1984 Miners' Strike', *English Historical Review*, 134, no. 566 (2019): 121–50.

Dror Wahrman, 'The New Political History: A Review Essay', *Social History*, 21, no. 3 (1996): 343–53.

William Waldegrave, *A Different Kind of Weather: A Memoir* (London: Constable, 2015).

George Walden, *Lucky George, Memoirs of an Anti-Politician* (London: Allen Lane, 1999).

Alan Watkins, *A Short Walk down Fleet Street: From Beaverbrook to Boycott* (London: Gerald Duckworth and Co. Ltd., 2000).

Antonion Weiss, 'The Religious Mind of Mrs Thatcher' (www.margaretthatcher.org/document/112748, accessed 31 May 2024).

Martin Westlake, *Kinnock. The Biography* (London: Little, Brown and Company, 2001).

William Whitelaw, *The Whitelaw Memoirs* (London: Aurum Press, 1989).

Kevin Williams, *Read All About It! A History of the British Newspaper* (London: Routledge, 2010).

Philip Williamson, *Stanley Baldwin: Conservative Leadership and National Values* (Cambridge: Cambridge University Press, 1999).

Woodrow Wyatt, *The Journals of Woodrow Wyatt*, Vol. 1 (London: Pan Books, 1999).

David Young, *Inside Thatcher's Last Election. Diaries of the Campaign That Saved Enterprise* (London: Biteback Publishing, 2021).

Hugo Young, *One of Us: A Biography of Margaret Thatcher* (London: Macmillan, 1990).

Philip Ziegler, *Wilson: The Authorised Life* (London: Weidenfeld & Nicolson, 1993).

Index

Abramsky, Jenny 103
ad hoc statements 3, 42, 93, 116, 134, 143
Aitken, Ian 83, 118
Aitken, Jonathan 154 n.26
Alexander, Michael 31
Allen, Peter 99
Antconc software 7–8
Armstrong, Robert 24
Ashford, Nicholas 89
Atkinson, Max 73
    Our Masters' Voices: The Language and Body Language of Politics 168 n.36
Austin, J. L., speech acts 152 n.57

Baker, Kenneth 36, 105
Baldwin, Stanley 35, 134–5
Bale, Tim, *Margaret Thatcher* 10
BBC (radio)
    Analysis 106–7
    Farming Today 99
    On the Hustings 174 n.3
    Six O'Clock News 102–3, 108
    The World This Weekend 99, 142
    Today programme 98–9, 103–4, 142
    Woman's Hour 79
BBC (television)
    Good Morning 144
    Nationwide 53–5, 98
    News at One 107
    News at Ten 37
    Nine O'Clock News 73, 102–3, 110–11
    Tonight 101, 103–4
Beesley, Sonia 79
Belgrano (Argentine warship) 54–5, 175 n.9
Bell, Tim 57, 123, 127, 175 n.11
Benn, Tony 100, 134
Biffen, John 83, 173 n.80
Birmingham Press Club 85
Birt, John 101

Blair, Tony 134–5
Blake, Robert 4
Blaxill, Luke 7–8, 53
Boddy, David 92
Bottomley, Virginia 99
Boyle, Edward 16
Briggs, Raymond, *The Tin-Pot Foreign General and the Old Iron Woman* 117
The British Genius report 74
Brittan, Sam 91
Bruce-Gardyne, Jock 30
Brunson, Michael 73, 105, 107
Buerk, Michael 102, 107–8
Burns, Gordon 36, 137
Butskellism 71
Butt, Ronald 118

Callaghan, James 23, 64, 82
Cambridge School 7
Camp David 71, 141, 167 n.25
Campbell, John 10, 150 n.26
Cannadine, David 151 n.35
Carrington, Lord Peter 58
Central Policy Review Staff (CPRS) 49
Centre for Policy Studies (CPS) 97, 139
Chamberlain, Neville 35
Charlton, Michael 106
Chequers 16, 20, 85, 118
Churchill, Winston 27, 29, 76, 120, 134–5, 169 n.68
Churchill, Winston Jnr. 123
civil servants' contributions to Thatcher's speeches 11, 21, 23–6, 32, 50, 133
Clark, Alan 116, 151 n.49
Clarke, Peter 6
Cold War 89
Cole, Michael 89
Coles, John 22–3, 73
Collins, Philip 134–5
Colville, John 134

Index

Commandos Anfibios 131
Community Charge 118–19, 129, 146
Conquest, Robert 43
Conservative Campaign Guide Supplement (1978) 38
Conservative Central Council Speech
  1975 126
  1981 17
  1982 70
  1983 121–3, 182 n.72
  1990 119
Conservative Central Office 91, 92
Conservative Councillor Conferences 72
Conservative Party 4–5, 8, 16, 20, 23, 38,
  50, 61, 63, 66, 69, 73, 86, 95, 115,
  119–120, 122–4, 129, 138
  band of revolutionaries 139
  economic policy 45
  electoral advantages 122
  moderation and quietness 39–40
  policy-agenda 38–9, 51, 95, 128, 137–8,
  145
  policy platform 10–11, 36–7, 115
  trade unionism/union reform 11, 51,
  70, 120–1
Conservative Party Conference Speech
  69, 85, 101, 135, 141, 154 n.29,
  173 n.61
  1975 19, 48, 74, 133
  1976 32, 37, 49
  1978 37, 82, 120
  1979 49, 82, 162 n.134
  1980 26, 28, 78–80, 102, 169 n.59
  1981 9, 45–6, 89, 125, 141, 179 n.123
  1982 49, 85
  1983 30–1, 43, 102–3, 143
  1984 77
  1985 25, 127
  1986 82, 86, 93
  1987 36, 128, 158 n.1
  1988 75
  1990 50, 119
Conservative Research Department
  (CRD) 18–20, 23, 44, 96,
  154 n.26
corpus analysis techniques 2, 7–9, 13–14,
  72, 80, 122, 140
Cowling, Maurice, *1867, Disraeli, Gladstone and Revolution* 4
Cox, David 142

'Crawfie' (Cynthia Crawford) 57
Crisell, Andrew 98
Critchley, Julian 51, 163 n.146
Curtois, Brian 103

Day, Robin 145
de Gaulle, Charles 113
Deedes, Bill 83–4, 171 n.17
Dickson, Niall 99
Disraeli, Benjamin 67
Donoughue, Bernard 121
Douglas-Home, Charles 31, 86–7
Downing Street 1, 16, 22, 74, 138

Education Reform Bill (1987) 36
'Election strategy' document (1979) 60
electioneering platform 53, 55, 79
  critical seats 61
  draft outline programme 60
  importance of television 66
  Labour and election 62
  'love-'em-and-leave-'em' approach 59
  speechmaking and 56, 58–9
Elizabeth I, Queen 106
Emery, Fred 82, 142
Employment Act (1980, 1982 & 1984)
  39–40
Eton College 18, 22, 138
Europe/European 62–3, 102
  Britain's relationship with 40, 110
  integration 110
  super-state 102, 110
Evans, Harold 86–7
Everett, Kenny 88, 143, 172 n.53
extra-parliamentary speeches 13, 94

Falkland Islands
  Argentine invasion of 131
  Falklands Crisis 117
  Falklands Factor 116
  Falklands War 62
Filby, Eliza 150 n.34
Finance Bill 124
Finchley constituency 59, 140
Fleet Street journalism 84
Foot, Michael 24, 88, 100, 108–9, 116, 124
Foreign and Commonwealth Office (FCO)
  31, 40–2, 137
Franklin Street Methodist Church 114
Frost, David 118, 175 n.11

Gallup Political Index (1979) 115, 124
Galtieri, General Leopoldo 2, 12, 116
Gamble, Andrew 150 n.25, 152 n.53
Gang of Four 23
Gardiner, George 23
Garner, A. S. 60
general elections 13, 26, 68, 122, 124
 1970 20
 1979 15, 39–40, 56–7, 59, 62, 64, 66,
  74, 107, 115
 1983 53, 55, 57–8, 60–3, 65, 79, 93,
  115, 122, 125
 1987 3, 30, 57–9, 61–3, 66, 73, 122,
  139–40, 184 n.109
Genghis Khan 102
German reunification 41–2
Gilbert, W. S. 32
Gladstone, William Ewart 3, 13
 Midlothian campaign (1879) 53
Golden Age of speechmaking 53, 55, 68,
 80, 144
Goodison, Nicholas 31
Goodman, Geoffrey 84, 171 n.18
Gorbachev, Mikhail 71, 105
Gould, Diana 54–5, 175 n.9
governmental speeches 21, 40, 50, 70, 92
Gow, Ian 70, 86–7, 123
Grantham 114
Great Reform Act (1832) 53
Green, E. H. H. 152 n.54
Greene, Sarah 144
Griffiths, Brian 18
Gummer, John 43, 45–6, 49, 51, 65, 124,
 136, 139

Haines, Joe 82, 134
Hall, Stuart 150 n.25
Hannay, David 167 n.25
Hanrahan, Will 144
Harris, Kenneth 117
Harris, Robin 6, 17, 20, 51, 65, 76, 127–8,
 136, 185 n.133
Hart, David 30, 44, 56, 138
Hart, Roderick 60, 115, 127–8, 164 n.21
Haviland, Julian 37
Healey, Denis 142
Heath, Edward 15, 37, 45, 51–2, 100, 116,
 134
 free collective bargaining 37–8
heckling 78–9

Hennessy, Peter 117
Heseltine, Michael 117
high politics 4, 53, 55, 67, 79,
 140
Hoggart, Simon 83–4
Holland, Julian 103
Holmes, David 56
Home Team 15, 20, 33, 44–5, 51, 134
Hoskyns, John 17–18, 26, 29, 32, 39, 44–6,
 70–1, 109, 125, 135–6, 138–9,
 180 n.20
 Just in Time 27
 Political Survival 115
 Stepping Stones 120–1, 128
Howe, Derek 92
Howe, Geoffrey 36–7, 40–1, 70
 Budgets 122
Howell, David 62, 135
Hurd, Douglas 42, 83, 104–6

immigration policy 36–8
independent state schools 36, 137
Ingham, Bernard 12, 41, 79, 82, 88–92,
 95–9, 105–6, 108–11, 124, 142,
 172 n.57, 175 n.9
Ipsos MORI polls 123
ITN 73, 75, 100–1

Jackson, Ben 148 n.5, 150 nn.32–3,
 151 n.37, 152 n.52, 187 n.70
Jay, Peter 82–3, 87, 101
Jenkins, Peter 83
Jenkins, Simon 117, 138
Jephson, Henry, *The Platform* 53
Jessel, Stephen 103
jobs, Thatcher's discussion of 62–3, 69–70,
 166 n.2
Johnson, Frank 49, 109
Jones, Tom 35, 134
Jopling, Michael 124
Joseph, Keith 128, 145

Kennedy, Ludovic 111
Kenny, Mary 83
Kerr, John 40, 167 n.25
King, Anthony 35
Kinnock, Neil 42, 55, 109, 119, 132
 'The Kinnock Report' 101
 Policy Review 124
Kwarteng, Kwasi 179 n.6

Index

Labour Party 2, 4, 8, 55, 60, 62, 64, 69, 93,
119–24, 129, 167 n.20, 182 n.71,
183 n.84, 186 n.25
communications programme 120
Conference 69
jobs pledge (1986) 127–8
The New Hope for Britain manifesto
124
policy of unilateral disarmament 123
political labels 122–6, 128, 145–6
tax and defence 121–4, 182 n.80
trade union movement 120–1
Lancaster, Terence 84–5, 89, 116
Langdon, Julia 23
Lankester, Sir Timothy 26
Lawley, Sue 54–5
Lawrence, Jon 5, 53, 150 n.33
Lawson, Nigel 36, 41–2, 83, 119, 128,
179 n.1
The View from No. 11 127
lobby system 89–92, 94, 173 n.74,
173 n.80
London Weekend Television (LWT) 101,
142
The Walden Interview programme 97,
118–19, 143
Weekend World programme 96–7, 142,
173 n.80
low politics 53, 55, 68, 79, 140

Macleod, Iain 24, 100
Macmillan, Harold 112, 125
art of speaking 111
television election 111
Majorism 144
Major, John 182 n.79
Mansbridge, Peter 145
Mao, Madam 23
Marr, Andrew 172 n.57
Maude, Angus 22, 64
Maudling, Reginald (Reggie) 43,
49, 76
Maxwell, Robert 86
May, Theresa 57
McFarlane, Robert 71
McKay, Peter 137
media landscape 13–14, 56, 100, 102
of 1970s and 1980s 14, 111–12,
142–4
post-war 111–12

Meisel, Joseph 27, 149 n.8
Review of *Margaret Thatcher: Complete
Public Statements, 1945–1990* 7,
151 n.40
memorable phrases, Thatcher's 1, 97
the 'enemies' within 2, 12, 114
'The Lady is not for turning' 78,
89, 116
'The National Health Service is safe
with us' 43, 49, 63, 79, 136
'no, no, no' 22
'there is no alternative' 141
'frit' 24
Metro-Goldwyn-Mayer (MGM) Studios
20
Meyer, Anthony 128
Millar, Ronald 3, 13, 15, 19, 21, 26, 29,
32–3, 43–6, 48, 51–2, 65, 76,
109–10, 135, 138, 143
Blackpool experience 19, 133
Party Political Broadcast (PPB) draft 48
professional career 20
'Ronnification' 21
A View from the Wings 78
Monkhouse, Bob 73
Monty Python, 'Parrot sketch' 50
Moore, Charles 7, 10, 151 n.35
Morris, John 83
Mount, Ferdinand 6, 18–19, 26, 29–31,
43, 49, 51, 64–5, 70, 101–2, 131,
136, 138
Cold Cream 6
Murdoch, Rupert 85–7
Murphy, Peter 104
Musolf, Karen, *From Plymouth to
Parliament* 5

National Health Service (NHS) 43, 49, 52,
63, 79, 136–7
National Insurance Surcharge 121,
182 n.80
National Playing Fields Association 72
National Union of Mineworkers (NUM) 2
Naughtie, James 128
Neave, Airey 23, 113, 179 n.1
Nero, Emperor, speeches for 76
New Political History 5–8
news-agenda 13, 81, 88, 94–5, 97, 99, 104,
111–12, 132, 142–3
Northern Ireland 164 n.25, 166 n.20

Nott, John 95, 116
Number 10 Policy Unit 6, 13, 17–18, 26,
    31, 40–1, 45, 89, 91, 94–5, 97,
    102, 107, 109, 122, 131, 133–4,
    138, 142

Oakley, Robin 82, 93
Official Secrets Act 26
Old Rose pub 138–9
O'Sullivan, John 19–21, 36, 40, 43, 50,
    72–3, 143, 146, 160 n.51
Owen, David 82, 125, 132
    Time to Declare 184 n.109

Palliser, Michael 77
Parkinson, Cecil 60, 103, 123, 135, 183 n.85
parliamentary speeches 3, 13, 22–4, 27, 32,
    41, 82, 94, 103
Parris, Matthew 31
Parsons, Anthony 102
Party Political Broadcast (PPB) 43, 48, 115
Patten, Chris 11, 17, 19, 29, 44, 48, 51, 91,
    128–9, 133, 139
Pattie, Geoffrey 23
platform, non-election years 67–8, 79
    geographical importance 140
    set-piece speeches and 80
    and speechmaking 71
    use of celebrities 73, 80, 141, 168 n.43
    use of flags 73
    use of songs 13, 73, 80, 141
    verbal combat 139–42
policy-agenda, shaping of 11, 28, 47, 65,
    95, 124, 146
    newspapers 13, 42, 46, 50
    radio 13
    television 13, 36–7
    Thatcher's speeches 11, 35–6, 41, 95,
    137–8, 145
    wordsmiths 43, 48, 50–1
policy hostages 11, 49
political labels 2, 4–5, 12, 14, 117, 122–6,
    128–9, 145–6, 181 n.61
political language 1–2, 4–5, 7, 12, 36, 145,
    147
popular capitalism 86–7
post-Thatcherism 128
Powell, Charles 23–5, 31, 40, 99, 101, 108,
    167 n.26, 169 n.68
Powell, Enoch 76, 100

press releases 81, 91–4, 132, 143, 183 n.85
Preston, Peter 83
prime ministerial speeches 21, 25, 44, 46,
    60–1, 66, 72, 91–2, 107, 134, 146
Prime Minister's Questions (PMQs) 23–5,
    32, 42, 131
print media
    Birmingham Post 3
    Daily Express 45, 82, 85, 90, 137
    Daily Mirror 50, 82, 85–7, 89, 100, 116
    The Daily Telegraph 1, 90
    The Economist 49
    Evening Standard 104
    Faversham News 71
    Financial Times 83, 91, 94
    The Guardian 1, 46, 69, 83–4, 87, 108,
    118–19, 173 n.74
    Hebden Bridge Times 83
    The Herald 143
    Independent 119, 173 n.74
    Labour Weekly 23
    The Listener 107
    Marxism Today 5, 126
    The Observer 51, 116, 163 n.146
    Occult Gazette 116
    Red Star 88
    The Scotsman 173 n.74
    Socialist Worker 1
    Spectator 101
    The Sun 1, 85, 88, 90, 92
    Sunday Express 83
    Sunday Times 117
    The Telegraph 49
    The Times 44, 82, 85–7, 89–90, 93, 101,
    104, 109, 115–18, 127, 138, 142
    Varsity 83
    Wall Street Journal 42
Prior, Jim 38–9, 48, 84
public language 5–9, 12, 28, 32, 42, 56, 62,
    69, 80, 137, 147
Pym, Francis 46, 90, 94, 125

radio and television 53, 95–100, 102, 105,
    111–12, 142. *See also* BBC (radio);
    BBC (television); ITN; London
    Weekend Television (LWT); set-
    piece television interviews
    television interviews 96, 98, 105,
    111–12, 142
    use of 'the diary' 107

Ramsden, John 148 n.2, 169 n.67,
    184 n.124
Ranelagh, John, *Thatcher's People* 153 n.10
Readman, Paul 4
Reagan, Ronald 64, 71, 75, 132, 135
Redwood, John 18
Reece, Gordon 92–3, 96–8, 107, 111, 141
Rees-Mogg, William 94
rhetorical devices 68, 76, 110, 141,
    168 n.55
  anaphora 76
  epiplexis 75
  erotema 75, 77
  humour 50, 73–5
Rhodes James, Robert, *Winston
    S. Churchill: His Complete
    Speeches, 1897–1963* 7
Rickett, William 23–5, 43
  boundaries 26
Riddell, Peter 82, 114, 116, 145, 170 n.4
Ridley, Adam 17, 19, 22–3, 29, 31, 44–5,
    48, 76, 91, 133
Ridley, Nicholas 17, 51
Rifle Brigade 18, 138
The Right Approach (Conservative policy
    statement) 49
Roberts, Alfred 114
Roberts, Matthew, *Constructing a Tory
    World-View* 5
Rowe, Andrew, *The Way Ahead* 37
Ryder, Richard 60

Saatchi & Saatchi, *Life in Britain* 118
Saunders, Robert 10, 148 n.5, 150 n.32,
    152 nn.51–2, 187 n.70
Scholar, Michael 16, 21–3, 27–8, 70, 76
Scottish Conservative Party 93, 119
  Conference Speech 17, 131
set-piece speeches 3, 25–6, 29, 32, 36,
    42, 55, 62, 66–8, 72, 79–80, 88,
    93–6, 101–2, 104–7, 111–12,
    119–20, 122–3, 127, 129, 131,
    133–5, 139, 146, 174 n.3.
    See also Thatcher's set-piece
    speeches
  and media environment 12–13
  as political communication 143–4, 147
  symbolic importance of location
    167 n.26

set-piece television interviews 3, 95, 103,
    142
Sherbourne, Stephen 25, 127–8, 182 n.79
Sherman, Alfred 19–20, 22, 33, 44, 46, 65,
    96, 138–9, 183 n.88
  'Fragments for Central Council Speech'
    123
Shrimsley, Anthony 61
Sikorsky 117
Simpson, John 109
Skinner, Denis 74
Skinner, Quentin 4, 7
Slocock, Caroline 51, 70, 162 n.141
Smith, David 105
Social Democratic Party (SDP)/SDP-
    Liberal Alliance 86, 125–6,
    166 n.20
soundbites 108–9
speech(es) 2–3, 13, 57–8, 100, 140. *See also*
    Thatcher's set-piece speeches
  acts 11, 152 n.57
  analysis of 17–19
  and British political history 147
  definition of 3
  extra-parliamentary 13, 94
  Golden Era of 12
  governmental 21, 40, 50, 70, 92
  as historical source 4–7
  in media landscape (1970s & 1980s)
    14, 111–12, 142–4
  parliamentary 3, 13, 22–4, 27, 32, 41,
    82, 94, 103
  prime ministerial 21, 25, 44, 46, 60–1,
    66, 72, 91–2, 107, 134, 146
  public 2, 35, 52, 79–80, 122, 138
  scholars and sources 4–7
  set-piece (*see* set-piece speeches)
speechmaking process, Thatcher's
    1–3, 6–7, 9, 13, 19, 25–6, 28, 35,
    45–6, 50, 52, 64–5, 70, 72, 76,
    79–80, 92–3, 114, 131–2, 137–8,
    146–7, 151 n.38
  chaos 15–16, 26, 32, 133–6, 138
  'clap lines' 29, 76, 141
  classical rhetoric 76
  debate policy 136
  defies analysis 15, 33
  defined by 'general rules' 21–2, 134,
    136

drafting process 9, 11–12, 113, 147
  importance of 132–3
  non-election years 57, 59, 62, 67, 80
  and policy-agenda 10–11, 35–6, 41
  political influence 11, 43–4, 51, 113
  post-delivery 94
  Thatcher's lack of confidence in her
    own ability 12, 16, 29, 134
  tortuous scripting 13, 27, 32
  viewed as verbal combat 79, 139–42
speechwriters 9, 16, 25, 28–9, 32, 35, 45,
    134, 136, 152 n.59
  academic template, use of 76
  civil servants as 25–6, 136
  difficult to categorize 33, 50–1, 138–9
  overstated influence of 123, 125
  position of influence 43–4
  sleep (lack of) for 77
  Thatcher and 2, 11, 43–4, 48, 50–1,
    76, 114–15, 125, 129, 136, 141,
    184 n.109
  viewed as dental technicians 51, 136–8
St Lawrence Jewry Church, London 72, 97
standing ovations 73, 141
Stedman Jones, Gareth, *Languages of Class*
    4, 149 n.15
Steel, David 184 n.109
Stephens, Caroline 133
Stothard, Peter 44
Stowe, Ken 7, 21, 134
Strategic Defence Initiative (SDI) 71, 75
Strauss, Norman, *Stepping Stones* 120–1,
    128
Sutcliffe-Braithwaite, Florence 150 n.33

Tarbuck, Jimmy 73
Taylor, A. J. P. 114
Tebbitt, Norman 11, 39, 136, 146
template speeches 65, 70, 140
text mining software 2, 8
textual analysis 9–10
That Bloody Woman (TBW) factor 118
Thatcher, Carol 156 n.100
Thatcher, Denis 27, 75
Thatcher, Margaret 1, 6, 8, 10, 12, 24, 35,
    41, 129, 146–7
  ad libbing 79
  'Battle of Ideas' 120
  challenges 12, 14, 57, 135

childhood 114, 129, 145
conviction politics/politician 113–15,
    117–19, 129, 179 n.6
declarative leadership 35
The Downing Street Years 158 n.4
economic policy 45
electoral dominance 1, 6
euro-sceptic language 41
fondness of quotes 32
frailty 57
ideology 137
immigration 36–8
incomes policy 37–8
as 'a lady in distress' 38, 57, 85, 106
language of conviction 9, 115–20, 129,
    145–6
mandatory strike ballots 39–40
marginalia 7, 19, 27, 71, 137
'Milk snatcher' and 'Hoarder' 126
monetarist policies 87
The Path to Power 144
personal papers 6
philosophy and practice 116
political messages 2, 9, 13, 69, 71,
    87–8, 92, 94, 100–1, 108–9,
    111–12, 143
self-scripted speeches 74
sense of humour 73–5, 88
speechmaking of (*see* speechmaking
    process, Thatcher's)
speechwriters, relations with 11, 13, 32,
    44–5, 48, 76, 115, 129, 184 n.109
    (*see also* speechwriters)
tiredness 1, 28, 36, 57, 64, 87
use of religion 72, 97, 144–5, 151 n.34
'wets' and 11, 43, 49, 139
Thatcherism 1–2, 5, 8, 10, 12, 14, 16, 35,
    39, 113, 125–9, 132, 144–6,
    152 n.53, 184 n.114
development of 7, 11
Thatcher's set-piece speeches
  to 1922 Committee (1975/1984)
    73, 126
  'Action for Cities' speech (1988) 104
  Britain Awake (1976) 141
  British American Chamber of
    Commerce speech (1977) 100–1
  British Residence, Washington DC
    speech (1985) 75

202 *Index*

Bruges Speech (1988) 6, 40–1, 82, 103, 151 n.49
Conservative Central Council (*see* Conservative Central Council Speech)
Conservative Party Conference (*see* Conservative Party Conference Speech)
Conservative Trade Unionists Conference speech (1980) 56, 106
Fornham All Saints speech (1987) 3
Franco-British Council speech (1980) 31
Golden Book Ceremony speech (1982) 22, 156 n.96
Guildhall Speech (1980) 32
Institute of Directors speech (1983) 70
Institute of Socio-Economic Studies speech (1975) 92
in Kuala Lumpur (1985) 176 n.44
in Luxembourg (1988) 107–8, 110–11
Mansion House Speech (1990) 136
Small Business Bureau, Surrey (1984) 69
to Sri Lankan Parliament (1985) 82
St Francis Speech (1979) 3
United States Congress Speech (1985) 31
Washington speeches (1983) 87
Winston Churchill Foundation Award Dinner speech (1983) 30, 140
Women's Conservative Party Conference Speech (1981) 17, 92–3
Young Conservatives (*see* Young Conservatives speech)
Thomas, Caroline 99
Thomas, Harvey 70, 73, 77, 101, 141, 152 n.49
Thomas, Hugh 113
Thorneycroft, Peter 22, 73, 81, 128
tortuous scripting process 13, 27, 32
Tunstall, Jeremy 86, 88

unemployment 3, 63, 69–70, 90, 105–6, 141
United States of Europe 40, 107, 111, 137
University of Cambridge 4, 83, 100
   Cambridge Union 100
University of Oxford 18, 83, 100
   Oxford Union 100

Urban, George 27, 29–31
Utley, T. E. 26

van der Post, Laurens 31
Vinen, Richard 152 n.52, 152 n.60
Vernon, James 4

Wade, Richard 98–9
Wahrman, Dror 5–8
Waldegrave, William 99
Walden, Brian 38–9, 96–7, 118–19, 142–4, 173 n.80
Walden, George 51
Walker, Peter 124–5
Wall, Stephen 41
Walters, Alan 87
Watkins, Alan 83
Watt, David 87, 117
Westland affair 23–4, 118, 129
'wets' and 'dries' 11, 43, 49, 139
Whitehouse, Mary 114
Whitelaw, Willie 36–7, 98, 101
Whitmore, Clive 26, 45
Whittingdale, John 25, 50, 91–2, 109
Williamson, Philip 2, 113
   Stanley Baldwin 5
Williams, Shirley 84
Wilson, Harold 23, 28, 106, 134–5, 173 n.73
Winchester College 154 n.25
Witchell, Nicholas 88
Wolfson, David 26, 44
wordsmiths 2, 9, 11–13, 33, 44, 48, 51, 94, 109, 112–13, 115, 123, 129, 132, 134–5, 143, 145–6
   as outsiders 138–9
   political significance of 136–8
World in Action programme (Granada) 36
Wright, Patrick 41–2
Wyatt, Woodrow 19, 85–6, 138

Young, Andrew 100
Young, David 30
Young, Hugo 127–8, 150 n.25
Young Conservatives 65, 77, 116, 122
Young Conservatives speech
   1979 73, 77
   1980 116
   1983 84, 88

www.ingramcontent.com/pod-product-compliance
Ingram Content Group UK Ltd.
Pitfield, Milton Keynes, MK11 3LW, UK
UKHW021127130425
457181UK00001B/1